Towards Unders Religion

Volume 1

Collected Writings From the Archives of *Al-Basheer,* the Magazine

مجموعة مقالات جمال الدين زربوزو

Jamaal al-Din M. Zarabozo

1999

Towards Understanding Our Religion— Volume 1:
Collected Writings From the Archives of *al-Basheer*,
the Magazine
By Jamaal al-Din M. Zarabozo

Published by:
Al-Basheer Company for Publications and Translations
10515 E. 40th Ave. Suite #108
Denver, CO   80239-3264
U.S.A.
www.al-basheer.com

(Note: Not affiliated with Basheer Publications)

Printed in U.S.A.

Cover Design by Ahmed Ali Ansari, Al-Basheer Graphics

ISBN 1-891540-08-4 $17.00 softcover

Table of Contents

i

Introduction

In the name of Allah, Most Compassionate, Most Merciful. All praises are due to Allah; we praise Him; we seek His help; we seek His forgiveness; and we seek His guidance. We seek refuge in Allah from the evil in our souls and the badness of our deeds. For whomever Allah guides, there is none to lead him astray. And for whomever He allows to go astray, there is none to guide him. I bear witness that there is none worthy of worship except Allah, for whom there is no partner. And I bear witness that Muhammad is His servant and Messenger. O believers, have *taqwa* [fear] of Allah according to His right and die not save as Muslims. O mankind, have *taqwa* of your Lord, the One who created you from one soul and created from it its mate and from them spread forth many men and women. And fear Allah from whom you demand your mutual rights and [do not cut] familial ties. Surely, Allah is ever an All-Watcher over you. O believers, have *taqwa* of Allah and always speak the truth. He will direct you to do righteous deeds and will forgive you your sins. And whosoever obeys Allah and His Messenger has indeed achieved a great achievement.

To proceed: Verily, the truest speech is the Book of Allah. The best guidance is the guidance of Muhammad. The worst affairs are the innovated ones. Every innovated matter is a heresy. And every heresy is a going astray. And every astray act is in the Hell-fire.

The History of *Al-Basheer*

Al-Basheer was a bi-monthly magazine dedicated to Islamic sciences. It was produced for a total of eight years,

1

from 1987 to 1995. It was published by Basheer Publications.[1] The magazine published articles in different sections, including: "From the Quran," "From the Hadith," "Fiqh Issues," "*Khutbah*s," "Book Reviews," "Questions and Answers," "Short Articles" and "Feature Articles." Almost all of these sections are represented in this present collection.

Although it did build up a very modest following, the company was forced to close its doors and discontinue the magazine in 1995. Ever since that decision was made, numerous people have called for its revival or, at least, for reprints of the original issues. At the present time, for many reasons, neither option is viable.

Since *al-Basheer* never had a very large subscription base, these articles never reached many Muslims. This was also seen as a strong argument that something had to be done with respect to the numerous, hopefully beneficial, articles that the magazine contained.

However, many of the articles in *al-Basheer* were originally written with the intention that they would some day be turned into books. By the grace and mercy of Allah, in some cases, such has already been accomplished. The articles in *Al-Basheer*'s section entitled, "From the Hadith," were greatly enlarged and formed part of this author's *Commentary on the Forty Hadith of al-Nawawi*. A five-part series of articles originally in *al-Basheer* have also been revised, expanded and published under the title, *How to Approach and Understand the Quran*. Furthermore, most of the articles in the section entitled, "*Khutbahs*," have been gathered together, added to and published in the author's *The Friday Prayer: Khutbahs (I)* and *(II)*. At the same time, though, it has to be admitted that it may be years before some of the articles ever see the light of day in the form of rewritten, revised and expanded-upon books.

---

[1] Basheer Publications is not affiliated in any way with the publishers of this book, Al-Basheer Company for Publications and Translations.

Hence, a solution was arrived at: *Al-Basheer*'s articles will be published in book form in a series of volumes. This is the first set; if there is a demand, a second or third volume may follow, Allah willing. One should also note that all of the articles included in this collection were written by this author, Jamaal al-Deen M. Zarabozo, who worked as the editor of *al-Basheer* during all of its years. Numerous others, may Allah reward them bountifully, contributed to *al-Basheer* over the years. If possible, with all the necessary details worked out, a future volume will contain the articles contributed by others to the magazine.

The Present Collection

All of the articles in this present volume are from only the first two years of *al-Basheer*— with the exception of the first article on the disjoined letters of the Quran.[1]

It was decided to remain faithful to the original publication of the magazines. Therefore, no changes or revisions were made to the text except for adding Arabic text, revising the transliteration of Arabic words to make them consistent with the other books published by Al-Basheer Company, adding of footnotes with additional reference material, correcting typographical errors and making minor editorial changes.

The reader should keep in mind that the tone, style and nature of writing in a periodical can be very different from that of writing for a book— in fact, the reader may note some stylistic aspects of the writing in these articles that he would never note in the author's books (such as writing in the first person). Furthermore, the time constraints in editing and putting out a magazine on a timely basis does not allow one to gather together all the kinds of research and reference material

---

[1] The relevant information about the first article is given later.

as possible. Space constraints are also very important considerations when writing for a magazine. Despite these facts, it was still decided that it would be best here to remain as faithful to the original as feasible.

Acknowlegements

By the grace and mercy of Allah, many, many people assisted in the production and distribution of the magazine *al-Basheer*. It would be virtually impossible to recount all of them by name here but, at the very least, some must definitely be mentioned due to their outstanding assistance and help. Explicit thanks must be extended to Hamad ali-Shaikh, Fahd al-Yahya, Muhammad al-Osimi, Ahmad al-Teraiqi, Basim al-Hamer, Muhammad Tahlawi and Nahar al-Rashid. Indeed, all of the subscribers and distributors of *al-Basheer* deserve thanks. Of course, my wife deserves a great deal of credit for all of her assistance and patience throughout the years of *al-Basheer*. Last, but not least, thanks must be extended to Sr. Imaan for editing and proofreading the manuscript of this book. May Allah reward them all with a blessed life in both this world and in the Hereafter.

From the Quran:
Alif Lam Meem.[1]

Allah begins *soorah al-Baqarah* with the following letters,

آلٓمٓ

"*Alif. Lam. Meem*" (*al-Baqarah* 1). These letters in and of themselves do not form a word. They are referred to as the *muqatta'aat* or "the disjointed letters".

"The Disjointed Letters"

These disjointed letters form the beginning of a number of *soorah*s in the Quran. Unfortunately, they have been the source of a great deal of controversy and confusion. The attempt here will be to first mention all of the different theories concerning such letters. This will be followed by a summary of the conclusions of the leading Quranic commentators. After that, a detailed discussion will follow of

[1] This article was prepared for *al-Basheer*, vol. 9, no. 1 (May-June 1995). Just before going to press, it was decided to discontinue the magazine. So it is actually an article that was never published. It was published as part of Jamaal al-Deen Zarabozo, *The Methodology of the Quranic Commentators* (Falls Church, VA: American Open University, 1997). However, since that publication is also not widely disseminated, it was decided to include the article here as part of the *al-Basheer* heritage. In this article, the references without footnotes to different Quranic commentators refer to the relevant commentary mentioned in the bibliography.

what seems to be the strongest opinion concerning the correct stance towards these letters.

First View: They are from the *Mutashaabihaat*

One opinion expressed is that these verses are from the *mutashaabihaat* (ambiguous verses) and their meanings are known only to Allah. Abu Bakr is reported to have said, "Allah has in every book a secret aspect and Allah's secret aspect in the Quran are the beginning letters." Al-Qurtubi attributes this opinion to Abu Bakr, Umar, Ali and ibn Masood. This opinion is also said to be that of Ibn Zaid, al-Shabi, Abu Saalih, Sufyaan al-Thauri and it is the conclusion of Abu Haatim ibn Hibbaan.

It is very strange, however, that al-Tabari mentions this opinion and then does not ascribe it to anyone. This is against his normal pattern. Could this imply that he does not believe that those are acceptable narrations? One cannot conclude anything on this matter except that one would have expected him to have, at least, given the narration and chain from Abu Bakr on this opinion.

Usmani definitely has a twist on this opinion, although it does not originate with him,[1] when he writes, "Others cannot reach their real meaning as it is a mystery between God and the Prophet (peace be upon him), which is not disclosed due to some reason."[2] However, there is no evidence that the Prophet (peace be upon him) knew the meanings of these letters and did not disclose them.

Some commentators have not accepted this view. This view implies that there are some verses of the Quran that are not understandable or that have no meaning to them. Both of these concepts are rejected by some scholars. Hence, they insist that there must be some meaning or purpose to these

---

[1] Abu Hayyaan (1/59) mentions that "some people" state that opinion.
[2] Usmani, vol. 1, p. 3.

letters. Obviously, there must be some purpose— as opposed to meaning— for these letters, as it is inconceivable that they were revealed in vain without any purpose for them.[1]

A Second View: They are Letters that Form a Name of Allah

It is also narrated from some that these letters, when put together properly, form one of the names of Allah. The following statement is narrated from Ali ibn Abu Taalib, "They are disjoined names. If the people knew how to construct them, they would know the name of Allah by which if they supplicated, they would be responded to." Similarly, ibn Abbaas was asked about آل and حم and نون (which contain all of the letters of *al-Rahmaan*) and he answered, "They are the name *al-Rahmaan* spread out." This report from ibn Abbaas is mentioned both by ibn Abi Haatim and by al-Tabari through different chains. However, both of the chains are weak and, therefore, one cannot hold this as the opinion of ibn Abbaas.[2]

A Third View: They are Letters by Which Allah Swears and They are from His Names

This has been narrated from ibn Abbaas and Ikrimah. Al-Salafi, in a lengthy footnote, discusses the narrations that state from ibn Abbaas that these are one of the names of Allah

---

[1] The question of whether it is possible to have a verse whose meaning is not known at all is discussed at the end of this article.
[2] See Ahmad al-Salafi, Footnotes to Abdul Raoof al-Munaawi, *al-Fath al-Samaawi bi-Takhreej Ahadeeth Tafseer al-Qaadhi al-Baidhaawi* (Riyadh: Daar al-Aasimah, 1409 A.H.), vol. 1, p. 125, fn. 1.

and he concludes that they are all weak narrations.[1] Al-Huwaini concurs with that conclusion.[2]

It is also narrated that Ali used to supplicate, يا كهيعص اغفر لنا, ("Oh *kaf ha ya ain saad*, forgive us"); however that has been reported through *mursal* chains (chains that are broken). It has been narrated from al-Suddi al-Kabeer that such letters are from the names of Allah and, according to al-Huwaini, that narration has a good chain to it.[3]

A Fourth View: They are Letters by Which Allah Swears

Ibn Qutaiba stated (as quoted in ibn al-Jauzi),

It is possible that He is swearing by all of the disjointed letters, and He simply mentioned some of them. Like a person who has learned the alphabet who says, "I learned the a b c's," and he means by that the remaining letters. Like one who says, "I read *al-hamd*," and he means all of *soorah al-Faatihah*. He mentions it by the first words only. He has sworn by the letters of the alphabet due to their honor and they are what make up His revealed books.

However, al-Qurtubi (1/156) mentions that some scholars reject this notion because, in general, any kind of oath usually is stated in a certain form. For example, it should begin with the words, *inna, qad, laqad, ma* and *wa*. Since these do not exist here, it cannot be considered a kind of oath.[4]

An objection that arises to this interpretation is that the people who read the Quran are either believers in it or deniers of it. The believers in it believe in it without any need for the

---

[1] Al-Salafi, vol. 1, p. 128, fn. 12.
[2] Al-Huwaini, vol. 2, pp. 55-56.
[3] Al-Huwaini, vol. 2, p. 53.
[4] After stating this objection, al-Qurtubi goes on to refute it but his refutation does not seem as strong as the argument itself.

oath while the disbelievers are not affected by the oath. The reply to this simple objection is given by al-Qurtubi (1/156) who said that in the Arabic speech, when someone wants to emphasize something, it is done by swearing. Hence, Allah revealed the Quran in Arabic and is using that aspect of the Arabic language.

A Fifth View: They are the Greatest Name of Allah

This has been narrated from ibn Abbaas through the following chain: Shubah on the authority of al-Suddi that it had reached him that such was the statement of ibn Abbaas. It seems, though, that the chain for this narration is broken between al-Suddi and ibn Abbas.[1]

A Sixth View: They are Simply the Opening by which Allah Begins Specific Soorahs

This view was expressed by Mujaahid.[2]

A Seventh View: They are an Inference to the Remaining Letters of the Alphabet

This view states that these letters are in reference to the alphabet as a whole. In other words, in the same way that these letters are the source or essence of one's speech, they also make up the speech of the Quran. This opinion was that of al-Faraa.

Obviously, it is known that the words are made up of such letters. Therefore, what is the benefit of presenting them

---

[1] Cf., al-Huwaini, vol. 2, p. 54, fn. 3.
[2] According to al-Huwaini, the chain back to Mujaahid is acceptable. See al-Huwaini, vol. 2, p. 52, fn. 1.

in such a manner? Ibn al-Jauzi (1/16) has replied to this question with the following response,

> Allah makes an inference to them to demonstrate the Quran's miraculous nature. It is as if He were saying, "It [the Quran] is from these letters that make up your speech. What is the matter with you people that you are not able to make anything to oppose this Quran? If you are not able to do that, then you should know that [this Quran] is not the speech of Muhammad (peace be upon him) [but it is a revelation from Allah].

An interesting aspect of all the different letters of the different *soora*hs that begin with such letters is that they are fourteen in number, exactly half of the total Arabic alphabet. However, as al-Zamakhshari points out, they encompass all of the types of letters available in Arabic (المهموسة والمجهورة ومن الرخوة والشديدة والمطبقة والمفتوحة ومن الستعلية والمنخفضة ومن حـــروف القلقلـــة). After discussing them in more detail, al-Zamakhshari states, "Glory be to the One who is so particular and exacting in all of His decrees."

An Eighth View: They are a Type of Abbreviated Speech that the Arabs Used on Occasion

For example, one person may said to another, "هل تا؟" ("Are you com?" instead of "Are you coming?") and the person will reply certainly. The meaning of the first sentence was "هـــل تـــأني؟" ("Are you coming?"). Examples of this nature may be found in the poetry from the time of *jaahiliyyah*. Two examples (from al-Jauzi, 1/17) should suffice[1]:

قلنا لها قفي لنا فقالت قاف

أراد قالت أقف

---

[1] The following is not translated into English because it, like the previous example, would not make any sense.

10

نادوهم أن الجموا ألا تا   قالوا جميعاً كلهم بلى فا

يريد: ألا تركبون؟ قالوا: بلى فركبوا.

Attiyah ibn al-Haarith al-Hamadaani stated that the Prophet (peace be upon him) used to read the Quran aloud in all of the prayers. The polytheists would clap and make noise to drown out the Prophet's reading. Therefore, these opening verses were revealed and this would make them confused and quiet. Others have stated that they were addressed in words that they could not understand in order to make them listen, as people always will turn to the thing they do not understand. When they turned and listened, they were addressed by what they understood. Hence, this was a means of reaching them and making them listen.

However, ibn Katheer is not pleased with this opinion. He states that if that were the case, then these letters should appear at the beginning of every or the majority of the *soorah*s in the Quran while such is not the case. In addition, he states, these two *soorah*s (*al-Baqarah* and *ali-Imraan*) were not directed towards the *mushrikeen* (polytheists) and, therefore, there is no need for such a beginning to such *soorah*s.

A Ninth View: They are the Names of the *Soorahs*

This opinion has been narrated from a number of early scholars, including Zaid ibn Aslam and his son. Commenting on this opinion, al-Tabari (1/89) asks: "Is there anything in the Quran that does not have any meaning to it?" He states that in this case there is a meaning to the letters in that they distinguish one *soorah* from the other. Then he gives two lines of Arabic poetry in which the same approach was used, wherein disjointed letters were used simply to set off one speech from another.

However, if names are meant to clearly distinguish one thing from another, such as different names of different people, how could these letters be names for different *soorah*s when so many *soorah*s have the same sets of letters at the beginning? Al-Tabari (1/90) replies to this by saying that in the same way that many people may have the same name and can only be distinguished by reference to something else unique about them, such is the case with the different *soorah*s that begin with the same opening letters. Therefore, for example, one would say, "I read *Alif Lam Meem al-Baqarah*," "*Alif Lam Meem. Dhaalika al-Kitaab*," or "*Alif Lam Meem. Ali-Imraan*."

There seems to be some support for this interpretation in an authentic hadith concerning one of the other *soorah*s that begin with such letters. Abu Hurairah narrated that from the *soorahs* that the Messenger of Allah (peace be upon him) used to recite during the *Fajr* prayer on Fridays was *Alif Lam Meem Sajdah*. (Recorded by al-Bukhari.)

At the same time, though, ibn Katheer argues that they could not simply be meant to separate one *soorah* from another as some have claimed. He states that that is not true because such is accomplished without need for such letters, since there is the saying, "In the name of Allah, the Compassionate, the Merciful" in between the different *soorah*s.

A Tenth View: They are from the Names of the Quran

This was narrated from Mujaahid[1], al-Shabi, Qataadah and ibn Juraij. However, ibn Katheer (1/72) discounts this view stating that what is meant by that is that it is in reference to a portion of the Quran and not the Quran as a whole. He wrote,

> Perhaps this goes back for its meaning to the statement of Abdul Rahmaan ibn Zaid ibn Aslam who said that it is one of the names of the *soorah*.

---

[1]However the report from Mujahid is weak, according to al-Zahraani. Cf., Ahmad al-Zahraani, notes to Abdul Rahmaan ibn Abi Haatim al-Raazi, *Tafseer al-Quran al-Adheem* (Madinah: Maktabah al-Daar, 1408 A.H.), vol. 1, p. 29.

Every *soorah* may be termed the Quran but it is far-fetched to say that *alif lam meem saad* is a name for the Quran as a whole. It comes to a person's mind when he hears someone say, "I read *alif lam meem saad*" that he is referring to *soorah al-Araaf* and not all of the Quran. Allah knows best.

An Eleventh View: They Stand for Specific Meanings

For example, the meaning of *alif lam meem* is أنا الله أعلم "I am Allah, Most Knowing." This has been narrated from ibn Abbaas, ibn Masood and Saeed ibn Jubair. However, the chains of transmission for this narration from ibn Abbaas and Saeed ibn Jubair are both weak.[1]

One other interpretation is that the letters stand for names. In this case, الألف for Allah, اللام for Jibraaeel and الميم for Muhammad. Commenting on this opinion, al-Munaawi stated that that is not known [that is, through chains] from Ibn Abbaas or from any of the early scholars.[2]

Another interpretation is that the *alif* stands for Allah, the *lam* for *Lateef* and the *meem* for *Majeed*. This was stated by Abu al-Aliyah.

Al-Rabi' ibn Anas said,

All languages have in common these [three] letters out of the twenty-nine [of the Arabic alphabet]. Each one of them is the key of one of His names; each one of them is [one of the names of] His blessings and His trials; each one of them is in the duration and term of a people. Jesus, the son of Mary, said: "How wondrous! They speak [using the letters which stand for] His names, and they live through His sustenance.

---

[1] See al-Salafi, vol. 1, p. 125, fn. 5; al-Zahraani, vol. 1, p. 27, fn. 1; al-Huwaini, vol. 2, p. 56, fn. 2.
[2] Al-Munaawi, vol. 1, p. 126.

How can they deny Him. The *Alif* is the key of His name Allah, the *lam* of His Name *Lateef*, and the *mim* of His Name *Majid*; the *alif* stands for the blessings (*ala*) of God, the *lam* for His Gentleness (*Lutf*), and the *mim* for His Glory (*majd*); the *alif* is for one year, the *lam* thirty, and the *mim* forty...[1]

According to al-Salafi (1/124/fn. 3), this narration attributed to Isa (peace be upon him) is from the *Israaeeliyaat*[2] that has no basis whatsoever with respect to narrations from the Prophet Muhammad (peace be upon him).[3]

A Twelfth View: They are from the Posited, Man-Made Letters of the Arabic Alphabet Placed in Scrambled Form

They are simply letters of a posited, man-made alphabet. This has been narrated from Mujaahid. Perhaps it is this quote that led Abu Bakr al-Tabreezi to say, "Allah knew that some people of this nation would claim that the Quran was from pre-creation so He mentioned these letters to point to the fact that His words are from these same letters and therefore it could not be from pre-creation." Al-Tabreezi's explanation must be rejected outright because it is well-established that the Quran is from the eternal speech of Allah.

A Thirteenth View: They Represent Numerical Values

Al-Tabari states that he dislikes to mention the report of this nature because it is from a narrator who is not trustworthy. This is somewhat strange because al-Tabari

---

[1] Quoted from the English translation of al-Tabari.
[2] *Israaeeliyaat* refers to stories that originated with the Jews and Christians, as opposed to incidents that are proven by the Quran or sunnah.
[3] Al-Salafi, vol. 1, p. 124, fn. 3.

mentions many weak and even fabricated narrations in his commentary. However, just a few pages later, after the above comment, he produces the story in question.

The major argument of this group is that no other meaning is known for these letters. It is inconceivable that there are verses with no known meanings. Therefore, the only possible meaning is the numerical representations of these letters. Note, however, that this is a far cry from claiming, as many of them do, that the numbers represented in these letters stand for specific events that will occur. That is, one may be able to determine what numerical values they represent but one will never be able to claim to know what event or aspect those numbers are in reference to.

Ibn Katheer writes, "There are those who claim that the letters are indications of the knowledge of periods of [history] form which can be deduced the times of events, tribulations, and eschatological happenings; such men have claimed things of which they have no knowledge." This approach is most likely based on the following hadith that ibn Katheer records and points out is weak:

> Abu Yaasir ibn Akhtab with a group of his fellow Jews passed by the Messenger of Allah as he was reciting the beginning of *Soorah al-Baqarah.* He went with his brother Hayy ibn Akhtab and Ka'b ibn al-Ashraf to speak to the Prophet about the letters *alif lam meem.* They said, "We adjure you, by Allah, [to tell us]: Is it true that these came to you from heaven?" He answered, "Yes, thus did they come down." Then Hayy said, "It is the truth you tell, for I know the number of years of the duration of this community." Then he said, "How can we enter into the religion of a man, the duration of whose community shall be 71 years according to the computation of these letters?" The Messenger of Allah smiled. Then Hayy asked, "Is there more?" He

said, "Yes, *alif lam meem sad.*" Hayy said, "That means 161. Is there still more?" He said, "Yes, *alif lam ra.*" Hayy said, "We bear witness that if you really speak the truth, your community will have dominion for no more than 231 years. Is there more still?" The Prophet said, "Yes, *alif lam meem ra.*" Hayy then said, "We do not know which of your statements we should accept." Abu Yaasir said, "As for me, I bear witness that our prophets foretold the dominion of this community but did not say how long it would endure. Thus if Muhammad speaks the truth, I see that all this shall be granted to him by God."[1]

This view is also attributed to Muqaatil ibn Sulaimaan who is reported to have said, "We have computed the numerical values of the letters which are at the heads of the *soorahs*, discounting repetitions, and they came to 744 years, which is the remainder of the history of this community."[2] Historical reality alone demonstrates that Muqaatil's statement is unacceptable.

A Fourteenth View: Sufi-Esoteric Interpretation of the Letters

Another approach to these letters is the approach of the Sufis or esoteric commentaries. Their explanations are often baseless, many times obviously contradicting what the Quran itself clearly states. Even when their commentaries contain some wisdom, the effort needed to sift through what may be acceptable from what is truly meaningless and false is not worth the effort. However, with respect to the letters at the beginning of the *soorahs*, an example from their

---

[1]This translation was based on Ayyoub, vol. 1, p. 61.
[2]Quoted by Ayyoub, vol. 1, p. 61 from al-Tabarsi (1/69-70).

commentaries, which demonstrates their way of thinking, is given below.[1]

> Nisaaburi, in his popular work *Ghara'ib al-Quran*, collects several such exegetical interpretations. "Every one of these letters signifies one of God's names or attributes. This *alif* means that He is One [*Ahad*], Eternal without beginning [*azali*] or end [*abadi*]. The *lam* means that He is most Gracious [*Latif*] and the *mim* that He is most Glorious [*majid*]... *alif* signifies Allah, *lam* Jibril [Gabriel] and *mim* Muhammad; that is to say, God sent down this book through the mediation of Gabriel to Muhammad" (Nisaaburi, I, p. 135). Nisaaburi reports that Sufis said, "*Alif* is *ana* [I], *lam li* [mine] and *mim minni* [from me]." They also say, "The *alif* is an allusion to the necessity of following the straight path of the *shariah* at the beginning [of the disciples' course of initiation]... the *lam* signifies the bowing down which the disciple experiences at the time of *mujahadat* [spiritual struggles, or struggles with the carnal soul]; this is the heeding of the *tariqah* [Sufi path]... The *mim* signifies the servant's becoming in the station [*maqam*] of love like a circle, whose end is its beginning and whose beginning is its end. This can be achieved only through complete annihiliation [*fana*] in God. This is the station of *haqiqah* [absolute reality]"... "The letters also mean '*alastu bi rabbikum?*' [Am I not your Lord?] [Q. 7:172], and that is the sealing of the Book of Covenant [*'ahd*] on the day of the primordial covenant [*mithaq*]".

Ibn Arabi offers yet another Sufi interpretation of the unconnected letters. God, according to ibn Arabi,

---

[1]This is taken from Ayyoub, vol. 1, pp. 58-60.

"has referred in these three letters to the entire existence from the point of view of its totality. Thus *alif* refers to the divine essence which is the First of existence... *lam* refers to the active intellect which is called Gabriel. It is the middle point of existence, receiving the emanation of the First, and itself overflowing upon the end of existence. *Mim* refers to Muhammad, who is the end of existence. Through him the circle of existence is completed. Thus he [the Prophet] said, "Surely, time has turned about back to its original form on the day when God created the heavens and the earth.'" Ibn Arabi then argues that *alif*, as the name of the divine essence, is the basis of all letters, so that the *lam* composed of two *alifs* and the *mim* includes it. Thus "every name is a reference to the essence which includes one or another of the attributes; it is as well a reference to the actions which became hidden in it in the Muhammadan image which is the greatest name of God." Hence, according to ibn Arabi, Muhammad and Gabriel, as concrete expressions of the divine essence, each represents one of God's names. "Gabriel is the manifestation of knowledge; he is His name the All-Knowing [*a-alim*]; Muhammad is the manifestation of wisdom; He is His name the All-wise [*al-Hakim*]."

Ibn Arabi concludes his interpretation with a typical Shi'i exegesis of the letters.[1] He writes, "The meaning of the verse *'alif lam mim'* is: this is the Book promised as the all-encompassing form alluded to in the *jafr* and *jami'ah* which contains everything."

---

[1]Unfortunately, many people either do not see or do not wish to see the strong connection between Sufism and Shiism and how both have clearly deviated from the teachings of the Prophet Muhammad (peace be upon him) and the practices of his Companions.

The *jafr* is a receptacle or a book which Ali is said to have inherited from the Prophet and passed on to his descendants the imams. The *jafr* contains knowledge of what has already passed and what is yet to come until the day of resurrection. The *jami'ah* is a scroll which contains knowledge of lawful and unlawful things. It was dictated by the Prophet to Ali, who passed it on to the imams as part of their inheritance of prophetic knowledge. Ibn Arabi continues, "It is a promised [book] in that it shall be with the Mahdi [expected messiah] at the end of time. No one shall read it truly as it is except him. The *jafr* is a tablet of the great void [*fada*'], which is the world of intellect. The *jami'ah* is the tablet of destiny, which is the world of the universal soul.

Certainly, a portion of Abdullah Yusuf Ali's comments to these letters must also go here. He wrote (p. 17, fn. 25):

If we look to the nature of the sounds which the letters represent, A is a breathing and comes from the throat, L is a lingual-palatal-dental sound from the middle of the mouth, and M is a labial or lip-sound. Can we not take them as symbolical of the Beginning, Middle and End? If so, are they not appropriate to the Suras which treat specifically Life, Growth, and Death- the Beginning and the End? In the New Testament Greek scripture, the first and the last letters of the Greek alphabet, Alpha and Omega, are symbolical of the Beginning and the End, and give one of the titles of God: "I am Alpha and Omega, the beginning and the ending, saith the Lord, which is, which was, and which is to come, the Almighty," (Rev. i. 8). The symbolism of the three things is better with three letters.

A Fifteenth View: Abbreviations of the Scribes Who Recorded or Codified the Soorahs

Some Orientalists have made the outlandish claim that these letters are not actually part of the Quran but actually refer to the name of the scribe who recorded the *soorah* during the Prophet's time or the name of the person who codified the *soorah* at a later date. Asad (p. 992) has replied to these authors by writing,

> None the less [*sic*], it is established beyond any possibility of doubt that all the Companions-obviously following the example of the Prophet-regarded the *muqatta'at* as integral parts of the *soorahs* to which they are prefixed, and used to recite them accordingly:[1] a fact which disposes effectively of the suggestion advanced by some Western orientalists that these letters may be no more than the initials of the scribes who wrote down the individual revelations of the Prophet's dictation, or of the Companions who recorded them at the time of the final codification of the Quran during the reign of the first three Caliphs.

---

[1] It would have been best had Asad mentioned the hadith concerning the reward for reading the Quran in which the Prophet (peace be upon him) stated, "I do not say that *Alif Lam Mim* is a *harf* but *Alif* is a *harf*..."

20

The Conclusions of the Major Quranic Commentators on This Question

Al-Tabari's Views

Al-Tabari makes the following conclusion (from translation 1/88-89)

> According to me, the proper interpretation of those openings of the suras which are letters of the alphabet is that Allah, exalted is His praise, made them discrete letters and did not join them together... because He wished their pronunciation to signify many meanings, not [just] one meaning, for each one of them. [This is] just what al-Rabi' ibn Anas said, although al-Rabi' confined himself to three meanings, without adding any more.

> The correct interpretation of them, according to me, is that every one of these letters comprises what al-Rabi' said, and also what the rest of the exegetes have said, except the opinion of the Arabic expert I mentioned who said that the interpretation is that they are [just] letters of the alphabet [with no meaning, like ABC]... For this latter is a pernicious error, because it is foreign to what all the Companions, the Followers, and the experts in exegesis and interpretation who followed in their footsteps have said.

Then he is forced to answer the following question: How can a single letter comprise the signification of many different meanings? He says that this is permissible in the same way that one word may have many meanings to it. For example, the word *ummah* is used throughout the Quran to mean many different things. Hence, there is no harm if one letter, like one word, could possibly have many different meanings.

Therefore, he concludes that almost all of the interpretations of these opening letters that he mentioned in his *tafseer*, such as names of the *soorah*, a swearing, and so forth, are all possible and acceptable and compatible with his conclusion of the interpretation of these disjointed letters. He further states (1/94) that if Allah had desired to mean only one of those possible interpretations, then He would made have made that clear and the Prophet (peace be upon him) would have explained such. Then he states (1/94),

> The fact that the Prophet (peace be upon him) left them without explaining them so that it would not be understood that it meant part of its possible meanings is the greatest evidence that they mean all of their possible meanings. Logically, this is not impossible at all. It is not illogical that a word with one lettering and one spelling could have lots of meanings to it.

He tries to further support his argument by saying that if that opinion is objected to, then the person has to prove the one opinion that he supports while there is no evidence to support one opinion over the other.

However, there seems to be a number of problems with al-Tabari's approach. First, it is true that a word may have many different connotations in different places but what is not the case or what he does not prove is the possibility of one word meaning many different things at one place or usage. This is something that is in need of proof and al-Tabari does not offer any such proof. Second, to imply that all of the views are acceptable and correct is untenable. Al-Tabari seems to accept any number of interpretations and explicitly states that the meanings stated by al-Rabi ibn Anas are all correct—but they are not the only ones that are correct. But how can he make such a statement when there is absolutely no evidence for al-Rabi's interpretation for the letters? If someone comes along today and thinks of new meanings for the three letters, should one understand from this that al-Tabari would accept that new meaning even though there is no evidence for that new meaning?

It seems that al-Tabari was simply trying to encompass all of the different opinions into one general approach. However, he has failed to do so because, in essence, he offers no proof for his approach except to say that any other approach is in need of evidence.

In general, al-Tabari's approach to this question has been fairly strongly refuted by ibn Katheer (1/73-74).

Al-Zamakhshari's Views

Al-Zamakhshari has an extraordinarily lengthy discussion of these letters, considering them in detail from a linguistic point of view. In fact, Abu Hayyaan (1/60) had the following to say about al-Zamakhshari's lengthy discussion, "Al-Zamakhshari and others spoke a great deal about those letters in a way that does not lead to much benefit from a *tafseer* point of view and for much of what they say, there is no evidence."

However, the gist of his argument and conclusion is the following: These assorted letters, placed in such a fashion, posed a challenge to others and a way to invite them to witness the unique structure of the Quran. It was meant to pique their curiosity and to realize that what they were hearing was a true miracle that was in its essence unique and different from what humans compose. Even though they considered themselves the greatest when it came to language and eloquence, all of their works could not come close to what they were now hearing.

He points out that the sounds in these letters encompass all the kinds of possible sounds from the point of view of speech, as was mentioned earlier. Ibn Katheer (1/75) further summarizes some of al-Zamakhshari's lengthy discussion by saying,

> Al-Zamakhshari has said that not all of them were stated at the beginning of the Quran. Instead, they were spaced out in order to make the challenge even greater in the same way that many of the stories in the Quran are repeated throughout and in the same way that the challenge to produce something similar to the Quran is found in different places. Sometimes only one letter is mentioned, as in *Saad, Noon,* and *Qaaf.* Sometimes two letters are mentioned, as in *Ha-Meem.* Sometimes, three, as in *Alif-Lam-Meem.* Sometimes four, as in *alif-lam-meem-ra* and *alif-lam-meem-saad.* And sometimes five, as in *kaf-ha-ya-ain-saad* and *ha-meem-ain-seen-qaaf.* This is because their words [that is, the Arabs' words] are made up from such wordings and roots, one letter, two letters, three letters, four letters and five letters, and none more than that.

Ibn Katheer points out that this is also the view of ibn Taimiyyah and al-Mizi. Al-Qaasimi (1/32) quotes al-Zamakhshari at length and seems to support or be satisfied with his view. The commentator on the *Aqeedah* of al-Tahaawi, ibn Abu al-Izz (2/205), who was greatly influenced by ibn Taimiyyah, also seems to support this view of the letters. Al-Zuhaili also supports this opinion. This opinion is also advanced by Sayyid Qutb who wrote,

> These letters are an allusion to the fact that this book is composed of these and similar letters which were familiar to the Arabs to whom the Quran was addressed. Yet in spite of this, it is the Book; a

miracle the like of which they were unable to compose out of these same letters. For such is the way of God with all His creatures; all that men can produce from the particles of this earthly soil are different shapes and devices. God, the Originator, makes from it life endowed with movement and reason.[1]

Al-Raazi's View

After reviewing twenty-one different opinions on this question, Al-Raazi concludes that these verses or disjointed letters must simply stand as names for the *soorahs*. His argument is the following: The best interpretation among the detailed scholars is that those letters are the names of the *soorahs*. This is because those letters are either understandable or they are not. The latter is definitely false, as otherwise one could speak to an Arab in a foreign tongue. Furthermore, Allah has described the entire Quran as guidance. Therefore, it could not possibly be something that is not understood. Now, Allah either meant by them a specific title or a specific meaning. The second is false because those letters, in the way they are presented, do not make up any meaning in the Arabic language, especially those meanings that are mentioned by some of the Quranic commentators. Therefore, these letters cannot be understood in such a way because the Quran is in Arabic and they do not have such meanings in Arabic. Furthermore, those commentators mention many different meanings and there is no proof to prefer one of those meanings over any other ones. One could only accept them all— but that is impossible because they cannot all be reconciled and none of the commentators accepted all of their meanings, they only

---

[1] From Ayyoub, 1/ pp. 58-59.

accepted one of their meanings. Therefore, the only thing that is left is that they are some kind of name or title.

However, he also states that there may be another wisdom in those letters: These letters were meant to attract the attention of the people who were refusing to listen to the Quran. When they heard those letters, they immediately became quiet and listened to what was being recited.

Afterwards al-Raazi presents many objections to his view that these letters act as names for the *soorahs* but he goes on to refute all of those possible objections (2/9f).

Ibn Katheer's View

As noted, ibn Katheer was not very pleased with al-Tabari's conclusions concerning this matter. He himself, however, took a much more cautious approach. He stated that there is no question that Allah did not reveal those letters in vain or sport. He continued,

> Those ignorant people who say that there is some wordings in the Quran that one worships by and that have no meaning to them are very wrong. They certainly have some meaning to them. If we have something authentic from the Prophet (peace be upon him), we would state that. Otherwise, we stop at what we know and we say, "We believe in all of as coming from our Lord." The scholars have not agreed upon any specific meaning to them. They have differed. If a scholar has some evidence for an opinion, then he should follow that opinion. Otherwise, he should not express an opinion until the matter becomes clear to him.

After refuting a number of different views of these letters (mentioned above), ibn Katheer seems to lean towards the view of his teacher ibn Taimiyyah that these letters were placed there as a sign of the miraculous nature of the Quran that it is made up of the same letters that the Arabs use in their everyday speech. After quoting al-Zamakhshari on this point, ibn Katheer adds that it is the case that every *soorah* that opens with such letters is then followed by a reference to the Book itself, such as the case with *soorah al-Baqarah.*

Abu Hayyaan's View

Abu Hayyaan also argues that the meaning of these letters is not known and that they form the *mutashaabihaat* of the Quran. He wrote (1/60), "The opinion I follow is that those letters at the beginning of the *soorahs* are from the *mutashaabihaat* concerning which Allah has concealed their knowledge. As for the rest of His speech, it is from the *muhkam* (whose meanings are known)."

Al-Shaukaani's View

Al-Shaukaani (1/32) is of the same view as ibn Katheer that it is best not to speak about these verses since there is nothing authentically recorded from the Prophet (peace be upon him) on this matter. He wrote, "What I follow for myself and for anyone who wants to be safe and follow the way of the early scholars is not to say anything about that, while recognizing that there is some wisdom in their revelation that has not reached our minds and which our understandings have not been guided to."

Al-Shaukaani also has a long discussion showing why the opinions of the Companions should not be followed on this issue. He says that they are so contradicting that this is an evidence that their own statements were simply based on *ijtihaad* and not on something coming from the Messenger of Allah (peace be upon him). He points out that not all of their opinions can be accepted since they are contradicting. In addition, there is no possible way to determine which of their different opinions should be accepted. Instead, one must resign himself to the fact that they were speaking based on their own opinion on this matter and they, like the later generations, had no true knowledge of the meanings of these verses. They will be, Allah willing, rewarded for their *ijtihaad* in this manner as they were people who were qualified to make *ijtihaad*.

Actually, the situation is not as bad as al-Shaukaani makes it seem. If one distinguishes between the authentic and weak narrations coming from the different Companions, one will then note that much of what is narrated from them is not authentic. And, in addition, the remainder that is authentic is not necessarily completely contradictory, as shall be noted later.

Al-Saadi's View

Al-Saadi must also be considered one of those scholars who consider it best not to comment on these letters and who believe that their real meaning is known only to Allah. In fact, his short passage on this topic is very similar to ibn Katheer's passage. He wrote (1/39), "As for the disjoined letters at the beginning of the *soorahs*, it is safest to remain silent and not to express their meanings without any *Shareeah* basis— with the firm conviction that Allah did not reveal them in vain, but due to a wisdom that we do not know."

Maudoodi's View

Concerning these letters, Maudoodi wrote (1/45) (apparently borrowing heavily from ibn al-Jauzi, however, without any reference to ibn al-Jauzi),

> The names of letters of the Arabic alphabet, called *huruf muqatta'at*, occur at the beginning of several

soorahs of the Quran. At the time of the Quranic revelation the use of such letters was a well-known literary device, used by both poets and orators, and we find several instances in the pre-Islamic Arabic literature that has come down to us.

Since the *muqatta'at* were commonly used, the Arabs of that period generally knew what they meant and so they did not present a puzzle. We do not notice, therefore, any contemporaries of the Prophet (peace be upon him) raising objections against the Quran on the ground that the letters at the beginning of some of its *soorahs* were absurd. For the same reason, no Tradition has come down to us of any Companion asking the Prophet about the significance of the *muqatta'at*. Later on this literary device gradually fell into disuse and hence it became difficult for commentators to determine their precise meanings.[1] It is obvious, however, that deriving right guidance from the Quran does not depend on grasping the meaning of these vocables, and that anyone who fails to understand them may still live a righteous life and attain salvation. The ordinary reader, therefore, need not delve too deeply into this matter.

Al-Dausiri (2/1), who did not wish to enter into a long discussion of this question, seems to be of the exact same view as Maudoodi.

---

[1] This aspect of his discussion is questionable because very early scholars had also debated the meanings of these verses. Hence, it was not a process that occurred over time and that confused later commentators.

Al-Adawi's View

After presenting many of the earlier stated opinions concerning the disjointed letters, al-Adawi makes the following astute and pertinent comment:

> To the best of my knowledge, concerning these letters, nothing authentic has been narrated concerning their meanings from the one who is protected from error [the Prophet Muhammad (peace be upon him)]. The scholars have also not agreed upon any specific interpretation. They have differed, as you have seen, and their statements are numerous. Therefore, the matter is as some of the scholars have stated: If, in someone's view, a specific opinion appears to have some evidence for it, he should follow that opinion. Otherwise, he should refrain from any opinion until the correct stance is made clear to him.[1]

Conclusions

Before concluding, a quick listing of the above fifteen views would be appropriate:

(1) They are from the *mutashaabihaataat* whose meanings are not known;

(2) They are letters that make up a name of Allah;

(3) They are letters by which Allah is swearing and they are from His names;

(4) They are letters by which Allah is swearing;

(5) They are Allah's greatest name;

---

[1] Mustafa ibn al-Adawi, *Al-Tasheel li-Taweel al-Tanzeel—al-Tafseer fi Suaal wa Jawaab (Soorah al-Faatihah wa Awal Soorah al-Baqarah)* (Riyadh: Daar al-Qaasim, 1996), vol. 1, p. 148.

(6) They are the opening by which Allah begins specific *soorah*s;

(7) They are an inference to the remaining letters of the alphabet;

(8) They are from the abbreviations that the Arabs used in their speech;

(9) They are names for the *soorahs*;

(10) They are from the names of the Quran:

(11) They stand for specific meanings;

(12) They are from the posited, man-made letters of the alphabet;

(13) They represent numerical values;

(14) Sufi-esoteric interpretation of the letters;

(15) Abbreviations of the names of the scribes who recorded or codified the *soorahs*.

The different opinions concerning the interpretation of the disjointed letters at the beginning of different *soorahs* of the Quran may be divided into different categories. Basically these are three categories: (1) Those opinions that are baseless and those that are based on weak narrations from the Companions; (2) Those opinions that are plausible but not very likely due to some defect; and (3) Those opinions that seem to have some support for them.

From among the first category are the following opinions:

(1) They are letters that form the name of Allah.

(2) They are Allah's name that He is swearing by.

(3) It is the greatest name of Allah.

(4) They stand for specific meanings.

(5) They represent numerical values.

(6) The Sufi-esoteric interpretations of the letters.

(7) They are abbreviations of the names of the scribes who recorded or codified the *soorahs*.

The second category would include the following:

(1) They are letters that Allah is swearing by. The defect in this opinion is that the letters, al-Qurtubi pointed out, do not appear in the manner in which oaths appear.

(2) They are names of the Quran. This is rejected because, as ibn Katheer pointed out, the correct interpretation of this view is that they are names of parts of the Quran and cannot be considered names for the Quran as a whole.

(3) They are letters of a posited alphabet. This actually is not an explanation for these letters but simply a statement of fact concerning them.

This leaves the following plausible explanations for these letters:

(1) They are from the *mutashaabihaat* and only Allah knows their exact meanings. This concept will be discussed in more detail below.

(2) They are the manner in which Allah begins specific *soorahs*. In this manner, they set off different *soorahs* from one another. They may have been placed at the beginning of different *soorahs* to attract the attention of the listeners as was sometimes practiced in the time of *jaahiliyyah*.

(3) They are an inference to the alphabet as a whole. That is, Allah is pointing out to mankind that the Quran is made up of the same kind of speech and letters that mankind uses yet it is impossible for mankind to create anything similar to the Quran.

(4) They are names for the *soorahs*.

(5) They are similar to the abbreviations that were commonly used by the Arabs in their poetry.

Note that there is no contradiction between these last three opinions. That is, these letters are certainly letters that Allah begins certain *soorahs* with and they were never questioned by the people, so they might have been treated like the disjointed letters used in Arabic poetry by the people. In addition, however, they certainly are used and continue to be used, at least some of them, to refer to specific *soorahs*. Hence, it cannot be denied that they are viable names for different *soorahs*. At the same time, however, there may be an additional wisdom which Allah has put in these letters. And that is that these letters form the language of the Arabs, which is the same language as the Quran, yet the disbelieving Arabs, who used all their resources to fight the Prophet (peace be upon him), could not possibly produce anything as miraculous as the Quran. Finally, it must also be noted that in addition to all of the above, these letters may have some meaning to them and that meaning is known only to Allah.

That is, one must distinguish between the use of these letters (used as openings for different *soorahs*, as titles for the different *soorahs*), the role these letters may have played (to make the listener attentive to what follows it), the wisdom behind these letters (pointing out the miraculous nature of the Quran), and the meaning of these letters (which are known only to Allah). When looked at in this manner, analyzing the different functions or roles of these letters, more than one explanation can be given as to their meaning, purpose or role without any contradiction whatsoever.

Is it Necessary for Every Verse to Have a Meaning that is Understood by the Creation?

As was already noted, there are some quotes from different Companions that state that the meanings of these letters are known only to Allah. Again, these quotes are: From Abu Bakr al-Siddeeq, "Allah has for every book a secret aspect and the secret aspect in the Quran is the beginning of the *soorahs*." And Ali is reported to have said, "Every Book has a special characteristic and the special characteristic of this book is the assorted letters." Some have even claimed that this is the interpretation that has been passed on from most of the early scholars.

These quotes may be found in the *Tafseer* of al-Thalabi which is not available to this author. Unfortunately, all of the *tafseer*s that make a reference to these quotes do not present the chains for the quotes. Therefore, it was not possible to ascertain the authenticity of these narrations.[1]

Al-Raazi (2/3ff) discussed the question of whether it is possible that there are certain verses in the Quran whose meanings are not known in great detail. The *mutakalimoon* (scholastic theologians) present arguments from the Quran, hadith and rational arguments to show that it must be the case that every verse has a meaning that can be understood by the creation.

They quote fourteen verses from the Quran to support their contention. Among the verses they quote are the following:

$$ أَفَلَا يَتَدَبَّرُونَ الْقُرْآنَ وَلَوْ كَانَ مِنْ عِنْدِ غَيْرِ اللَّهِ لَوَجَدُوا فِيهِ اخْتِلَافًا كَثِيرًا $$

"Have they not pondered over the Quran. If it were from other than Allah they would certainly have found therein lots of contradictions" (*al-Nisaa* 82).

$$ أَفَلَا يَتَدَبَّرُونَ الْقُرْآنَ أَمْ عَلَى قُلُوبٍ أَقْفَالُهَا $$

"Do they not ponder over the Quran or is over their hearts a seal" (*Muhammad* 24). The argument from these verses is that it is not possible for someone to ponder over the Quran or note if there are any discrepancies in the Quran when part of the Quran is not understandable.

$$ وَإِنَّهُ لَتَنْزِيلُ رَبِّ الْعَالَمِينَ نَزَلَ بِهِ الرُّوحُ الْأَمِينُ عَلَى قَلْبِكَ لِتَكُونَ مِنَ الْمُنْذِرِينَ بِلِسَانٍ عَرَبِيٍّ مُبِينٍ $$

---

[1] Even al-Huwaini did not discuss their chains but simply referred the reader to al-Qurtubi's commentary, in which these reports also do not appear with their complete chains.

"And truly, this [Quran] is a revelation from the Lord of the Worlds which the trustworthy spirit has brought down upon your heart that you may be of the warners in the plain Arabic language" (*al-Shuaraa* 192-195). If the Quran is not understood, then the Prophet (peace be upon him) would not be a warner with it. Similarly, the last portion states that it is in clear Arabic. This by necessity implies that it must be understood.

The rest of their arguments are similar to the two verses mentioned above. With respect to the hadith of the Prophet (peace be upon him), they quote, for example, the following hadith:

تَرَكْتُ فِيكُمْ أَمْرَيْنِ لَنْ تَضِلُّوا مَا تَمَسَّكْتُمْ بِهِمَا كِتَابَ اللَّهِ
وَسُنَّةَ نَبِيِّهِ

"I have left among you two matters that if you adhere to them you will never be misguided: the Book of Allah and the sunnah of His prophet."[1] Again, the argument here is how can the people stick to and follow the Quran if it is not understandable?

As for rational arguments, they state that if there is something in its speech that is not understood, it would be like speaking to the Arabs in a foreign language and that is inconceivable of the Quran. Secondly, the purpose of speech and communication is understanding. If the speech itself is not understandable *in toto*, then that speech is vain and nonsense. Obviously, one would not say that of the Quran. Third, the Quran challenges mankind to produce something similar to it, yet if it is not understandable, this challenge does not make any sense.

---

[1] Recorded by Maalik. Al-Haakim has something similar that al-Albaani graded *sahih*. See Muhammad Naasir al-Deen al-Albaani, *Saheeh al-Jaami al-Sagheer* (Beirut: al-Maktab al-Islaami, 1986), vol. 1, p. 566.

However, the proponents of the other view also present their arguments. They begin with the Quranic verse,

وَمَا يَعْلَمُ تَأْوِيلَهُ إِلاَّ اللَّهُ وَالرَّاسِخُونَ فِي الْعِلْمِ يَقُولُونَ آمَنَّا بِهِ كُلٌّ مِنْ عِنْدِ رَبِّنَا وَمَا يَذَّكَّرُ إِلاَّ أُوْلُوا الأَلْبَابِ

"No one knows its *taweel* [explanation] except Allah. And those well-grounded in knowledge say, 'We believe in all of it as coming from our Lord.' And none will grasp the message except those of understanding" (*ali-Imraan* 7). This shows the special place of the scholars in that they believe in all that is revealed although they realize that some of what is revealed is unknown to them. Furthermore, if the interpretation of the verses referred in this passage was meant to be sought, why does Allah blame those who seek such interpretations in the preceding portion of the verse,

فَأَمَّا الَّذِينَ فِي قُلُوبِهِمْ زَيْغٌ فَيَتَّبِعُونَ مَا تَشَابَهَ مِنْهُ ابْتِغَاءَ الْفِتْنَةِ وَابْتِغَاءَ تَأْوِيلِهِ

"As for those in whose hearts is deviance, they seek what is not entirely clear, seeking thereby trials and seeking its *taweel*" (*ali-Imraan* 7).

Furthermore, and this is one of their strongest evidences, if these narrations are authentic, there are narrations from the Companions stating that the meaning of these verses are not known or are secrets of Allah.

Finally, with respect to rational arguments, these scholars claim that what Muslims are ordered to do or believe in falls into two categories: those acts whose wisdom is understood, like the prayers, fasting and so forth, and those acts whose wisdom is not known, such as some of the acts of the pilgrimage. Then, al-Raazi writes (2/5) that it is right and proper that Allah orders his believers to do both types of acts. This is because the first category of acts does not demonstrate one's real willingness to submit to Allah. Instead, the person may be submitting only to what his mind accepts. If this is true with respect to acts that one must perform, may that also be a possibility for the wordings that Allah asks one to believe in? In other words, Allah sometimes reveals what humans understand as well as some aspect that they do not understand. The goal or purpose would be for them to demonstrate that they accept all of it, not just what their minds understand. There could be another point here. If man understands all of something completely, the worth of that thing in his heart falls. However, when there is some aspect that he still cannot grasp, although he is certain that such speech has come from Allah, his heart will always be attuned to it, trying to achieve what it has not yet achieved. He will always be thinking about it and pondering over it; hence, his heart remains attached to it. That may be a great wisdom and benefit to these letters of the Quran.

The following quotes are also of extreme value:

Rabee ibn Khuthaim said, "Allah has revealed this Quran and He has kept hidden of its knowledge whatever He willed and He has exposed to you of its knowledge whatever He willed. As for what He has kept hidden, you will not be able to achieve it, so do not ask about it. As for what He has shown you, this is what you are going to be asked about and tested concerning. You do not know everything there is to know of the Quran and [however] not all that you know do you actually act upon."

Abu Bakr al-Anbaari then said, "This makes it clear that the meaning of those letters in the Quran has been hidden from all of mankind as a trial from Allah and a test. Whoever believes in them will be rewarded and made happy. Whoever disbelieves in them or doubts them commits a sin and will be turned further away from Allah's mercy."

Abdullah ibn Masood said, "There is no faith of a believer better than his faith in the Unseen." Then he recited the verses at the beginning of *al-Baqarah*, "Those who believe in the Unseen."

Related Points

(1) Allah begins the Quran, His Book of Guidance, with these letters that should always remind humans of their limited knowledge and their need for Allah to guide them. Although the Quran is a book of guidance, without Allah's help and assistance, no one will achieve the knowledge and guidance of the Quran.

(2) Furthermore, no human can encompass all of the knowledge of this world. However, everyone will be asked about the knowledge that he did have and how he applied it. Hence, it is important to realize that the goal of knowledge is not knowledge in itself but application. One must always seek to increase his knowledge but he must be more concerned with applying the knowledge that he already possesses than pondering knowledge that he does not possess.

(3) Some scholars consider these letters a separate verse while others do not (combining them with the next words as one verse). This is one reason why there is a slight difference in the numbering of verses in different copies of the Quran. The people from Kufah consider them separate verses standing by themselves while the Basrans and others consider them part of the following words.[1]

Bibliography

Ali, A. Yusuf. *The Glorious Quran: Translation and Commentary.* American Trust Publications. 1977.

---

[1] Cf., Abu Hayyaan, vol. 2, pp. 60-61.

Asad, Muhammad *The Message of the Quran.* Gibraltar: Daar al-Andalus. 1980.

Ayoub, Mahmoud M. *The Quran and its Interpreters.* Albany, NY: State University of New York Press. 1984.

Al-Baghawi, al-Hussain. *Tafseer al-Baghawi: Maalim al-Tanzeel.* Riyadh: Daar Taibah, 1409 A.H.

al-Baidhaawi, *Anwaar al-Tanzeel wa Israar al-Taweel.* In *Kitaab Majmuaat min al-Tafaaseer.* Beirut: Daar Ihyaa al-Turaath al-Arabi.

Cooper, J., trans. *The Commentary on the Quran: al-Tabari.* Oxford, England: Oxford University Press. 1987.

Daryabadi, Abdul Majid. *The Holy Quran.* Karachi, Pakistan: The Taj Company Limited. 1971.

al-Dausiri, Abdul Rahmaan. *Sifwat al-Athaar wa Mafaaheem min Tafseer al-Quran al-Adheem.* Al-Kuwait: Daar al-Arqam. n.d.

Al-Huwaini, Abu Ishaaq. Footnotes to Imaad al-Deen Ismaaeel ibn Katheer. *Tafseer al-Quran al-Adheem.* Al-Damaam, Saudi Arabia: Daar ibn al-Jauzi. 1997.

ibn Abi Haatim, Abdul Rahmaan. *Tafseer al-Quran al-Adheem Musnadan an Rasoolillah wa al-Sahaabah wa al-Tabieen.* Makkah: Maktabah Nazaar Mustafa al-Baaz. 1997.

ibn al-Adawi, Mustafa. *Al-Tasheel li-Taweel al-Tanzeel—al-Tafseer fi Suaal wa Jawaab (Soorah al-Faatihah wa Awal Soorah al-Baqarah).* Riyadh: Daar al-Qaasim. 1996.

ibn Katheer, Ismaaeel. *Tafseer ibn Katheer.* Beirut: Daar al-Qalam. n.d.

ibn Qutaiba, Muhammad. *Taweel Mushkil al-Quran.* Madinah: al-Maktabah al-Ilmiyyah. 1981.

Maudoodi, Abul Ala. *The Meaning of the Quran.* Lahore, Pakistan: Islamic Publications, 1982.

Al-Munaawi, Abdul Raoof. *Al-Fath al-Samaawi bi-Takhreej Ahadeeth Tafseer al-Qaadhi al-Baidhaawi.* Riyadh: Daar al-Aasimah, 1409 A.H.

Al-Qaasimi, Jamaal al-Deen. *Mahaasan al-Taweel.* Beirut: Daar al-Fikr. 1978.

Al-Qurtubi, Muhammad. *Al-Jaami Li-Ahkaam al-Quran.* Beirut: Daar Ihyaa al-Turaath al-Arabi. 1965.

Al-Raazi, Fakhr al-Deen. *Al-Tafseer al-Kabeer.* Beirut: Daar Ihyaa al-Turaath al-Arabi. n.d.

al-Salafi, Ahmad. Footnotes to Abdul Raoof al-Munaawi. *al-Fath al-Samaawi bi-Takhreej Ahadeeth Tafseer al-Qaadhi al-Baidhaawi.* Riyadh: Daar al-Aasimah, 1409 A.H.

Al-Suyooti, Jalaal al-Deen. *Al-Durr al-Manthoor fi al-Tafseer bi-l-Mathoor.* Beirut: Daar al-Marifah. n.d.

al-Tabari, Muhammad ibn Jareer. *Jaami al-Bayaan an Taweel Ayi al-Quran.* Beirut: Daar al-Fikr, 1988

Tafsir ibn Katheer: Abridged by Sheikh Muhammad Nasib ar-Rifai. London: Al-Firdous, Ltd., 1996.

al-Zahraani, Ahmad. Notes to Abdul Rahmaan ibn Abi Haatim al-Raazi. *Tafseer al-Quran al-Adheem.* Madinah: Maktabah al-Daar, 1408 A.H.

al-Zamakhshari, Mahmood. *al-Kashaaf an Haqaaiq Ghawaamidh al-Tanzeel.* Beirut: Daar al-Kutub al-Arabi. 1987.

From the Quran:
Allah's Description of the Hypocrites[1]

al-Baqarah 8-9

Allah says in the Quran,

وَمِنَ النَّاسِ مَنْ يَقُولُ آمَنَّا بِاللَّهِ وَبِالْيَوْمِ الآخِرِ وَمَا هُمْ
بِمُؤْمِنِينَ يُخَادِعُونَ اللَّهَ وَالَّذِينَ آمَنُوا وَمَا يَخْدَعُونَ إلاَّ
أَنفُسَهُمْ وَمَا يَشْعُرُونَ

"And of mankind are some who say, 'We believe in Allah and the Last Day,' and they believe not. They think to beguile Allah and those who believe. And they beguile none save themselves, yet they do not perceive this fact" (*al-Baqarah* 8-9).

Allah began *soorah al-Baqarah* by describing the believers and then their absolute opposites, the unbelievers. Now, Allah moves on to another group of disbelievers, the hypocrites. Allah has used more verses to describe the hypocrites than the other two groups perhaps due to the fact that the hypocrites are much more dangerous for the Muslim society.

---

[1] This article appeared in *al-Basheer*, vol. 1, No. 3 (September 1987). The purpose of these articles in the early years of *al-Basheer* was to present some of the lessons of the verses of the Quran. They were not meant to be a detailed discussion of *tafseer* (Quranic commentary). Hence, they are not heavy in references and footnote material. References to well-known Quranic commentators imply that the discussion was taken from the relevant *tafseer*'s commentary on the respective verse.

41

Concerning these verses Qataadah said, "These verses describe the hypocrites. They accept (the religion) with their tongues and reject it with their hearts. The testify to it with their tongues and deny it with their actions. They appear in one way although they are following a completely different way." In this verse, Allah clearly says that they do not believe although they claim belief. This proves that the sect called al-Karramiya (and others who hold the same beliefs today) are wrong in their claim that *imaan* (faith and belief) is only a statement of the tongue and it has nothing to do with the heart. Indeed, *imaan* is not just a statement of the tongue but it is foremost the belief in the heart in conjunction with the actions of the tongue and the body.

In these verses Allah makes it clear to us that the hypocrites are different from the believers and they are also different from the people who are openly disbelievers. The disbelievers are clear and staunch concerning their disbelief and thus they are not as great a harm for the Muslims since they are so easily definable and noticeable. What is much more dangerous and harmful for the Muslims are those who do not truly believe yet they claim to be believers and, therefore, the Muslims trust them and take them as friends, allies and so forth. Such hypocrites actually have a hatred in their hearts for Islam and for the Muslims although the Muslims think he is their sincere friend. Such people are afraid or are too cowardly to present their real feelings and to show their actual disbelief. It is no coincidence that, as some of the commentators such as al-Dausiri pointed out, throughout the history of the Muslims this group of hypocrites has always been supported by the Jews—during the time of the Prophet (peace be upon him) until our present day. This is because the Jews share with the hypocrites their hatred for Islam and their fear of Islam becoming supreme. In Allah's mercy, He has clearly described their behavior to us and has clearly warned us that they are simply trying to deceive us.

In their ignorance the hypocrites thought that they were fooling the Prophet (peace be upon him) and the Muslims but, in fact, they were only deceiving themselves into thinking that they had found the perfect way to live and that no one would become aware of their evil actions and plots. Actually, Allah is aware of them and He will punish them for their evil doings. Since the hypocrites did not really believe in Allah and what the Messenger (peace be upon him) taught, they thought that they would be safe by their outward acts of faith. But out of ignorance they had deceived themselves, although they were not aware of the reality of their situation, as Allah not only knows their seemingly pious acts that they did in front of the Muslims but He also knows the evil acts that they did behind the believers' backs. Most importantly, Allah knows the intention behind their pious acts—and since those acts were done solely for the sake of show, Allah will punish them severely.

One may note that all of the verses in the Quran that refer to the hypocrites were revealed after the Prophet (peace be upon him) migrated to Madinah. This is very much consistent with the nature of the hypocrites. They were trying to get the best out of their actions (of course, all that they perceive is of this life). In Madinah, they could achieve some benefits by claiming to be Muslims as the Muslims were ruling Madinah at that time. Such was not the case in Makkah. If one claimed to be a Muslim in Makkah he would have to face the wrath of the Quraish and the other unbelievers. Therefore, during the Makkan period of the Prophet's life there were no such people as hypocrites. So Allah did not reveal anything concerning them until the Prophet (peace be upon him) moved to Madinah.

The case, Allah knows best, is similar today with the modern day hypocrites. Since they do not truly believe in Allah, they will only claim to be Muslims and act like Muslims if they see some worldly benefit for themselves in doing so. Whenever the Muslims face any affliction the hypocrites will be the first to abandon the religion and join arms with the unbelievers if the unbelievers are victorious against the Muslims. During the Prophet's time we find the hypocrites consorting with the unbelievers of Makkah and the Jews thinking that the Muslims would be defeated and these unbelievers would then support their old friends, the hypocrites. Similarly, if Islam should gain a stronghold anywhere, the hypocrites are the first to come out to say that they supported Islam their entire lives. Or they are the first to "repent and become pious" whenever the Muslims become powerful.

As a final note, we would like to quote Hudhaifa who was asked what hypocrisy is and he stated, "It is to speak by Islam and not to act by it."

We Muslims should study these verses concerning the hypocrites very carefully as the hypocrites will always be a thorn in the Muslim society and we must be aware of hypocrisy in order to stay away from it as the hypocrites will be in the lowest depths of Hell.

Al-Baqarah 10

Allah says in the Quran,

$$فِي قُلُوبِهِمْ مَرَضٌ فَزَادَهُمُ اللَّهُ مَرَضًا وَلَهُمْ عَذَابٌ أَلِيمٌ بِمَا كَانُوا يَكْذِبُونَ$$

"In their hearts is a disease and Allah increases their disease. A painful doom is theirs because they lie" (*al-Baqarah* 10).

Again, we must point out that, in the same way that the description of the true believers does not change through the ages, the general description of the hypocrites stays the same at all times. We must thank Allah for exposing them to us so clearly in these opening verses of the Quran.

Allah describes the hypocrites as having a disease in their hearts. The meaning of the word "disease" can give us a clue to their situation. Ibn Faaris, a scholar of the Arabic language, said that disease or illness is any condition that is outside of the realm of health due to some sickness or shortcoming.

Some say that this disease in their hearts is their sticking firmly to this life and their love of this life and their forgetfulness of the Hereafter and their turning away from the events of the Hereafter. Some say that Allah increases their disease by increasing their love for this world which leads to nothing but increased worries and anxieties concerning this world. They ignore the fact that problems cannot be solved save by looking to the Hereafter.

Allah says that He increases the disease in their hearts. Some scholars say that this verse is like a supplication against them due to their wickedness and their refusal to accept the truth. This is due to a number of reasons: (i) Since the disease in their hearts is due to their doubts about the sources of this religion, every time there is another principle explained or ruling laid down, their doubt increases and, thereby, the disease in their hearts also increases. (ii) Their hatred for Allah's revelation is so great that if anything new comes from Allah, it just increases their hatred and, thereby, increases the disease in their hearts. (iii) It is Allah's *sunnah* (law) in this creation that if there is an illness and the solution or ailment to that illness is not found, the illness will just continue to get worse. The same is true for the diseases of the heart. Since the hypocrites continue not to heal their hearts by *imaan*, the illness in their hearts continues to grow until they die and are thrown into the hell-fire. In a similar fashion, a healthy body is made even healthier through proper diet, exercise and so on. This is similar to the believer whose faith continues to increase as he reads more Quran, turns to Allah more often and so forth, until finally he is entered into paradise. (iv) Their disease is increased due to their actions towards Allah and His Prophet (peace be upon him) which take them farther and farther away from *imaan* or a healthy heart. (v) If Allah makes it seem as if they have garnered some success from their deceptions, then they become convinced of their correctness and begin to practice their hypocrisy more and more fervently. They think they are getting ahead while in reality Allah is recording what they are doing and only giving them respite until their appointed time.

"And theirs will be a lasting, painful punishment due to what they denied." They deserve the punishment due to their behavior in this world and their refusal to accept the call to Islam although they were free to accept it and were not coerced away from it. The Arabic word, *"yakdhiboon,"* implies that they continually and repeatedly denied the truth.

In these verses, the disease in their hearts is both of a physical sense and of a spiritual sense. In the spiritual sense, they suffered from doubts and a wrong *aqeedah* (belief system). In a physical sense, they suffer from anxiety, rancor, resentment, malice and so forth. If one looks through the Quran, one will find twenty-some-odd diseases of the heart that the unbelievers and hypocrites suffer from.

The reason for their hypocrisy is their personal goals and desires. This, and the people they are with, prevent them from accepting the truth. Through every generation or every time, it is not uncommon to find that those who support the hypocrites in their selfish goals are the Jews. Hypocrisy first appeared in Islam when Islam first came face to face with the Jews. The Jewish leaders did their best to flatter and support Abdullah ibn Ubayy ibn Abi Salool. It was this Abdullah who had sought to become the leader of all Madinah. Yet when the Prophet (peace be upon him) came to Madinah and the people embraced Islam, Abdullah saw that the chances of him achieving his selfish and egotistical goal were very small, unless he got support from some group in Madinah. He found that support in the Jews of Madinah. The Jews actually hoped that the Prophet (peace be upon him) would be forced to kill some of his so-called "followers," thus turning people away from Islam. Instead, Allah simply sent down verses of the Quran that gave all of the Muslims until the day of Resurrection the clear and concise description of these hypocrites and the evil that they attempt to spread as the selfish and egotistical goals of man will always exist in every land and time.

It should further be noted that Allah completely and absolutely states that they possess no *imaan* whatsoever. [This is stressed by the Arabic of the verse, "*Wa maa hum bimumineen.*"] This means that they are not part of the believers at all. This is actually an answer to a statement: "There are some of them who believe in Allah and the Day of Judgment and they do not deny *tauheed*." Allah's response to this, as we can conclude from the Arabic structure of the verse, is their *aqeedah* or belief is just one of tradition or convention and their belief has no affect on their actions; otherwise, they would not perform their actions out of show and deceit just to fool the Muslims. The fact is that whatever little recognition of Allah they may possess is completely overshadowed by their personal desires and therefore they have chosen the road of hypocrisy instead of that of *imaan*.

These verses, which are a blessing to us in that they show the way and characteristics of the hypocrites, are also a strong warning and lesson for us to be away from their path and an admonition for us to fight against the desires and goals in our own selves that may go against what Allah has revealed to be lawful for us. If our personal desires overtake us, we may fall from the highest levels of *imaan* to the lowest levels of creation. These verses describing the hypocrites also clearly show us that we must be absolutely sincere in our relationship to Allah. And we should do all of our deeds solely for His sake and not due to any lower desires.

It should be noted that Imam Maalik once said, "The hypocrites at the time of the Prophet (peace be upon him) are the same as the *zandiqa* among us today." This is very true.

The *zandiqa* are those people who appear as Muslims yet their sole desire is to keep people away from the true Islam. In the days of Maalik, it was these people who were forging hadith and spreading innovations in Islam. Today, we have similar people who use clever arguments to convince other Muslims that interest is permissible, or that there is nothing in the Quran concerning women wearing *hijaab*, or that there is nothing wrong with alcohol, or that we do not have to pray. As we stated before, the characteristics of the hypocrites are always the same and these modern day hypocrites are doing nothing new: their own selfish desires keep them from following Islam and, therefore, out of jealousy, they want to keep others from practicing Islam.

Al-Baqarah 11-13

Allah says in the Quran,

وَإِذَا قِيلَ لَهُمْ لَا تُفْسِدُوا فِي الْأَرْضِ قَالُوا إِنَّمَا نَحْنُ مُصْلِحُونَ أَلَا إِنَّهُمْ هُمُ الْمُفْسِدُونَ وَلَكِنْ لَا يَشْعُرُونَ وَإِذَا قِيلَ لَهُمْ آمِنُوا كَمَا آمَنَ النَّاسُ قَالُوا أَنُؤْمِنُ كَمَا آمَنَ السُّفَهَاءُ أَلَا إِنَّهُمْ هُمُ السُّفَهَاءُ وَلَكِنْ لَا يَعْلَمُونَ

"And when it is said unto them: Make not mischief in the earth, they say: We are peacemakers only. Behold they are indeed the mischief makers but they perceive not. And when it is said unto them: Believe as the people believe, they say: Shall we believe as the foolish believe? Behold they are indeed the foolish but they know not" (*al-Baqarah* 11-13).

In these verses Allah describes one of the biggest problems of the hypocrites: Everything that they see as good in this life (since it is based on following their own desires and lusts) is actually evil for both themselves and the world as a whole yet they cannot perceive that fact—if they would listen closely to the clear texts of the Quran and sunnah, they would realize that fact, but they have opted not to do so. They claim that they are doing good throughout the world, yet they are spreading nothing but corruption and evil throughout the world. This can be seen today in the words of the hypocritical leaders of the world who claim to be working on behalf of "mankind" yet all they ever do is spread evil and benefit themselves and their parties at the expense of all of mankind.

This is the way it is with every hypocrite. He claims to be doing good while, in fact, he is doing evil. One of the most recent examples of this type of behavior is that of those people who, in the name of the religion, say that it is not necessary to follow the *Shareeah* (Islamic Law) exactly and that Allah did not mean to set down laws for us but simply general principles for us to live by and to spread peace and love on this earth. By such speech they claim to be doing "good" by abolishing the *Shareeah* that was meant for the happiness of mankind, and replacing it with manmade laws which, as we can see in the West, lead to a great deal of evil. They claim that they simply want progress and freedom, but actually they just want freedom from serving Allah to serve their own desires. Another such claim from such hypocrites is that religion is to play no role in politics. They claim that by freeing the people from religion they will be able to rule and vote according to the real utility of the people. Actually, it is just another excuse not to apply the *Shareeah* upon themselves or upon others.

Actually these people are (openly) denying that Allah has the knowledge of all things and is able to reveal to us what is the best for all of mankind until the Day of Judgment. So some of them honestly believe that the *Shareeah* is outdated; therefore, they spread evil (in the form of their manmade laws) at the expense of the *Shareeah* that was revealed for the benefit of all of mankind. By doing so they are also denying that Allah is compassionate and merciful enough to have revealed such a perfect way of life to us. Instead, according to what they claim, Allah would leave us wandering to find our own ways. But the Muslim realizes that Allah sent the Prophet (peace be upon him) and his message as a mercy for all of mankind until the Day of Judgment.

We need only look to some of the laws or customs that such people have either introduced or have attempted to introduce in the Muslim countries to see if Allah was true in His statement that they claim to be spreading good yet they are actually spreading evil. In Turkey now it is forbidden, in many cases, for a woman to be dressed in the proper Islamic dress. In many Muslim countries alcohol is not illegal. The hypocrites encourage the free mixing of the sexes, music, discos, adultery. According to the laws of some Muslim countries adultery is not a crime unless the wife wishes to prosecute. These are some of the things that these "well-doers" have introduced into our Muslim lands. Their actions have shown that they are, in fact, spreaders of evil as Allah describes them in the above verse. Allah begins the verse with the word *alaa* ("is it not certain") (ﺍﻻ) to emphasize the fact that they are certainly evildoers.

Then Allah says that they are not aware of the evil that they spread, yet previously Allah described them as deceiving liars. This shows us that there are actually two types of such hypocrites: (1) Those who introduce such evil into the Muslim lands knowing full well what they are doing and what evil they are introducing. They are the leaders of such hypocrites. In many cases, these people spread this evil due to their great hatred of Islam. (2) Then there is a second group of people who claim to be believers yet they only wish to follow their desires and lusts, and they follow the lead of those who introduce these evils into the lands of the Muslims, while they are not fully aware of the evil that they are doing—they may have a clear understanding that what is being implemented is not consistent with the teachings of Islam. They think that they are just enjoying this world and having fun and they do not consider the harm that they are doing as important. They do not care to consider their actual situation with respect to Allah and they don't care to seriously consider what Islam is and what it means to be a Muslim. Such people will be punished in a fashion similar to the first group due to the evil of the fact that they did not care if they pleased Allah or not.

Then Allah informs us of the evil of their actions and beings in the form of a question and a reply; this is one of the styles used in the Quran as it is one of the easiest ways for the person to understand clearly the meaning and intent of the speaker. This way the characteristics of the hypocrites will be made even clearer to those who ponder the Quran.[1]

Allah tells us about a very obvious characteristic of the hypocrites. If one goes to them and asks them to believe as they should believe and to behave as one should behave, they always respond in a rude manner and arrogantly, such as, "Shall I behave like so and so" or "Shall I believe like these fools." This is how Allah described them in the Quran and this is exactly how we find them today. The "fools" (Ar., *sufahaa*) refers to those people who have poor reasoning or always hold weak opinions, exactly like that person who cannot weigh the difference between this life and the Hereafter and cannot see which is more important. This is exactly the case with the hypocrites and therefore they are truly the fools. Again, Allah begins the clause with *alaa* (ألا), stressing the fact that they are truly the fools and to encompass all of them and all of their actions. Another aspect of their foolishness is that they follow their desires and the footsteps of the Satan instead of behaving in the manner that the human, as opposed to the animal, is supposed to behave.[2] That is why Allah says in the Quran,

---

[1] When Allah uses *idha* with a question it is a case where the reason is very strongly related to the action and it cannot be refuted. If Allah uses *in* then there is a weak connection between the reason and the action.

[2] Some commentators note that this is why Allah uses the term *an-Nass* for them instead of *insaan* (human) as non-believers are not deserving of being called humans since their behavior is more akin to that of animals. Allah knows best.

وَلَقَدْ ذَرَأْنَا لِجَهَنَّمَ كَثِيرًا مِنَ الْجِنِّ وَالإِنسِ لَهُمْ قُلُوبٌ لا
يَفْقَهُونَ بِهَا وَلَهُمْ أَعْيُنٌ لا يُبْصِرُونَ بِهَا وَلَهُمْ آذَانٌ لا
يَسْمَعُونَ بِهَا أُوْلَئِكَ كَالأَنْعَامِ بَلْ هُمْ أَضَلُّ أُوْلَئِكَ هُمُ
الْغَافِلُونَ

"Many are the jinn and men We have made for Hell: they have hearts wherewith they understand not, eyes wherewith they see not, and ears wherewith they hear not. They are like cattle, nay more misguided: for they are heedless (of warning)" (*al-Araaf* 179).

It is not abnormal for the hypocrites to call the believers "fools." This has been an action of the hypocrites and unbelievers since the very early times as we can find the unbelievers saying something similar to the Prophet Noah. Nowadays they not only call them fools but they also say that they are uncivilized people, backwards people, savages and so forth, while they call themselves progressive, advanced, civilized. This has always been a characteristic of the hypocrites: they always call the good things by insulting names and the evil things by complementary names.

Al-Baqarah 14-15

وَإِذَا لَقُوا الَّذِينَ آمَنُوا قَالُوا آمَنَّا وَإِذَا خَلَوْا إِلَى شَيَاطِينِهِمْ
قَالُوا إِنَّا مَعَكُمْ إِنَّمَا نَحْنُ مُسْتَهْزِئُونَ اللَّهُ يَسْتَهْزِئُ بِهِمْ
وَيَمُدُّهُمْ فِي طُغْيَانِهِمْ يَعْمَهُونَ

"And when they fall in with those who believe, they say: We believe, but when they go to their devils they declare: Lo! We are with you, we were just joking. Allah (Himself) does mock them, leaving them to wander blindly on in their contumacy" (*al-Baqarah* 14-15).

In these verses Allah describes the fourth type of evil action that the hypocrites perform.

In the first verse recorded above, Allah makes it clear that the earlier stated question, "Should we believe as the fools believed?" was a question that they had asked each among themselves and not in front of the true believers.

Their statement that they believe is actually their implying that they have the true faith and sincerity in their hearts as their outward actions already had shown that they were following the laws of Islam. Therefore, to mislead the believers they try to stress the fact that they are truly believers.

This is how the hypocrites behave: When they meet the believers they claim to be believers. And then when they meet with their "devils,"[1] they tell them clearly that they are not believers. Their leaders are not satisifed with this declaration alone; the hypocrites must stress that they are mocking or making fun of the believers in the same way that their leaders attempt to deceive and make fun of the believers. By pretending to be believers and by making false acts of belief, they are just trying to make fun of the believers.

There is a difference of opinion concerning whom exactly these devils are. Some Companions of the Prophet (peace be upon him) said that they referred to the unbelievers, some said it meant the Jews who were leading the hypocrites on, while others said that it referred to the hypocrites who were leading the other hypocrites. In any case, the meaning or the message of the phrase is very clear.

[In another article in this collection,] we discuss those acts that take one from Islam to *kufr*. One of those acts is

---

[1] Allah calls their leaders "devils" because they follow the way of the Satan in going farther away from Allah and in not obeying Allah.

making fun of Islam or of the Muslims. In fact, in *soorah at-Taubah* Allah says,

وَلَئِنْ سَأَلْتَهُمْ لَيَقُولُنَّ إِنَّمَا كُنَّا نَخُوضُ وَنَلْعَبُ قُلْ أَبِاللَّهِ وَآيَاتِهِ وَرَسُولِهِ كُنْتُمْ تَسْتَهْزِئُونَ لَا تَعْتَذِرُوا قَدْ كَفَرْتُمْ بَعْدَ إِيمَانِكُمْ

"If you were to ask them [about their statements], they would declare, 'We were just talking idly and joking.' Say [to them]: Is it Allah or His signs or His Messenger that you are mocking? Make no excuses for yourself. You have made *kufr* after you have had faith" (*al-Taubah* 65-66).

Allah, therefore, mocks them. But when Allah mocks someone it is not like that of a created being mocking another. The mocking of Allah involves both punishment in this life and the Hereafter. One of the ways that Allah mocks them is by showing the Muslims clearly the characteristics of the hypocrites such that they can be easily recognized, even though they think they are following the Muslims. Allah also mocks them by the fact that if they want to fool the Muslims they have to perform the actions of faith (for example, prayer, charity and so on) which, in reality, they hate to perform. And in the hereafter, the believers will be reclining upon couches looking at and laughing at the hypocrites who will be punished in the fire. Also Allah mocks them by allowing them to increasingly believe that they are doing good and are actually being rewarded (in a material, worldly sense) for their deeds while in the hereafter all of their actions will be for naught. Allah says in the Quran,

وَلَا يَحْسَبَنَّ الَّذِينَ كَفَرُوا أَنَّمَا نُمْلِي لَهُمْ خَيْرٌ لِأَنْفُسِهِمْ إِنَّمَا نُمْلِي لَهُمْ لِيَزْدَادُوا إِثْمًا وَلَهُمْ عَذَابٌ مُهِينٌ

"And let not those who disbelieve imagine that the rein We give them brings good unto their souls. We only give them rein that they may grow in sinfulness. And theirs will be a shameful doom" (*ali-Imraan* 178). And,

$$فَلَمَّا نَسُوا مَا ذُكِّرُوا بِهِ فَتَحْنَا عَلَيْهِمْ أَبْوَابَ كُلِّ شَيْءٍ حَتَّى$$

$$إِذَا فَرِحُوا بِمَا أُوتُوا أَخَذْنَاهُمْ بَغْتَةً فَإِذَا هُمْ مُبْلِسُونَ$$

"Then, when they forgot that whereof they had been reminded, We opened unto them the gates of all things till, even as they were rejoicing in that which they were given, We seized them unawares, and lo they were dumfounded" (*al-Anaam* 44).

The enemies of Islam are constantly trying to find "mistakes" or inconsistencies in the Quran. With respect to these verses there is a question that might arise that we should know the answer to. "How could Allah be characterized as mocking them when it is confirmed that mocking involves deception or frivolty, both of which cannot be said of Allah?" The scholars of the Quran have given five answers to this question. For the sake of brevity I shall mention only two of them here. (1) What Allah does to them is a reward for what they have done and the reward takes on the same description or name as the deed. Allah says,

$$وَالَّذِينَ كَسَبُوا السَّيِّئَاتِ جَزَاءُ سَيِّئَةٍ بِمِثْلِهَا$$

"But those who have earned evil will have a reward of like evil" (*al-Shooraa* 27). (2) They are attempting to harm the believers by their mockery but in fact they are only harming themselves; therefore it is as if Allah is mocking them. In any case, the previous paragraph demonstrates how Allah mocks them and there is no deception or frivolty involved whatsoever.

And Allah says in these verses, "And [He] will leave them for a while in their overweening arrogance, blindly stumbling to and fro." That is, Allah leaves them free to increase their evil deeds and their belief that what they are doing is good and sound. Allah states the punishment for their mocking in phrases or terms that imply repetition, ever-present and eternal punishment. Allah does not originally make them go astray blindly, but they have chosen that way for themselves and Allah allows them to continue in the path that they have chosen for themselves.

This is an important point: Allah allows them to live the way they do and then He will judge them with justice.

Al-Baqarah 16

Allah says in the Quran,

أُوْلَئِكَ الَّذِينَ اشْتَرَوُاْ الضَّلالَةَ بِالْهُدَى فَمَا رَبِحَتْ تِجَارَتُهُمْ وَمَا كَانُوا مُهْتَدِينَ

"These are they who purchase error at the price of guidance, so their commerce does not prosper and they are not at all rightly guided [in their deal]" (al-Baqarah 16).

In these verses Allah continues to give us an in-depth description of the hypocrites who will be of the most severely tormented people in the Hereafter and who inflict a great deal of damage upon Islam. Concerning the Hereafter, Allah says about them,

إِنَّ الْمُنَافِقِينَ فِي الدَّرْكِ الأَسْفَلِ مِنَ النَّارِ وَلَنْ تَجِدَ لَهُمْ نَصِيرًا

"The hypocrites will be in the lowest depths of the Fire; no helper will you find for them" (al-Nisaa 145).

These are the people, as Allah has described them, who claim to be believers but who are unbelievers; who claim to be doing good but who are doing evil; who call the believers backwards and foolish while, in fact, they are the ones who are backwards as they always return to every type of misguidance that the world has ever known.

In these verses Allah clearly tells us that these people have purchased or have preferred disbelief instead of belief in the same way that one trades one thing for another thing that he prefers.[1] This is their choice in the same way that a person freely makes a business dealing according to his choice. The hypocrites are those people who see the truth of Islam around them yet they refuse to follow it sincerely. Yet the guidance is right there in front of them and if they wish to follow it they are free to do so, yet they refuse to follow it and instead substitute misguidance for Allah's guidance.

This is the plight of all "Muslims" of today who refuse to follow the Quran yet who claim to be such good Muslims. They have clearly given up the true guidance for misguidance. By doing so they lose the blessings of being along the straight path and they do not get any benefit from the "deal" that they have made. This is why Allah mentions that they get no gain from their trade (of belief for disbelief) and that they have no guidance whatsoever. In fact, we can see how misguided their "deal" is by noting the fact that not only do they get no gain from their deal but they also lose whatever they had before they made the deal. Qataadah said, "They go from guidance to misguidance, from obedience [to Allah] to disobedience, from being in the community to being separate, from a life of safety to that of fear and from the sunnah to innovations." Since, by their deal, they are left with no proper guidance they are left to follow their own desires, the commands of the human devils among them, the way of their fathers or some other source of misguidance. Such people can lead to no good in society since they are void of guidance. Yet they are sometimes able to fool

---

[1] The commentators point out that the verse does not mean that they used to be guided and then they changed, but it is simply referring to the fact that the truth is right in front of them if they desire to follow it.

sincere Muslims who are not completely aware of the teachings of the Quran regarding the hypocrites and therefore they are able to penetrate into the Muslim society and cause evil and immorality among the Muslims.

All of the verses that we have discussed to date clearly show us the behavior of the hypocrites and the emptiness of their promises and claims to the Muslim believers. If the believers are sincere to Allah and earnestly seek to understand His teachings, found in the Quran and the sunnah, they will be able to protect themselves from the likes of the unbelievers and the hypocrites and they will be able to save themselves from the Hell fire. In the same way that Allah teaches us how to save ourselves from the tricks of the Satan, by describing to us Satan and how he behaves, He has also shown us how to save ourselves from the human devils (for example, the hypocrites and disbelievers) by describing the way they behave so we will be aware of them and we will not fall prey to their evil plots.

These verses should increase the *imaan* of the believers as through these verses Allah clearly shows the believers the different types of people and how they behave. Throughout all the ages, the believer can read the opening verses of *soorah al-Baqarah* and find that they do, in fact, perfectly describe the believers, disbelievers and hypocrites. They also serve as a warning to the believers that they should not, in any way, behave in a manner similar to that of the hypocrites. For example, they should never say things that they do not do, they should never stand against the truth for the sake of worldly gain while claiming to be implementing the truth and so on.

But Allah did not stop there in His lengthy description of the hypocrites. Instead, Allah gave us two parables of the hypocrites that can further our understanding of them, not of their behavior so much, but of how badly misguided and foolish these people are.

Al-Baqarah 17-18

Allah says in the Quran,

مَثَلُهُمْ كَمَثَلِ الَّذِي اسْتَوْقَدَ نَارًا فَلَمَّا أَضَاءَتْ مَا حَوْلَهُ ذَهَبَ اللَّهُ بِنُورِهِمْ وَتَرَكَهُمْ فِي ظُلُمَاتٍ لا يُبْصِرُونَ صُمٌّ بُكْمٌ عُمْيٌ فَهُمْ لا يَرْجِعُونَ

"Their likeness is as the likeness of one who kindles a fire, and when it sheds its light around him, Allah takes away their light and leaves them in darkness, wherein they cannot see. They are deaf, dumb and blind; and they return not" (*al-Baqarah* 17-18).

In these verses from the first portion of *soorah al-Baqarah*, Allah gives us two parables of the hypocrites. In verses 17-18 is the first parable.

Allah describes the hypocrites as being like a group of travelers who have lost their way on the road due to the darkness. They light a fire, hoping that by its light they will be able to find the path. Then when they think that they have found the way, the fire goes out and they are left in a darkness that is even greater than before as now they are void of the three senses, hearing, seeing and feeling, that could show them to the truth. They did not benefit from their hearing, seeing and feelings and, therefore, they have become deaf, dumb and blind. "And they return not," due to their increased darkness after they had a glimpse of the light.

Allah says, "And Allah takes away their light," instead of saying, "their light left them." This is a special sign for the believers in that Allah preserves His light only for those who truly believe in Him and He takes it away from those who do not believe in Him or who do not apply His guidance.

There are a number of subtle points that we can note from the fact that Allah uses "fire" in this similitude:

(1) Getting guidance or light from a fire is getting guidance or light from something else and not from one's self and when that fire goes the person is left in darkness. When the hypocrites attest to the faith with their tongues yet they have no belief in their hearts it is as if they are borrowing some light that does not belong to them.

(2) Fire always requires other things, such as wood, to keep it going. In the same manner the true faith always requires sincerity, devotion and good deeds from the person. Since the hypocrites do not have these characteristics they return to darkness in the same way that the fire goes out when there is no more oxygen.

(3) A darkness that occurs after light has been spread is harder upon the human than darkness where there was never any light. Therefore, Allah describes the hypocrites as returning to darkness after light has been shed.

(4) Allah says that he takes the "light" away from them and He did not say that he takes the fire away from them. That is because a fire has brightness to it and also burning, smoke and so forth. The light has been taken from them but they are left in the smoke and rubbish.

(5) Allah uses the singular for "their light" yet he uses the plural for their "darkness." That is because the truth is one path, the straight path of Allah, and beyond that there are many paths and all of them are paths of darkness and misguidance. This is why Allah says,

اللّهُ وَلِيُّ الَّذِينَ آمَنُوا يُخْرِجُهُمْ مِنَ الظُّلُمَاتِ إِلَى النُّورِ وَالَّذِينَ كَفَرُوا أَوْلِيَاؤُهُمُ الطَّاغُوتُ يُخْرِجُونَهُمْ مِنَ النُّورِ إِلَى الظُّلُمَاتِ

"Allah is the Protecting Friend of those who believe. He brings them out of darknesses into light. As for those who disbelieve, their patrons are false deities. They bring them out of light into ways of darkness" (*al-Baqarah* 257).

(6) The hypocrites replace the light of recognition and sight for the darkness of doubt and disbelief for after he has seen he actually becomes blind.

(7) This verse is related to the previous one, "They purchase error by the price of guidance..." In this verse their trade is made even clearer as they have chosen the path of darkness over the path of light.

(8) This verse also describes the plight of the hypocrites in the Hereafter. There is a hadith in *Sahih Muslim* that states that on the Day of Judgment all of the believers and hypocrites will be given a light and told to follow their Lord. But Allah will then extinguish the lights of the hypocrites and they will be thrown into the Hell-Fire.

They are left deaf, dumb and blind. The word Allah uses for "deaf" is actually stronger than just meaning that they cannot hear as the word used completely denies any use for the ears. The word used for "dumb" or not able to speak means that one has a deficiency in speaking or in the heart, that is, in one's feelings and grasp of what is happening around him. And the hypocrites will not return from their misguidance or from the attributes described above because they have turned away from the truth and they have deliberately chosen the path of error due to being overcome by their own desires or love of this world.

The hypocrites are not like the people who are openly unbelievers. The unbelievers have openly turned away from the truth and they have refused to listen to it or pay attention to it from the beginning. They refuse to listen in fear that they may become convinced by the truth. If the hypocrites were like the openly unbelieving people, the Muslims would not be so greatly harmed by their evil. But the hypocrites are different; they appear to be believers although they have no belief in their heart. They do this after they have recognized the truth of Islam but refused to follow it. It is for this reason that Allah describes them to be like a people who did have some light but who refused to benefit from the truth and signs that they saw and who therefore made themselves deaf, dumb and blind. They have turned their hearing to things other than the guidance of Allah and their tongues are busy with useless talk that is void of guidance. They refuse to listen to the revelations of Allah anymore as they have put their trust in their own desires; and when they are called to the signs of Allah, they act deaf and dumb.

Al-Baqarah 19-20

Allah says in the Quran,

أَوْ كَصَيِّبٍ مِنَ السَّمَاءِ فِيهِ ظُلُمَاتٌ وَرَعْدٌ وَبَرْقٌ يَجْعَلُونَ أَصَابِعَهُمْ فِي آذَانِهِمْ مِنَ الصَّوَاعِقِ حَذَرَ الْمَوْتِ وَاللَّهُ مُحِيطٌ بِالْكَافِرِينَ يَكَادُ الْبَرْقُ يَخْطَفُ أَبْصَارَهُمْ كُلَّمَا أَضَاءَ لَهُمْ مَشَوْا فِيهِ وَإِذَا أَظْلَمَ عَلَيْهِمْ قَامُوا وَلَوْ شَاءَ اللَّهُ لَذَهَبَ بِسَمْعِهِمْ وَأَبْصَارِهِمْ إِنَّ اللَّهَ عَلَى كُلِّ شَيْءٍ قَدِيرٌ

"Or [their parable is] like a rainstorm from the sky wherein is darkness, thunder and the flash of lightning. They thrust their fingers in their ears by reason of the thunder, for fear of death. Allah encompasses the disbelievers. The lightning almost snatches away their sight from them. As often as it flashes forth for them they walk therein, and when it darkens against them they stand still. If Allah willed, He could destroy their hearing and their sight. Lo! Allah is Able to do all things" (*Al-Baqarah* 19-20).

This is the second parable that Allah has given concerning the hypocrites in these opening verses of *soorah al-Baqarah.* These verses are also the ending of Allah's description of the hypocrites in the beginning of the Quran.

Of course, with any parable in the Quran, one must be very careful in stating what is meant by such verses as only Allah knows the complete lessons and truths of any parable in the Quran. Here we shall mention the interpretation of some scholars of the Quran. It should be noted that it may be the case that a number of different interpretations are all correct in essence; the important aspect is to learn and to apply the lessons of these parables.

Allah describes the hypocrites with respect to a rainstorm which is a rain that descends from the higher places to the lower elevations in the same way that the guidance is revealed from the heavens to the earth. Similarly, the revelations and guidance give life to the heart of man in the same way that the rain gives life to the earth. But the hypocrites are like a type of people who get nothing from the rain except fearing its darkness, noise and severity; in the same way they get nothing from the revelations from Allah save a fear of the Muslims and a fear that their true situation will be revealed in the revelations. The darkness may represent their blindness to the truth and the thunder is like a warning to them. The flash of lightning is like the clear proofs that should have overwhelmed them and have taken them to the straight path. The noise of the thunder is what Allah has commanded them to do but they refuse to listen or obey what they have been commanded.

The parable also shows the plight of the completely ignorant person who cannot see the reality behind something. He just acts according to the outward appearance of something or from what he has experienced. From the rainstorm, for example, such a person can only note the darkness, thunder and lightning without being able to see the benefit that this rainstorm has in reviving the dead earth. The weak minded person can only see the outward things and therefore he cannot possibly note the positive aspects of many actions. For example, most of the people see in jihad only the hardship and the loss of lives and wealth, and therefore, they hate to go for jihad and possibly lose their lives. But they do not see the positive aspects of jihad which include making the Word of Allah supreme, wiping out injustice and oppression, and its promised rewards in the Hereafter. Therefore, they conclude it is better not to participate in jihad.

Similar is the situation of the hypocrites with respect to the Quran. To them, the Quran is a burden and they try to flee from its orders and prohibitions or promises and warnings.

In general, we may say that the hypocrites view the revelations of Allah that bring life to the heart and purify the soul in the same way that they view a rainstorm in which they only note its wetness, lightning and thunder.

In their ignorance they think that they can just close their eyes to the truth that is around them but when the truth comes they will see that the actions that they performed will not be able to benefit them in any manner. This parable shows people in the most extreme state of helplessness and fear. Also, the hypocrites are in the extreme state of helplessness with respect to the religion and in the extreme state of fear with respect to this world as the hypocrites are always afraid that if the reality of their hypocrisy is discovered, they would be greatly harmed in this world or they would be killed. This anxiety and this fear of the reality will always stick with the hypocrites as they must always fear the revelations of Allah and they must always fear the true believers in Allah.

Another interpretation of this parable is that the rain is usually beneficial to mankind yet when it comes in severe storms it can also be harmful to mankind. In the same way *imaan* or faith is beneficial to mankind if that faith is true. If it is just on the tongue and it is not mixed with sincerity and love for Allah, then it will be harmful to the person in the same way that such "faith" will lead to the ultimate destruction of the hypocrites.

These verses again point to the fact that the hypocrites are just concerned with the outward aspects of events. They think that by thrusting their fingers into their ears they can be protected from the storm. In the same way, they think that by their outward show of faith and by fooling the believers they will be safe from any punishment.

Yet another interpretation of this parable is that the rain refers to *imaan* and the Quran while the darkness, thunder and lightning refers to the obligations of Islam that are hard upon the hypocrites, such as the prayers, fasts, zakaat, jihad, leaving the misguided customs and so forth. In the same way that one protects himself from a rainstorm, the hypocrites do their best to protect or fortify themselves from the *imaan* and the Quran due to those related aspects that they dread so much. Allah describes them, "As often as it flashes forth for them they walk therein." This refers to those cases where they get some benefit from the religion, in which case they stick to the religion, for example, protection of life and wealth, distribution of zakaat and charity. But then Allah says, "And when it darkens again, they stand still." This refers to those aspects of the religion that they dislike and that they don't wish to be a part of. At that point, they stop as if they never had anything to do with Islam at all. Ibn Masood and Qataadah narrated that when the hypocrites received any blessings they would say that this is a good and blessed religion. If any test or hardship would befall them they would become upset with the religion and their hypocrisy would increase. An-Nihaas said that this is an excellent interpretation as it is supported by the Quranic verse,

وَمِنْ النَّاسِ مَنْ يَعْبُدُ اللَّهَ عَلَى حَرْفٍ فَإِنْ أَصَابَهُ خَيْرٌ اطْمَأَنَّ بِهِ وَإِنْ أَصَابَتْهُ فِتْنَةٌ انقَلَبَ عَلَى وَجْهِهِ خَسِرَ الدُّنْيَا وَالآخِرَةَ ذَلِكَ هُوَ الْخُسْرَانُ الْمُبِينُ

"And among mankind is he who worships Allah upon a narrow verge such that if good befalls him he is content therewith, but if a trial befalls him, he falls away utterly. He loses both the world and the Hereafter. That is the sheer loss" (*al-Hajj* 11).

Then Allah says, "If Allah willed, He could destroy their hearing and sight." According to some commentators, the meaning of this is that Allah could, if He desired, make the believers aware of each hypocrite and thereby they could kill them or throw them out of their homes.

Obviously, this second parable is much more far-reaching than the first one as this parable shows how extremely lost or helpless the hypocrites are.

These fourteen verses of *soorah al-Baqarah*, as well as other verses in *ali-Imraan*, *al-Nisaa*, *al-Maaidah*, *al-Anfaal*, *al-Taubah*, *al-Noor*, *al-Ahzaab*, have been revealed by Allah to clearly explain the ways of the hypocrites and to disclose their foolishness and to make clear their attributes. The hypocrites can be much more dangerous to the Muslims than those who are openly unbelievers. This fact was true during the time of the Prophet (peace be upon him) and it will be true for every time and age. This is why we have spent so much time in discussing in detail these verses at the beginning of *soorah al-Baqarah* that so completely describe the attributes and machinations of the hypocrites.

Also with this passage we conclude the opening verses of the Quran in which Allah gives a clear description of the Believers, the unbelievers and the hypocrites. We must learn the attributes of each group and do our best to make sure that we fulfill the attributes of the believers.

From the Quran:
"There is No Compulsion in the Religion"[1]

Allah says in the Quran,

لا إِكْرَاهَ فِي الدِّينِ قَدْ تَبَيَّنَ الرُّشْدُ مِنْ الغَيِّ فَمَنْ يَكْفُرْ بِالطَّاغُوتِ وَيُؤْمِنْ بِاللَّهِ فَقَدْ اسْتَمْسَكَ بِالْعُرْوَةِ الْوُثْقَى لا انْفِصَامَ لَهَا وَاللَّهُ سَمِيعٌ عَلِيمٌ

"There is no compulsion in religion. The right direction is henceforth distinct from error. And he who rejects false deities and believes in Allah has grasped a firm handhold which will never break. Allah is Hearer, Knower" (*al-Baqarah* 256).

The early missionaries and colonialists of the past two centuries attempted to attack Islam openly— trying to show that Western civilization and religion was more advanced than Islam and, therefore, the Muslims should abandon their backwards and retarding religion of Islam. Their onslaughts were met by a number of Muslims scholars who showed that Islam is superior to Christianity and the Western way of life and, furthermore, that Europe's renaissance only came about when the Europeans revolted against the Christian Church.

The intellectual defeat of the missionaries and colonialists led to a new approach. No longer could they openly attack Islam and claim that their religion or way of life was better. They found that such was not successful for both intellectual reasons (as they were refuted by Muslims scholars) and emotional reasons (the Muslims were too attached to Islam

---

[1] This article appeared in *al-Basheer*, vol. 2, no. 4 (Nov.-Dec. 1988).

to give up their religion). Therefore, they started a new approach towards the Muslims.

In 1902, a missionary leader delivered a speech to other missionaries and stated, "The premise upon which the work in Africa is to be based must be different from the premise that the colonialist governments used to base their actions upon." He stated that they must now approach the Muslims through propagating peace and security. He stated, "We must deal with them with justice and peace as we must deal with them with religious tolerance. We must not openly point to those important matters that stir the emotions of the people but we must use an inconspicuous approach." He stated that the people of North Africa could not be pulled away from their religion by force and, therefore, "We must be tolerant in this matter. And not just tolerant but we must study this religion and strive our best to understand it. And we can use the Islamic statement of 'there is no compulsion in religion' as a slogan whose limits we will not go beyond. We must respect the religion of Islam."[1]

So their approach changed. They decided to change the thinking of the Muslims instead of overtly pulling them away from Islam. One of the means by which they would accomplish this is by using the slogan, "There is no compulsion in religion." That is, everyone is free to follow any religion he wishes and, therefore, no one should object to the presence of Christian missionary work and the spread of Christianity among Muslims. They, most likely knowingly, were misinterpreting this verse and tried to use it against the stronghold of Islam in Africa.

Unfortunately, many current and past Muslim thinkers have been adversely affected, either consciously or subconsciously, by the writings and teachings of missionaries

---

[1] Quoted in Mahmood Uthmaan, *Juhood al-Mufakkkireen al-Muslimeen al-Muhdatheen fi Muqawamat al-Tayyaar al-Ilhaadi* (Riyadh: Maktabah al-Maarif, 1981), pp. 157-8.

and Orientalists. Many of them also interpreted this verse in the same or similar manner that the enemies of Islam interpreted it. They believe that jihad has no place in the spreading of Islam and that jihad is only called for when the Muslims must defend their homeland.

Another mistake with respect to this verse is alluded to by al-Dausiri who stated that many Muslim writers of this era, in their attempt to "defend" Islam from the onslaught of the enemies of Islam, have interpreted verses of the Quran in ways that clearly contradict many principles of the Shareeah. One example is interpreting this verse to mean that the atheists and apostates are free to follow their own way of life in an Islamic state.

Given below is the correct interpretation of this verse, Allah willing, according to the scholars of *tafseer*.

"There is no compulsion in religion."

There is a specific reason for the revelation of this verse. Abu Daawood and others recorded from ibn Abbaas that this verse was revealed concerning the Ansaar. If an Ansaari woman's children all died in infancy, she would swear that if she were to have children who lived, she would raise them as Jews. When the Jewish tribe of al-Nadheer was expelled they had many of the children of the Ansaar and they said that they would not leave their originally Ansaari children behind although the Ansaar wanted the children to stay with them and embrace Islam; then Allah revealed, "There is no compulsion in religion. The right direction is henceforth distinct from error."[1]

This incident shows that this verse means that the people of the Book (and those who are to be treated like the People of the Book, such as the Magians) are not to be forced

---

[1] Cf., Muqbil al-Waadi'ee, *Al-Saheeh al-Musnad min Asbaab al-Nuzool li-Ayaat wa Soor al-Quraan al-Kareem* (al-Maktab al-Salafi, 1401 A.H.), p. 20.

to follow Islam but this does not apply to every unbeliever. For example, the apostate is forced to return to the religion of Islam according to the consensus of the Muslim scholars. Thus, he does not fall under the generality of this verse.

Some scholars say that this verse is general and applies to every unbeliever save the apostates and whoever refuses to pay the *jizyah*. Some say that this verse is abrogated by the verses that instruct the Muslims to fight the unbelievers. Al-Tabari is of the opinion that its application is specific (*khaass*) and it is not abrogated. In other words, it is to be applied to the People of the Book and the Magians, but concerning the apostates and idol worshippers, the evidence of the Quran and sunnah shows that they must be forced to submit to the law of Allah. Some scholars are of the opinion that the statement is an enunciative statement (Ar., *khabr*) and does not imply disapproval. If that is true, the meaning of the verse is that the one who is compelled to follow Islam will not benefit at all from his practice on the Day of Judgment as long as he never sincerely embraced Islam although in this life he will benefit as his life will be spared and protected due to his outward embracing of Islam. This last opinion has been narrated from ibn al-Anbari.

Therefore, the four opinions concerning this verse may be summed up as follows:

(1) This verse has been abrogated by the verses commanding the Muslims to fight the unbelievers. Al-Dausiri rejects this statement because of the following: A verse cannot abrogate another verse unless it completely removes the ruling of the earlier verse and there is no way to reconcile the contradictory meanings of the verses. In this case, the generality of the verse implies that it applies to all non-believers while, in fact, it really only applies to a special section of the people. Therefore, it is not abrogated by the verses of jihad or *qitaal* because those verses do not remove the ruling of this verse completely; that is, the ruling of this

verse still applies to the people who accept the Islamic law and pay the *jizyah* although they remain Christians or Jews.

(2) The verse is an enunciative statement and not one of disapproval; hence, no ruling is to be derived from the verse.

(3) The verse applies to all unbelievers save the apostates and those who refuse to pay the *jizyah*.

(4) The verse is in particular reference to the People of the Book and the Magians as they are not forced to enter Islam as long as they submit to the Islamic state and pay the *jizyah*. Al-Tabari states, "The most likely to be correct of the statements [concerning this verse] is that of those who say: This verse was revealed with respect to a particular group of people. And they say, 'Who is referred to by, 'There is no compulsion in religion,' are the People of the Book and the Magians as it is accepted from them to stay with their established religion which differs from the religion of truth.' And the *jizyah* is to be taken from such people. And it is rejected that any part of this verse is abrogated."

This last statement seems to be the correct interpretation of this verse. As al-Shanqeeti pointed out, this interpretation is consistent with other verses in the Quran. Such as,

أَفَأَنْتَ تُكْرِهُ النَّاسَ حَتَّى يَكُونُوا مُؤْمِنِينَ

"Will you compel the people until they become believers" (*Yoonus* 99). And,

وَمَا جَعَلْنَاكَ عَلَيْهِمْ حَفِيظًا وَمَا أَنْتَ عَلَيْهِمْ بِوَكِيلٍ

"We have not sent you as a keeper over them, nor are you set over them to dispose of their affairs" (*al-Anaam* 107). But there are other verses that give different meanings, such as,

وَقَاتِلُوهُمْ حَتَّى لا تَكُونَ فِتْنَةٌ وَيَكُونَ الدِّينُ لِلَّهِ

"Fight them until there is no more *fitnah* (that is, idolatry) and the religion is all for Allah" (*al-Baqarah* 193). Furthermore, the Prophet (peace be upon him) said,

$$أُمِرْتُ أَنْ أُقَاتِلَ النَّاسَ حَتَّى يَقُولُوا لا إِلَهَ إِلَّا اللَّهُ$$

"I have been commanded to fight the people until they say there is no one worthy of worship except Allah." (Recorded by al-Bukhari.) In fact, this is further evidence that the fourth interpretation stated above is the correct interpretation of the verse. As al-Shanqeeti stated, these other verses show that this verse is particular for the People of the Book and it means that they are not forced to embrace Islam as long as they submit to the laws of Islam and pay the *jizyah*.

But this does not mean that the People of the Book are free to do whatever they wish in an Islamic state. In particular, they must abide by certain laws of the Islamic state, such as cutting the hand of the thief, stoning of the married adulterer and so forth (that is, those laws that are related to general social welfare). And they are not free to spread their corrupted beliefs in the Islamic state because their beliefs are *kufr* and it is the purpose of jihad to eradicate this world of *kufr*. Obviously, therefore, their *kufr* must be eradicated as much as possible in the Islamic state and this implies not allowing the non-Muslims to make propaganda for their *kufr* in the Islamic state.[1]

"There is no compulsion in religion" does not mean that they are left free in an Islamic state to establish their own army or national guard. This would go against the Quranic command of having them pay the *jizyah*,

---

[1] Unfortunately, some Muslim activists seem to be ignorant of this point. At a recent convention, a speaker even stated that the Socialists and Communists should be free to propagate their anti-Islamic beliefs in the Muslim state.

قَاتِلُوا الَّذِينَ لا يُؤْمِنُونَ بِاللَّهِ وَلا بِالْيَوْمِ الآخِرِ وَلا يُحَرِّمُونَ

مَا حَرَّمَ اللَّهُ وَرَسُولُهُ وَلا يَدِينُونَ دِينَ الْحَقِّ مِنْ الَّذِينَ أُوتُوا

الْكِتَابَ حَتَّى يُعْطُوا الْجِزْيَةَ عَنْ يَدٍ وَهُمْ صَاغِرُونَ

"Fight against such of those who have been given the Scripture as believe not in Allah nor the Last Day, and forbid not that which Allah has forbidden by His messenger, and follow not the religion of truth, until they pay the tribute readily, being brought low" (*al-Taubah* 29).[1]

It is not unusual that a people of a different ideology would have to sacrifice part of their beliefs when living in a society based on a different way of life. As Al-Ulyani pointed out, every society preserves its own beliefs and forces others to submit to the aspects of its society that deal with social welfare. He says that most people must give up at least ninety percent of their beliefs and way of life when living under a foreign or hostile regime. There is no doubt that in "civil matters" there is "compulsion" to abide by the laws of the present society.[2] Even in so-called "free" or "democratic" societies, one must submit to the laws that are presently being enforced in the society.[3] This is something natural with respect to any nation-state.

On a parenthetical note, from an Islamic perspective, everything of this world belongs to Allah and those people who misappropriate the material goods of this earth and who refuse to recognize the sovereignty of Allah are actually

---

[1] For a complete discussion of the position of the non-Muslims in an Islamic state, based on sound reports from the Prophet (peace be upon him), Companions and Followers as well as sound Islamic principles, see ibn al-Qayyim al-Jauziya, *Ahkaam Ahl al-Dhimma* (Beirut: Daar al-Ilm al-Malayeen, 1983), two volumes.

[2] Ali al-Ulyaani, *Ahamiyyat al-Jihaad* (Riyadh: Daar Taiba, 1985), p. 285.

[3] An example from the United States are the polygamists who have been sent to prison simply because they believe in polygamy that violates American law.

evildoers or *dhaalimoon* but out of Allah's mercy He allows them to live in an Islamic state and in their own states in this world. More than that, He even allows them to continue to live in their *kufr* and continues to grant them their material needs of this world.

But, at the same time, Allah obliges the Muslims to strive and struggle to establish an Islamic state and to allow the people to see Islam as it really is and to be able to choose Islam freely. This cannot become a reality without the jihad that opens the lands for the spreading of Islam. Al-Ulyaani, in *Ahamiyyat al-Jihaad*, convincingly argues that Islam would not have spread to the other present-day Muslim lands without this jihad. T. W. Arnold, in his book *The Preaching of Islam*, claims that Islam spread completely in many parts of the world through peaceful means. Although his work (which was translated into Arabic) has been able to fool many Muslims, his intention is obvious. He is trying to remove jihad from the arena of *dawah* (propagation of Islam). This is a grave mistake. It was actually the opening of the lands by the Muslim armies that led to the great numbers of people who embraced Islam in those countries after the Muslims ruled over them for some time. The importance of this aspect of jihad can be appreciated by looking at the United States. The media, educational systems and government are completely in the hands of anti-Islamic forces. Through these institutions they are able to spread anti-Islamic propaganda and present an evil picture of Islam. Is it conceivable that under such circumstances the people of the United States would embrace Islam *en masse* in the same manner that the people of North Africa did in the early history of Islam? Obviously, this is hardly conceivable. This author has met many Americans who believe in Islam but due to social pressures and so forth are not able to embrace and practice Islam in this society.[1] This same

---

[1] Obviously, in many cases, when one first embraces Islam, the person's faith is not as strong as it is after living Islam for a period of years. Hence, these people

point can be made for all of the countries of Europe, Russia, many countries in Africa and elsewhere. Hence, the need for jihad as an instrument of *dawah* is evident today as it was when Islam first flourished.

Therefore, what "There is no compulsion in religion" means is that the People of the Book (Jews, Christians- and this verse also refers to Magians according to the majority of the scholars) are allowed to stick to their religion as long as they submit to the Islamic state. This is an exception for them because, as ibn Taimiyyah pointed out in discussing the reasons why a Muslim man may marry a woman from the People of the Book, they possess fragments of a Divine revelation which, if they read them closely and they sincerely follow them, will lead them to believing in the message of Islam and the truth of the message of the Prophet Muhammad (peace be upon him). In the history of the Middle East, many of the Christian tribes of al-Shaam embraced Islam after living under the Islamic authority for a number of years. The Messenger of Allah (peace be upon him) said,

$$ عَجِبَ اللَّهُ مِنْ قَوْمٍ يَدْخُلُونَ الْجَنَّةَ فِي السَّلاسِلِ $$

"Allah is pleased by those who enter paradise through chains,"[1] that is, they are first slaves of the Muslim populous and then over time they see the truth of Islam, embrace it and by the mercy of Allah are entered into Paradise.

It is confirmed from the Prophet (peace be upon him) that this same treatment was not accorded the polytheists of the Arabian peninsula. Qataadah narrated that the Arabs were compelled to embrace Islam or be killed as they had no book (that is, they were *ummiyeen*) and therefore they had no religion except polytheism. Thus, nothing but Islam was

---

who cannot overcome the obstacles of these social pressures may have been able to embrace Islam and increase their faith in an Islamic environment.
[1] Recorded by al-Bukhari.

75

accepted from them. According to some scholars, this principle extends to all people who are void of any revelation, such as the materialists, atheists, capitalists, socialists, Marxists and communists. Further historical evidence is Abu Bakr's fighting against the apostates after the death of the Prophet (peace be upon him) and Ali's burning alive of those people who had preached the divinity of Ali.

The important conclusions that can be made concerning this one phrase of the Book of Allah are the following:

(1) Its meaning is not that people are allowed to spread *kufr* in an Islamic society. This is a type of *munkar* or evil that the Islamic state is obliged to eradicate.

(2) This phrase does not contradict the Quranic commandments to struggle against the unbelievers and to make the Law of Islam supreme. They are not contradictory because this phrase simply means that if they submit to the Law of Allah, by paying the *jizyah*, then they are not forced to accept Islam but are allowed to remain as Jews and Christians.

(3) Jihad is to be made against any people who set up laws other than those of Allah. But the purpose of the jihad is not to force them to accept Islam—belief is something internal and there is no way to force someone to believe in something that he does not believe in—but the jihad against them is to eradicate the laws that do not originate with Allah, to force them into allowing the religion of Allah to be propagated freely in their land, to allow them to witness the beauty of Islam and to allow the people to accept Islam freely.

"The right direction is henceforth distinct from error"

Both al-Zamakhshari and al-Raazi point out that Allah did not compel or force anyone to accept Islam as this world is one of trial and testing: He left man free to choose the path of truth or the path of evil. Also, at the same time, Allah has made it very clear, through proofs, signs and evidence, that the path of Islam is the true path and it is very distinct from all of the paths of falsehood that the unbelievers follow. This fact alone demonstrates that Allah's throwing people into the Hell-fire is due to Him being the Just as such people who refuse to follow what is clearly the truth deserve the eternal damnation that they will receive. There is no excuse for such people who refuse to follow something that is so evidently true.

This is even more so the case if this verse is addressed to the People of the Book as some scholars have stated. In what Allah revealed to the Prophet Muhammad (peace be upon him), He has made the straight path very clear to the Christians and the Jews and He has plainly shown the mistakes in their beliefs and way of thinking. Eighty-four verses of *soorah al-Baqarah* are dedicated to them; furthermore, Allah, in the same *soorah*, shows that the religion of Abraham, whom both the Christians and Jews claim to believe in, was Islam. Therefore, there is no need to compel them to embrace Islam. If they refuse to embrace Islam in the light of the clear evidence that Allah has presented to them, then forcing them to embrace Islam will not have any positive effect on them. They refuse to embrace Islam not because they are following evidence and proofs but because they prefer to follow their own false gods or desires or to blindly follow the ways of their fathers. These are all types of *taaghoot* (false gods) that are referred to in the following phrase of this verse.

"And he who rejects false deities (Ar., *taaghoot*) and believes in Allah..."

Al-Raazi wrote, "This points to it being a must that the unbeliever must repent first from *kufr* and then attain belief after that." Similarly, Abu Saood stated that denial of *taaghoot* precedes belief in Allah because "evacuation [of the heart] comes before the quality of [faith in the heart]." This is part and parcel of the testimony of faith: "I bear witness that there is none worthy of worship except Allah." This testimony in itself is both a negation and an affirmation. One must negate all other false objects of worship and then affirm that only Allah is worthy of worship.

This is an important point for those who are calling to Islam. The convert to Islam must realize that his former beliefs are *kufr*—no matter whether his old way be that of Judaism, Christianity, Hindusim, atheism, materialism—and he must repent from his wrong beliefs and sincerely affirm his faith in Allah. Many who embrace Islam feel that their old beliefs or way of life were not "wrong" but simply not as "guided" as that of Islam. This demonstrates an incomplete understanding of the essence of faith in Islam.

A number of opinions have been expressed regarding what the word *taaghoot* is referring to in this verse. Perhaps the best statement on this question is al-Tabari's who said, "It refers to any usurper of the right of Allah who is worshipped other than Allah, either by coercion over the one who worships him or through obedience [submission] of the one who worships him. [And it does not matter] if the worshipped is a human, devil, idol, statue or whatever it might be."

It is essential that this part of this verse be understood and applied correctly. Any being that goes over the limit that Allah has set for him as being His slave and subservient to His commands is a type of *taaghoot*. If anyone sets himself up as someone to be worshipped other than Allah, he is a *taaghoot*. If anyone makes laws that contradict the *Shareeah* (law) of Allah, he is a *taaghoot*. It is a must for the believer to recognize such people as *taaghoot*s and to despise and to oppose them and to also despise and oppose those who support that *taaghoot*. If someone knowingly supports a *taaghoot* or loves what they do or accepts what they do of making the prohibited permissible and vice-versa and he still claims to be a believer in Allah, then he is from those people who Allah described in the verse,

$$وَمَا يُؤْمِنُ أَكْثَرُهُمْ بِاللَّهِ إِلاَّ وَهُمْ مُشْرِكُونَ$$

"And most of them believe not in Allah except that they attribute partners (unto Him)" (*Yoosuf* 106). If anyone has even the slightest aspect of *shirk* (associating partners with Allah) in his deeds, then all of his deeds will be of no avail unless he repents from such *shirk*. Allah says about such deeds,

$$وَقَدِمْنَا إِلَى مَا عَمِلُوا مِنْ عَمَلٍ فَجَعَلْنَاهُ هَبَاءً مَنْثُورًا$$

"And We shall turn unto the work they did and make it scattered motes" (*al-Furqaan* 23). It is absolutely essential for a believer to free himself (Ar., *baraa*) from loving or supporting anyone who opposes the way of Allah and to attach himself (Ar., *walaa*) and to love those who follow the way of Allah.

As al-Dausiri wrote, "How can a man claim to adhere to Islam while he supports and loves the opponents of Allah and His Messenger who discard the Islamic *Shareeah* by allowing what Allah has forbidden of alcohol and lewd acts? Could the love for Allah and the love for those *taaghoots* who follow that path be combined in the one heart of a Muslim?... Whoever actualizes denying *taaghoots* in all their forms and actualizes the true faith in Allah by completing his love for Him, for His sake and in His way, and hating everything that Allah hates of humans or deeds has '...grasped a firm handhold which will never break.'"

"...has grasped a firm handhold which will never break."

There is a difference of opinion concerning what "the firm handhold" is. Mujaahid said that it is faith while al-Suddi said it is Islam and Saeed ibn Jubair said it is the statement, "There is no God but Allah." As ibn Katheer pointed out, there is no contradiction between these three statements and all of them are correct.[1]

Al-Dausiri explains grasping on to the firm handhold as sticking to the path of Allah by fulfilling the love for Him and not opposing Him by loving His enemies and *taaghoot*s. The expression also includes fulfilling His orders and avoiding those acts that He prohibits and so on. If anyone does not fulfill these obligations of this religion, then he has not grasped on to the firm handhold from Allah.

Al-Dausiri states that most of the people who claim to be Muslim today have, in their hearts, some aspect of *shirk* and love for the present-day *jaahiliyyah* or ignorance. This is why Allah ends the verse by saying, "Allah is Hearer, Knower." That is, He hears the statement of those who claim to be free of any *taaghoot* yet at the same time He knows what is in their hearts of love and pleasure in the different *taaghoot*s of the present day.

Concerning the last part, "which will never break," Mujaahid explained it by the verse,

$$\text{إِنَّ اللَّهَ لَا يُغَيِّرُ مَا بِقَوْمٍ حَتَّى يُغَيِّرُوا مَا بِأَنفُسِهِمْ}$$

"Allah does not change the condition of a people until they change what is in themselves" (*al-Raad* 11). That is, as long as the person denies all of the different types of *taaghoot* and confirms his faith in Allah, then Allah will continue to support him, love him and bless him.

---

[1] This is a classic example of a common type of "difference of opinion" that existed among the early Quranic commentators. At first glance, it seems like they might be expressing different opinions as to the meaning of the verse. In reality, though, they are simply expressing the same truth in different terms or expressing different aspects of one reality.

"Allah is Hearer, Knower."

There are two reports about the meaning of this phrase. The first is that Allah hears the statement of those who claim belief as well as those who refuse to believe. More than that, He knows the faith in the heart of the believers and He knows the lack of faith in the hearts of the unbelievers and hypocrites. Second, it has been narrated from ibn Abbaas that the Messenger of Allah (peace be upon him) longed for the Jews around Madinah to embrace Islam. Therefore, he used to ask Allah, publicly and privately, to guide them. This phrase means that Allah hears and knows of the Prophet's longing and striving to bring them to Islam.

Fiqh Issues: Daily Congregational Prayers and Combining the Prayers[1]

The Daily Congregational Prayers: Obligatory or Sunnah?

A number of scholars have addressed this question. In *Fataawa al-Kubra*, ibn Taimiyyah discusses this question in a number of places (for example, vol. 1, pp. 112-124 and vol. 2, pp. 430-440). In *Nail al-Autaar* (vol. 3, pp. 150-159), ash-Shaukaani also discussed this question. Basically there are four opinions on this question. We shall first mention each opinion and then derive a conclusion.

The First Opinion: The Congregation is a Condition for the Validity of the Prayer

The congregation is a condition for the validity of the prayer and the prayer is not acceptable if it is not said in a

---

[1] This article appeared in *al-Basheer*, vol. 1, no. 4 (November 1987). It began with the following paragraph, "In this issue, we are actually combining two sections, *Fiqh Issues* and *Questions and Answers* to answer two questions that we have received a number of times now. The two questions are: (1) Concerning performing the five daily prayers in a congregation, is this obligatory or a sunnah or just something that is permissible? (2) Here in Boulder (and other similar places) we often combine the prayers in the mosque due to rain or snow. What exactly is the legal position of the different schools of thought concerning the combining of prayers?"

congregation unless the person has some acceptable excuse for not attending the congregation. (Of course, this is not referring to women or children who are not obligated to attend the prayers in the mosque.) This statement has been made by ibn Taimiyyah (in one of the reports from him), ibn al-Qayyim (ibn Taimiyyah's student), ibn Aqeel, ibn Abu Moosa, Ahmad ibn Hanbal (in one narration) and the Dhaahiri school of thought. The evidence for this opinion is in the following: Ali stated, "There is no prayer for a neighbor of the mosque except in the mosque." (Recorded by al-Baihaqi.) The Prophet (peace be upon him) said,

مَنْ سَمِعَ الْمُنَادِيَ فَلَمْ يَمْنَعْهُ مِنِ اتِّبَاعِهِ عُذْرٌ قَالُوا وَمَا الْعُذْرُ قَالَ خَوْفٌ أَوْ مَرَضٌ لَمْ تُقْبَلْ مِنْهُ الصَّلَاةُ الَّتِي صَلَّى

"If someone hears the call to prayer and does not have any excuse to prevent him from attending the prayer," [the people asked what an acceptable excuse is and he answered "fear or illness"] "then his prayer will not be accepted." (Recorded by Abu Daawood with a weak chain.) Al-Daaraqutni also recorded that the Prophet (peace be upon him) made the same statement that was quoted from Ali above but it is with an unacceptable chain.

Ibn Hazm (in *al-Muhalla*, vol. 3, p. 188) wrote,

The obligatory prayer said alone by any man is not sufficient. If he can hear the call to prayer, he must pray in the mosque with the Imam. If he intentionally does not do so, without any valid excuse, his prayer will not be valid. If he cannot hear the call to prayer, he must still pray in a congregation with one or more persons. If he does not do so, it would be as if he did not pray—unless he cannot find anyone to pray with, in which case his prayer would still be valid. Also, if he has some valid excuse not to attend the prayer of the congregation, his prayer said alone will still be valid.

The Second Opinion: It is an Obligation and Any Man Who is Able to But does Not Perform the Prayer in a Congregation Has Sinned

The congregation is an obligatory part of every prayer for every free, adult, sane capable man. Any such man who performs any prayer outside of a congregation without any valid excuse for doing so has sinned. The people of this opinion cite a number of verses and hadith in support of this conclusion. For example, Allah says,

وَإِذَا كُنتَ فِيهِمْ فَأَقَمْتَ لَهُمُ الصَّلَاةَ فَلْتَقُمْ طَائِفَةٌ مِنْهُمْ مَعَكَ وَلْيَأْخُذُوا أَسْلِحَتَهُمْ فَإِذَا سَجَدُوا فَلْيَكُونُوا مِنْ وَرَائِكُمْ وَلْتَأْتِ طَائِفَةٌ أُخْرَى لَمْ يُصَلُّوا فَلْيُصَلُّوا مَعَكَ

"And when you are among them and arrange their worship for them, let only a party of them stand with you to worship and let them take their arms. Then when they have performed their prostrations let them fall to the rear and let another party come that has not worshipped and let them worship with you...." (*al-Nisaa* 102) This verse is a description of how the prayer is to be performed in the face of the enemy. This verse is related to the question at hand in that Allah shows that even in the time of battle the Muslims are not excused from performing their prayers in congregation, unless there was no possible way to perform it in the manner prescribed in the above verse. If the congregational prayer is so important during the time of the battle itself imagine how important it must be during the rest of the times.

Also Allah says,

وَأَقِيمُوا الصَّلاةَ وَآتُوا الزَّكَاةَ وَارْكَعُوا مَعَ الرَّاكِعِينَ

"Establish worship, pay the zakaat and bow your heads with those who bow (in prayer)" (al-Baqarah 43). The command in this verse is in the imperative form and, as is known from the field of *usool al-fiqh* (Islamic legal theory), the imperative means that the act is obligatory.

Other verses that have been cited in favor of this opinion are: *al-Noor* 37, *al-Taubah* 18 and *al-Araaf* 29.

From the hadith, there are the following: Abu Hurairah reported that the Prophet (peace be upon him) said,

لَيْسَ صَلاةٌ أَثْقَلَ عَلَى الْمُنَافِقِينَ مِنَ الْفَجْرِ وَالْعِشَاءِ... لَقَدْ هَمَمْتُ أَنْ آمُرَ الْمُؤَذِّنَ فَيُقِيمَ ثُمَّ آمُرَ رَجُلاً يَؤُمُّ النَّاسَ ثُمَّ آخُذَ شُعَلاً مِنْ نَارٍ فَأُحَرِّقَ عَلَى مَنْ لا يَخْرُجُ إِلَى الصَّلاةِ بَعْدُ

"There is no prayer heavier upon the hypocrites than the night prayer and the dawn prayer....I have thought to ask someone else to lead the prayer and I would go with someone to kindle a fire and burn the houses of those who do not go out to attend the prayers." (Recorded by Muslim and al-Bukhari.) In Ahmad's version the Prophet (peace be upon him) is reported to have said, "If it were not for the women and the children in the houses I would..." In these hadith the Prophet (peace be upon him) has severely threatened those who stay away from the congregational prayer and, again according to the principles of *usool al-fiqh*, such a grave threat means that the referred to act is sinful; that is, staying away from the congregational prayer in the mosque is sinful.

In another hadith the Prophet (peace be upon him) stated that Allah may seal the hearts of those people who remain away from the congregation. (Recorded by Muslim and al-Bukhari.) Sealing of the hearts is one of the greatest torments that Allah metes out and Allah has used such a term in His description of the hypocrites. Furthermore, the Prophet (peace be upon him) did not give ibn Umm Maktoom (who was blind) permission to stay away from the daily congregational prayers although he had no guide to take him to the mosque. Abdullah ibn Masood also stated that the only people who remained away from the daily congregational prayers were the hypocrites who were well-known for their hypocrisy. (Abu Daawood records from ibn Masood that if they prayed in their houses they would be considered unbelievers but this narration is weak and not acceptable.) In a hadith quoted earlier, Ibn Abbaas related that the Prophet (peace be upon him) said, "If anyone hears the call to prayer and does not respond to it [by attending the prayer], then his prayer would not be acceptable unless he had some valid excuse." (Recorded by Abu Daawood, ibn Hibbaan, ibn Maajah and al-Baihaqi.) However, this hadith is not a sound hadith.

All of the above points to the fact that the daily prayers in congregation are obligatory and if one does not have a valid excuse for missing the congregational prayer, then he has sinned. This is the opinion of the majority of the scholars from among the Companions and those who followed them (for example, Ata, al-Auzaaee, Ishaaq, Abu Thaur, ibn Khuzaima, ibn Hibbaan and ibn al-Mundhir) and it is also the opinion of Ahmad and ash-Shafi'ee. Abu Hanifah and Maalik say that the congregational prayer is only a *sunnah muakada* ("an emphasized sunnah") but they also say that it is sinful for one to leave a *sunnah muakada* and this is actually the same thing as saying that the act is obligatory. Also Ibn Rushd, in *Bidaayah al-Mujtaahid* (vol. 1, p. 198), stated that continually leaving a sunnah is sinful. Thus the four Imaams agree that prayer in congregation is obligatory; in other words, leaving it is sinful. Abdul Azeez ibn Muhammad ibn Daawood wrote, "From what has proceeded, it is clear that all four of the Imaams agree, although they use different terms in their statements, that the performing of the prayers in a congregation is an obligation and if one fails to do so without a valid excuse, he has sinned. And the clear texts from the Quran and sunnah prove that it is obligatory as has been shown and no one may dare speak in the face of the statements of Allah and His messenger (peace be upon him)."

The Third Opinion: The Congregation is an Obligation on the Community (*Fardh Kifaayah*) But Not on Each Individual Muslim

The performance of the five daily prayers in a congregation is a *fardh kifaayah*, meaning, if one group of the Muslims perform it, the others are absolved of any sin but if none of them perform the act then they are all guilty of the sin. This group argues from the general meaning of the verses and hadith that point to the importance of the congregation and they state that the congregation is one of the "signs" of Islam that may not be dispensed with. A number of Shafi'ees are of this opinion. They argue that the hadith of ibn Umm Maktoom, the blind man whom the Prophet (peace be upon him) ordered to attend the prayer, was referring to the Friday prayer only and not the daily congregational prayers. [Ibn Rushd (p. 178) says that this interpretation of the hadith concerning Umm Maktoom is definitely not acceptable.]

The Fourth Opinion: The Congregation is Only a Recommended Aspect and is Not Obligatory

The performance of the five daily prayers in a congregation is a *sunnah mu'akadah* (a stressed sunnah). The people of this opinion use the following hadith (and other hadith similar to them) as the evidence for their position: The Prophet (peace be upon him) said,

$$صَلاةُ الْجَمَاعَةِ تَفْضُلُ صَلاةَ الْفَذِّ بِسَبْعٍ وَعِشْرِينَ دَرَجَةً$$

"The prayer said in a congregational is twenty-seven degrees superior to a prayer said on an individual basis." (Recorded by al-Bukhari.) And,

$$صَلاةُ الرَّجُلِ فِي الْجَمَاعَةِ تُضَعَّفُ عَلَى صَلاتِهِ فِي بَيْتِهِ وَفِي سُوقِهِ خَمْسًا وَعِشْرِينَ ضِعْفًا$$

"The prayer of a man in a congregation is superior to his prayer in his house or in his market by twenty five degrees." (Recorded by al-Bukhari.) There are yet other hadith of an exhortative nature.

The point of the argument here is that if the prayer said alone by the individual was not of great merit why is it that the prayer in congregation is only superior to it by a number of degrees? In other words, both of the acts, congregational or solitary, must satisfy the requirement for the prayer but one of them is simply superior or preferred to the other. This is the opinion of al-Shaukaani (vol. 3, p. 158) and he also says that it is the opinion of ibn Taimiyyah's grandfather.

Conclusion on the Question Concerning Congregational Prayers

From the above it is clear that the strongest opinion, that is, the one with the strongest support from the evidence available, is the second opinion which states that the congregation is an obligation for each of the five prayers upon every individual, male, adult, free Muslim. One of the strongest evidences, as mentioned above, is the fact that even during times of war Allah still obliged the Prophet (peace be upon him) and his companions to pray in a congregation. Furthermore, from the principles of *usool al-fiqh* (Islamic legal theory), it is clear that if the Prophet (peace be upon him) threatens a people for not performing an act, like burning down their houses for not praying in a congregation, then that act must be an obligatory act as the Prophet (peace be upon him) would not make such a threat for an act that is simply preferred.

The first opinion stated above is not strong since the hadith that they quote to support their opinion are all of a doubtful status and therefore they cannot be used as evidence in Islamic law. Furthermore, it is also known that the Prophet (peace be upon him) never ordered some people who had prayed by themselves to repeat their prayers in a congregation. If the congregation was a condition for the validity of the prayer he would have ordered them to do so.

If the congregation was just *fardh kifaayah* (opinion number three above), then Allah would not have ordered each group to perform the prayer behind the Prophet (peace be upon him) during the time of battle as it would have been sufficient for just one group to pray behind the Prophet (peace be upon him) and for the others to pray by themselves. Furthermore, the Prophet (peace be upon him) did not permit ibn Umm Maktoom, as mentioned above, not to attend the congregational prayers. Had the prayers in congregation just been *fardh kifaayah* there would have been no need for the Prophet (peace be upon him) to refuse ibn Umm Maktoom's request.

As for the last opinion, that the congregation is *sunnah mu'akadah*, if this were true Allah would not have ordered the Muslims to pray in a congregation during the battle. Also, the Prophet (peace be upon him) would not have threatened those people who did not attend the prayers with burning down their houses.

Abdul Azeez ibn Muhammad ibn Daawood (p. 200) concludes his study by saying, "The strongest opinion, Allah knows best, is the second opinion that states that the congregation is an obligation upon each individual and one who leaves the congregation is committing one of the gravest sins and he is leaving himself to the hatred and punishment of Allah if he does not repent or he does not get forgiven by Allah."

Perhaps a good conclusion for this topic is the statement of ibn Masood who said, "Whoever wishes to meet Allah tomorrow as a Muslim should guard the prayers whenever he is called to them. The Messenger of Allah taught us the sunnah of guidance. And part of this sunnah is to perform the prayers in the mosques in which the call to prayer is given. If you pray in your houses like those people who stayed behind and prayed in their houses, you have left the sunnah of your Prophet. If you leave the sunnah of your Prophet, you will be misguided... In our view, no one would not attend the prayers accept for someone who was well known for his hypocrisy." (Recorded by Muslim.)

References for the Question of Daily Congregational Prayers

Abdul Azeez ibn Muhammad ibn Daawood. "Bayaan Hukm Salaat al-Jamaa." *Adhwa al-Shareeah*. Vol. 14. 1403.

Ibn Hazm, Ali. *Al-Muhalla*. Beirut: Al-Maktab al-Tijaariyyah. No date.

Ibn Rushd, Muhammad. *Bidaayat al-Mujtaahid wa Nihaayat al-Muqtasid*. Cairo: Daar al-Kutub al-Hadeethah. No date.

Ibn Taimiyyah, Ahmad. *Fataawa al-Kubra*. Beirut. Daar al-Marifah.

-----*Majmoo Fataawa Ibn Taimiyyah*. Riyadh: Daar al-Ifta. No date.

al-Shaukaani, Muhammad ibn Ali. *Nail al-Autaar*. Beirut: Daar al-Jeel. 1973.

Combining the Prayers

This question shall be dealt with in a different manner. First, a *fatwa* or verdict from Daar al-Ifta of Riyadh shall be quoted and then some points related to it will be discussed. The following is *fatwa* number 828, dated 8/13/1394 from Daar al-Ifta and published in *Majallat al-Buhooth al-Islaamiyyah*, vol. 17.

The *Fatwa*

The Question: A congregation combines the afternoon (*Asr*) prayer with the noon (*Dhuhr*) prayer and the night (*Isha*) prayer with the sunset (*Maghrib*) prayer due to rain during the time of the noon prayer and the sunset prayer. If the rain stops by the proper time of the afternoon prayer or the night prayer, does this mean that they must repeat the afternoon and night prayers?

The Answer: The scholars have stated that the rain that makes the clothing wet and that causes hardship when going through it is a valid excuse for combining the prayers. All are in agreement that it is allowed to combine the night prayer with the sunset prayer due to such rain. [This is not exactly correct, see the discussion below.] This is based on what has been recorded by Abu Salama ibn Abdul Rahmaan who said, "It is part of the sunnah to combine the sunset and night prayers in the case of rain." [Recorded by Al-Athram.] And also what is in *al-Bukhari* that the Prophet (peace be upon him) combined those prayers due to rain. There is a difference of opinion concerning combining the noon with the afternoon prayers. Some of them say that it is allowed based on the report from Al-Hasan ibn Widhaah from Moosa ibn Uqba on the authority of Naafi on the authority of ibn Umar who stated that the Prophet (peace be upon him) combined the noon and afternoon prayers in Madinah due to rain. This is the conclusion of al-Qaadhi, Abu al-Khitaab and the Shafi'ee school of *fiqh*. Some of the scholars say that it is not allowed to combine the noon and afternoon prayers due to rain. They say that it has only been recorded that it is permissible to combine the sunset and night prayers due to the greater hardship during the times of those prayers. In *al-Mughni*, ibn Qudaamah said, "Combining the noon and afternoon prayers is not permissible. Al-Athram said, 'I said to Abu Abdullah [Ahmad ibn Hanbal], 'What about combining the noon and afternoon prayers due to rain?' He said, 'No [it should not be done] as I have never heard anything about it.' That is the opinion of Abu Bakr [the disciple of Ahmad], ibn Hamid and Maalik." Then he states, after mentioning the opinion that says it is permissible, "For our opinion there is proof in what has been stated by Abu Salama and a consensus that nothing has been narrated save for the combining of the sunset and night prayers. Their hadith [about combining the noon and afternoon prayers] is not authentic as it has not been mentioned in any of the books of the *Sahih* or *Sunan*. And Ahmad's statement that he never heard of such a report means that it is not worth anything. It is not correct to argue by an analogy with the sunset and night prayers as there is much more of a hardship for these prayers due to darkness and possible harm. Also, one cannot make an analogy based on the combining of prayers during travelling as the reason for that combining is the travelling and missing the travelling group which is not present in this case."

From among the prerequisites for combining the prayers is the existence of the reason or excuse at the time of the beginning of the first prayer, its ending and the beginning of the second prayer. If the excuse is no longer present after the second prayer has begun, the prayer is still valid and it will not be affected by the change in conditions as the excuse was present at the beginning of the first prayer and at its ending and at the beginning of the second prayer. It will not be affected if the excuse is not present at other times. Therefore, the afternoon prayers, for those who consider it permissible to combine the noon and afternoon prayers, need not be repeated if the rain is no longer present at the [proper] time of the afternoon prayers. The same is true with respect to the night prayer.

[End of *fatwa*. The committee that made the *fatwa* was Abdul Razzaaq Afeefi, Abdullah ibn Abdul Rahmaan ibn Ghudyan and Abdullah ibn Sulaimaan ibn Manee.]

Comments

There are some further points that should be added to the response of the committee.

First is a discussion of the hadith used in the answer. The hadith concerning the combining of the noon and afternoon prayers during rain is in fact weak. In *Talkhees al-Habeer* (vol. 2, p. 50), ibn Hajr has stated that it has no known source. In *Irwa al-Ghaleel* (vol. 3, p. 39), al-Albaani has also called it weak. Therefore, as ibn Qudaamah pointed out, there is no authentic hadith stating that the Prophet (peace be upon him) ever combined the noon and afternoon prayers due to rain. The latter hadith from the Abu Salama ibn Abdul Rahmaan, concerning combining the evening and night prayers due to rain, is also not strong, as al-Albaani (vol. 3, p. 41) has pointed out. But there is an authentic hadith from ibn Umar, recorded by Imam Maalik in *al-Muwatta*, that states that the Companions did combine the evening and night prayers due to rain. Furthermore, many of the members of the following generation have been recorded to have combined their sunset and night prayers due to rain. Hence, it cannot be objected to if an Imam decides to combine the evening and night prayers due to hardships from rain.

Second is more detail about the combining of the prayers. There are two types of combining of the prayers. One is called *soori*, where it only looks like the prayers have been combined in each other's time, and the other is called *haqeeqi*, where the prayers have truly been combined during the proper time of one of the prayers. In the first case the noon prayer is delayed until the end of its time is closely approaching. The person then performs the noon prayer directly followed by the afternoon prayer in its *proper* time. Suppose the time for the afternoon prayer commences at 3:00. Then the person will delay the noon prayer until about 2:50 or so and then perform the noon prayer followed by the afternoon prayer at around 3:01. Although it is not mentioned in the above answer to the question, this is the only type of combining the prayers that the Hanafis allow. Hence, they do not allow an Imam to perform the sunset prayer with the night prayer before the beginning of the time for the night prayer. This is their interpretation of the hadith that state that the Prophet (peace be upon him) combined the prayers. But this interpretation is definitely wrong as some of the hadith stating that the Prophet (peace be upon him) combined some of his prayers clearly state that he prayed one of the prayers during the time of the other prayer.

There is still the question of whether or not it is permissible to combine the noon and afternoon prayers due to rain. The only possible proof that I could find for such an act is the hadith of ibn Abbaas who said, "The Prophet (peace be upon him) combined the noon and afternoon prayers and combined the sunset and night prayers in Madinah without any fear or rain." (Recorded by Maalik, Muslim and others.) This hadith has been the source of a great deal of discussion. Some scholars, such as al-Tirmidhi, say that it is not to be applied. Others say that it is referring to the *soori* type of combining and not the *haqeeqi* type. Both of these claims have been soundly refuted by ibn Taimiyyah in a lengthy passage in *Majmoo Fataawa ibn Taimiyyah* (vol. 24, pp. 73-84). (In one of the narrations of this hadith ibn Abbaas clearly states that the Prophet (peace be upon him) performed that act in order for their to be no hardship on his nation. Ibn Taimiyyah asks which is easier: performing each prayer at any time during its proper time or delaying the noon prayer until the afternoon time is just about to begin and then combining the prayer? Therefore, how could the hadith be referring to a *soori* combination of the prayers? Hence, based on this action of the Prophet (peace be upon him), it can be considered permissible to combine the noon and afternoon prayers due to rain.

It should be kept in mind that combining the prayers without any valid excuse (which is a common practice of the Shiahs), such as travelling, rain, snow, extreme cold, fainting spells, post-menstrual bleeding and so forth, is considered a grave sin. Ibn Abbaas said, "Whoever combines the prayers without any valid reason has opened the door to the grave sins." (This is sometimes narrated as a hadith of the Prophet but, in fact, it is a statement of ibn Abbaas.) It is up to the regular Imam of the mosque to decide if the Muslims should combine the prayers or not.

Finally, there is the question of the "intention" related to combining the prayers. According to the Hanbalis and Shafi'ees, the person must make the intention to combine the prayers before he combines them. But this opinion is not correct as both ibn Hajr and al-Suyooti have pointed out. When the Prophet (peace be upon him) combined his prayers, he never told the followers behind him that he would do so. If the intention was a necessity he would have informed his Companions that he was to combine the prayers in order to allow them to make the proper intention. (Cf., al-Ashqar, p. 210.)

Allah knows best.

[One final note: Hadith number 581 in *Irwa al-Ghaleel* has been misprinted. It should read, "The Prophet (peace be upon him) combined the noon and afternoon prayers during a rainy day."]

References for the Question of Combining the Prayers.

al-Albaani, Muhammad N. *Irwa al-Ghaleel*. Beirut: Al-Maktab al-Islaami. 1979.

al-Ashqar, Umar. *Muqaasid al-Mukallifeen*. Kuwait: Maktab al-Falaah. 1981.

Daar al-Ifta. *Fatwa* Number 828. 8/13/1394. Reprinted in *Majallat al-Buhooth al-Islaamiyyah*, vol. 17.

Ibn Hajr, Ahmad. *Talkhees al-Habeer*. Madinah. 1964.

Ibn Rushd, Muhammad. *Bidaayat al-Mujtaahid wa Nihaayat al-Muqtasid*. Cairo: Daar al-Kutub al-Hadeethah. No date.

Ibn Taimiyyah, Ahmad. *Majmoo Fataawa Ibn Taimiyyah*. Riyadh: Daar al-Ifta.

Fiqh Issues:
Zakaat and Jewelry[1]

The Permissibility of Wearing Gold and Silver Jewelry

The desire for *zeenah* or adornments seems to be rooted in human nature. Many men will even sacrifice some of life's necessities in order to save enough money to purchase nice clothing or some other type of adornment. The same is true for women. Islam recognizes this natural inclination of humans and permits certain types of adornment for both men and women. Yet at the same time, as one can note in many of the regulations of Islam, it sets limits to the use of such permissible items. Allah says in the Quran,

يَابَنِي آدَمَ خُذُوا زِينَتَكُمْ عِنْدَ كُلِّ مَسْجِدٍ وَكُلُوا وَاشْرَبُوا وَلَا تُسْرِفُوا إِنَّهُ لَا يُحِبُّ الْمُسْرِفِينَ قُلْ مَنْ حَرَّمَ زِينَةَ اللَّهِ الَّتِي أَخْرَجَ لِعِبَاده وَالطَّيِّبَات مِنْ الرِّزْقِ قُلْ هِيَ لِلَّذِينَ آمَنُوا فِي الْحَيَاة الدُّنْيَا خَالِصَةً يَوْمَ الْقِيَامَة كَذَلِكَ نُفَصِّلُ الآيَات لِقَوْمٍ يَعْلَمُونَ

"O Children of Adam, take your adornment at every place of worship, and eat and drink, but be not prodigal. Lo, He loves

---

[1] This article appeared in *al-Basheer*, vol. 2, no. 3 (Sept.-Oct. 1988).

not the prodigals. Say: Who has forbidden the adornment of Allah which He has brought forth for His bondmen and the good things of His providing? Say: Such, on the Day of Resurrection, will be only for those who believed during the life of the world" (*al-Araaf* 31-32).

According to Imam al-Nawawi there is a consensus (Ar., *ijmaa*) that it is permissible for women to wear gold and silver jewelry, be that jewelry necklaces, rings, bracelets, anklets and so forth. He says that there is no difference of opinion concerning such matters.[1]

The question that arises is: Since gold and silver jewelry are permissible for women, are they required to pay any zakaat on such gold and silver jewelry? This question will be answered in detail in the following pages.

A Warning Concerning Not Paying the Zakaat

The Messenger of Allah (peace be upon him) has given very strong threats concerning the failure to pay zakaat on jewelry. Abu Daawood, Ahmad, at-Tirmidhi, ad-Daaraqtuni and others relate from Umar ibn Shuaib from his grandfather that a woman, with her daughter, came to the Messenger of Allah (peace be upon him) and the daughter was wearing bracelets of gold on her wrists. The Messenger of Allah (peace be upon him) asked, "Did you give the zakaat on those?" She said, "No." He then said,

---

[1] For an opposing, and in this author's opinion weaker opinion, see Muhammad Naasir al-Deen al-Albaani, *Adaab al-Zafaaf* (Beirut: al-Maktab al-Islaami, 5th edition), pp. 132-142. A complete refutation of al-Albaani's opinion may be found in Ismaaeel ibn Muhammad al-Ansaari, *Ibaahat al-Tahulli bi-l-Dhahab al-Muhallaq li-l-Nisaa wa al-Radd ala al-Albaani fi Tahreemihi* (Riyadh: Daar al-Ifta, 1984).

$$أَيَسُرُّكِ أَنْ يُسَوِّرَكِ اللَّهُ عَزَّ وَجَلَّ بِهِمَا يَوْمَ الْقِيَامَةِ سِوَارَيْنِ مِنْ نَارٍ$$

"Would you be pleased if Allah would make, due to them, two bracelets of fire for you on the Day of Judgment?" She took them off and gave them to the Messenger of Allah (peace be upon him) and said, "They are for Allah and His Messenger."[1] Al-Khattaabi said that the words, "Allah will make by them on the Day of Judgment bracelets of fire," are the explanation of the Quranic verse,

$$يَوْمَ يُحْمَى عَلَيْهَا فِي نَارِ جَهَنَّمَ فَتُكْوَى بِهَا جِبَاهُهُمْ وَجُنُوبُهُمْ وَظُهُورُهُمْ هَذَا مَا كَنَزْتُمْ لِأَنفُسِكُمْ فَذُوقُوا مَا كُنتُمْ تَكْنِزُونَ$$

"On the day when it will (all) be heated in the fire of hell, and their foreheads and their flanks and their backs will be branded therewith (and it will be said unto them): Here is that which you hoarded for yourselves. Now taste of what you used to hoard" (*al-Taubah* 35).

An-Nasaai relates in *mursal* and *mutassil* form (meaning with both "broken" and "connected" chains) that two women came to the Messenger of Allah (peace be upon him) and on their wrists were bracelets of gold. The Messenger of Allah (peace be upon him) said to them, "Have you given the zakaat?" They said, "No." The Messenger of Allah (peace be upon him) said, "Do you love that Allah makes because of them bracelets of fire?" They said, "No." So he said, "Then pay the zakaat due on them."

---

[1] According to al-Albaani, this hadith is acceptable. See Muhammad Naasir al-Deen al-Albaani, *Adaab al-Zafaaf fi al-Sunnah al-Mutahhirah* (Amman, Jordan: al-Maktabah al-Islaamiyyah, 1409 A.H.), p. 256.

Abu Daawood, ad-Daaraqtuni and al-Baihaqi relate from Aishah that she was present with the Prophet (peace be upon him) and he saw on her fingers rings of gold. He said, "What is this, O Aishah?" She said, "They are put on as adornments for you, O Messenger of Allah!" He said, "Did you pay the zakaat (due on them)?" She said, "No...and whatever Allah wills." He said, "That is sufficient for you of the fire of hell!"[1] Al-Khattaabi said that those few rings by themselves were not enough to reach the minimum amount required to pay zakaat, therefore he must have been referring to those rings as well as whatever else she may have possessed of jewelry.

Ahmad records with a *sahih* chain that Asmaa bint Yazeed and her aunt came upon the Messenger of Allah (peace be upon him) and they were wearing bracelets of gold. He said, "Have you given the zakaat (due on them)?" They said, "No." He said,

أَمَا تَخَافَانِ أَنْ يُسَوِّرَكُمَا اللَّهُ أَسْوِرَةً مِنْ نَارٍ أَدِّيَا زَكَاتَهُ

"Do you not fear that Allah may make for you bracelets of fire. Pay the zakaat (due on them)."

Brief Review of the Opinions of Five Fiqh Schools

Although the above hadith seem to be clear, there is a difference of opinion among the scholars concerning whether or not a woman must pay zakaat on her allowable jewelry of gold and silver. And they also differ about when it becomes obligatory upon her to pay the zakaat. Below the opinions of the different schools of fiqh are given.

---

[1] Al-Albaani says that the chain of this hadith is *sahih*. See al-Albaani, *Adaab*, p. 264.

Abu Haneefah and ibn Hazm are of the opinion that a woman must pay zakaat on her gold and silver jewelry, once it reaches the minimum amounts (*nisaab*) that require one to pay zakaat. They give, as their proofs, the hadith that were recorded above. Aishah was ordered to pay the zakaat in the first hadith from Abu Dawood, al-Baihaqi and ad-Daaraqutni. In the hadith that Ahmad recorded, both Asmaa and her aunt were ordered to pay the zakaat on their bracelets. Similar is the case with the other hadith recorded by an-Nasaai.

The Malikis are of the opinion that there is no zakaat to be paid on gold or silver jewelry, except in the following cases: (1) The jewelry is broken and there is no chance to bring it back to its original state save by melting it and making new jewelry. (2) The jewelry is broken and could be repaired without melting it but the owner does not intend to repair it. (3) The jewelry is used for speculative purposes of possible future need, such as poverty. (4) It is being saved by someone for a future daughter. (5) The jewelry is being kept to be used as dowry in the future. (6) The jewelry is kept for the intention of making business. In these cases (where the jewelry is not really being kept as jewelry but for other reasons, such as speculative or business reasons), it becomes obligatory to pay zakaat on the jewelry.

The Shafi'ees are of the opinion that it is not obligatory to pay zakaat on the allowable jewelry that the woman knows of and that she posseses for a year. If she did not know that it belonged to her, that is, it is jewelry that she inherited and kept for a year without knowing its amount, then she must pay zakaat on it. Zakaat is also obligatory if the woman is amassing jewelry, for example, one hundred bracelets. One must pay zakaat on gold necklaces if they do not have a coil of gold or copper. If the jewelry does have a coil of one of those two, then there is no zakaat upon it. If the jewelry is broken, there is no zakaat if one has the intention to repair it and it can be repaired without resorting to a goldsmith. Otherwise, the zakaat is obligatory.

The Hanbalis are of the opinion that there is no zakaat on allowable jewelry that is used repeatedly or is lent out for use. If it is not used repeatedly then one must pay zakaat on it. If it is broken but can be worn, there is no zakaat on it. If it cannot be worn but could be put back into form, then there is zakaat on it. If it could not be put back into form, although one attempted to do so, there is no zakaat on it.

The Reasons for the Different Opinions

Ibn Rushd states that the difference of opinion revolves around the following two points: (1) Some of them make an analogy between such jewelry and those goods that are possessed for their own benefit (consumption goods) while others make an analogy between such jewelry and the goods that are possessed for the purpose of business (merchandise). In the former case, there should be no zakaat on the jewelry while in the latter case there would be zakaat. Therefore, those who say that gold and silver jewelry resemble consumer goods will argue that there is no zakaat on such goods and those who argue that such jewelry resembles merchandise will argue that there is zakaat on the jewelry.[1]

Regardless whether *qiyaas al-shabah* (discussed in the previous footnote) is acceptable or not, it is not acceptable to make *qiyaas* (analogy) when there is a text from the Quran or sunnah on a certain issue. Therefore, one cannot resort to

---

[1] This is known as *qiyaas al-shabah* where an object has two bases upon which an analogy could be made. For example, a slave is, in some aspects, treated as a slave while in other aspects he is considered as a human being who is subservient to the commands of Allah like anyone else. Therefore, if a new question arises, should an analogy be made on the basis of the slave as a slave or on the basis of the slave as a human who must obey the *Shareeah* in the same manner as other free humans? Due to the difficult foundation on which an analogy in this case would be structured, many scholars do not accept this type of *qiyaas* or analogy as a means of *ijtihaad*. Cf., Dr. Naadiyah al-Umari, *al-Qiyaas fi al-Tashri al-Islaami* (n.c.: Hajr, 1987), pp. 289-297.

qiyaas on this question of zakaat on jewelry. Hence, *qiyaas* cannot be considered a proof on this question.

(2) The second reason that ibn Rushd mentions are the contradictory reports from the Companions and Followers. This will be discussed in more detail in the following section.

The Proofs and Discussion

The Hanafis say that it is obligatory to pay zakaat on gold and silver jewelry once the amount reaches the minimum required for the payment of zakaat. The other three Imams say that, in general, it is not obligatory, whether or not it reaches the minimum. Their proof is the following: Al-Baihaqi reported that Asmaa bint Abu Bakr possessed gold jewelry for her daughter and did not pay zakaat on it even though it was a great deal of jewelry. In *al-Muwatta* there is a report that Aishah had some orphans with her who possessed jewelry and she did not pay zakaat on their jewelry.[1] The same is recorded concerning Abdullah ibn Umar and his daughter, and they possessed four hundred *dinaar*s worth of jewelry.

Al-Khattaabi says, summing up this question, "The clear meaning of the hadith bear evidence for those who say that it is obligatory (to pay zakaat on jewelry) and the reports support it. Those who say that it is not obligatory argue by reasoning and from reports in a circumstantial way. The safest thing to do is to pay (the zakaat)."

According to Khamees, if the woman has a purpose for the jewelry, such as making it an adornment for the husband then there is no zakaat on such jewelry no matter how much of it she may own. If the woman owns jewelry in order to pile up wealth, or she hoards it (for fame or for whatever reason) and

---

[1] It should be noted, though, that Aishah was of the opinion that it is not obligatory to pay zakaat on the wealth of orphans.

calls it jewelry, then there is no use or need for such jewelry and she is obliged to pay the zakaat on such jewelry.

Khamees continues by saying that those who have a great deal of God-consciousness are more willing to be on the safe side to give the zakaat if the gold or silver reaches the *nisaab* (minimum) and this is what the clear meaning of the hadith show and this is the opinion of Abu Haneefah and Ibn Hazm.

Ibn Uthaimeen's Discussion

Ibn Uthaimeen has also discussed this question of zakaat on jewelry. He stated that there are five opinions on this question: (1) There is no zakaat upon it no matter how much it is and this is the opinion of Maalik, ash-Shafi'ee and Ahmad. (2) There is zakaat on it in only one year (that is, not every year) and this has been related from Anas ibn Maalik. (3) Its zakaat is to lend it out whenever it is asked for and this has been related from Asmaa and also from Anas ibn Maalik. (4) It is obligatory to either pay zakaat on it or to lend it out when it is asked for and this is the opinion that ibn al-Qayyim concluded was the strongest. (5) Zakaat is obligatory on it for every year that its amount goes above the minimum level of *nisaab*. This last opinion is that of Abu Haneefah as well as one report from Ahmad. According to ibn Uthaimeen, this last opinion is the strongest opinion according to the Quran, sunnah and sound analogy.[1]

Ibn Uthaimeen begins his proof of (5) being the strongest opinion by quoting the Quranic verse,

---

[1] There is a sixth opinion that ibn Uthaimeen failed to mention and that is that it is best to pay the zakaat on jewelry in order to be on the safe side. This is actually the opinion of al-Khattaabi (note the quote above from him in this article), al-Sindi, al-Shanqeeti, Mahmood Khitaab al-Subki, Abu Bakr al-Jazaairi and Fakhr al-Deen al-Raazi. See al-Basaarah, pp. 27-28. The consequences of this opinion are the same as the opinion of those who say that it is definitely obligatory to pay zakaat on jewelry.

وَالَّذِينَ يَكْنِزُونَ الذَّهَبَ وَالْفِضَّةَ وَلَا يُنفِقُونَهَا فِي سَبِيلِ اللَّهِ
فَبَشِّرْهُم بِعَذَابٍ أَلِيمٍ يَوْمَ يُحْمَى عَلَيْهَا فِي نَارِ جَهَنَّمَ
فَتُكْوَى بِهَا جِبَاهُهُمْ وَجُنُوبُهُمْ وَظُهُورُهُمْ هَذَا مَا كَنَزْتُمْ
لِأَنفُسِكُمْ فَذُوقُوا مَا كُنتُمْ تَكْنِزُونَ

"They who hoard up gold and silver and spend it not in the way of Allah, unto them give tidings of a painful doom. On the day when it will (all) be heated in the fire and their foreheads and their flanks and their backs will be branded therewith (and it will be said unto them): Here is that which you hoarded for yourselves. Now taste of what you used to hoard" (*al-Taubah* 34-35). With support from reports from ibn Umar and others, ibn Uthaimeen states that what is hoarded or wealth in this verse is any type of gold or silver upon which one has not paid the zakaat, regardless of whether it be jewelry or something else. Then he recorded the hadith that was mentioned above in which the Prophet (peace be upon him) asked, on different occasions, "Have you paid the zakaat [on that jewelry]?" And he also recorded the hadith from *Sahih Muslim* which states,

مَا مِنْ صَاحِبِ ذَهَبٍ وَلَا فِضَّةٍ لَا يُؤَدِّي مِنْهَا حَقَّهَا إِلَّا إِذَا
كَانَ يَوْمُ الْقِيَامَةِ صُفِّحَتْ لَهُ صَفَائِحَ مِنْ نَارٍ فَأُحْمِيَ عَلَيْهَا فِي
نَارِ جَهَنَّمَ فَيُكْوَى بِهَا جَنْبُهُ وَجَبِينُهُ وَظَهْرُهُ كُلَّمَا بَرَدَتْ
أُعِيدَتْ لَهُ فِي يَوْمٍ كَانَ مِقْدَارُهُ خَمْسِينَ أَلْفَ سَنَةٍ حَتَّى
يُقْضَى بَيْنَ الْعِبَادِ فَيَرَى سَبِيلَهُ إِمَّا إِلَى الْجَنَّةِ وَإِمَّا إِلَى النَّارِ

"If any owner of gold or silver does not pay what is due upon them, when the Day of Resurrection would come, plates of fire would be beaten out for him; these would be heated in the hell-fire and his side and forehead and back would be branded with them. Whenever these cool down, the process would be repeated during a day the length of fifty thousand years, until judgment is pronounced among the servants and he sees whether his path is to take him to Paradise or to Hell." Again, ibn Uthaimeen says that this is a hadith whose meaning is general and applies to all types of gold or silver.

Concerning other hadith, those that intimidate people from wearing gold jewelry, he says that they do not mean that such jewelry is forbidden but they only mean that one must pay the zakaat on the jewelry. (Al-Albaani is one scholar who uses those hadith to prove that gold jewelry, with some exceptions, is forbidden for both men and women.)

Ibn Uthaimeen then discusses a well-known hadith that states,

$$\text{ليس في الحلي زكاة}$$

"There is no zakaat upon jewelry." Al-Baihaqi recorded this hadith and he himself said that it is not an authentic hadith (he, in fact, called it *baatil*). This is a sufficient refutation of the hadith but Ibn Uthaimeen also discussed how one must respond to the hadith if one is forced to accept it as authentic. Since the hadith is generally recognized not to be authentic, his discussion on that point has not been included here.

Ibn Uthaimeen then presents reports from Umar, ibn Masood, ibn Abbaas, Abdullah ibn Amr ibn al-As and Aishah which state that they were all of the opinion that zakaat is to be levied upon gold and silver jewelry. He says that al-Athram recorded from Ahmad that Anas ibn Maalik, Jaabir, ibn Umar, Aishah and Asmaa did not call for zakaat on jewelry. In any case, when such a difference of opinion occurs one must, as the Quran states, return to the Quran and the sunnah to find the definitive answer.

He then states that some may argue from the Prophet's statement, "O women, give charity even if it be from your jewelry," that this statement implies that zakaat must not be obligatory on their jewelry as otherwise the Prophet (peace be upon him) would not have made the statement in that manner. But this is no proof. If one is asked to give charity from one's wealth, as the Prophet (peace be upon him) had on occasion asked his followers, it does not mean that there is no zakaat obligatory on one's wealth.

In a lengthy discussion he argues that there is no sound analogy between permissible clothing, upon which there is no zakaat, and permissible jewelry, upon which zakaat is to be levied; one cannot use the fact that there is no zakaat on clothing (a consumption good) to argue, then, that there is no zakaat on jewelry either. (The reader should again note that there is no recourse to *qiyaas* if there is a text from the Quran and sunnah on any matter.)

He then concludes that if one's gold or silver (including jewelry) reaches their respective *nisaab*, then one must pay the zakaat upon such gold and jewelry every year that this occurs as there is no proof in the Quran or the sunnah that would lead one to conclude otherwise.

Conclusion

From the above, the conclusions that can be made are the following:

(1) There are explicit hadith from the Prophet (peace be upon him) that show that zakaat is to be levied upon such jewelry.

(2) In the face of those hadith, the different opinions of the Companions need not be considered as perhaps it was just the case that some of them did not hear about the Prophet's commands on this issue.

(3) There is no proof that the Prophet's orders for zakaat on jewelry were abrogated. Indeed, the original case was no zakaat at all, in general, and on jewelry, in particular. Therefore, the argument of abrogation is in need of proof.

(4) There is no call to resort to *qiyaas* (analogy) in the presence of explicit texts from the Prophet (peace be upon him).

Therefore, zakaat is obligatory on jewelry every year once the amount reaches the *nisaab* and has been in the possession of the woman for one year. This is the opinion of the following scholars: Abdullah ibn Masood, Aishah, Saeed ibn Jubair, Saeed ibn al-Musayyab, Jaabir ibn Zaid, Maimun ibn Mahran, Muhammad ibn Sireen, Mujaahid, al-Zuhri, Ata ibn Abu Ribah, Abdullah ibn Shidaad, Ibraaheem al-Nakhai, al-Dhuhaak, Abu Haneefah, Sufyaan al-Thauri, al-Auzaaee, Abdullah ibn al-Mubaarak, ibn Shibrima, al-Tahaawi, Daawood ibn Ali al-Dhaahiri, ibn Hazm, ibn al-Mundhir, al-Raazi, al-Sanaani, Abdul Azeez ibn Baaz, Muhammad ibn Uthaimeen and Ahmad al-Banna.[1]

The scholars are agreed, by the way, that there is no zakaat on diamonds, pearls, rubies, chrysolite and other similar precious stones, unless they are for the purpose of business in which case they fall under the category of zakaat on merchandise. Furthermore, the above difference of opinion is only concerning legal jewelry. If the woman owns, for example, men's jewelry or ornaments, such as a sword, then she is obliged to pay zakaat on them.

The *Nisaab* and Examples

The minimum amount that one must possess of wealth before the zakaat becomes obligatory is known in Arabic as

---

[1] See al-Basaarah, pp. 15-26, for the respective references for these scholars' opinions.

the *nisaab*. The *nisaab* of gold is twenty *mithqaal*s (= 85 grams). If someone possesses this amount of gold jewelry for a period equal to one lunar year, she must pay the zakaat on that jewelry. The zakaat on such jewelry is 2.5%. For example, if a woman owns 1000 grams of pure gold jewelry, which is above the *nisaab*, for one year, then she must pay 1000 grams X 2.5%, which equals 25 grams, as zakaat.

Many scholars are of the opinion that she may pay the dollar value of the gold instead of actually giving gold.

The *nisaab* of silver is two hundred *dirham*s which is equivalent to 595 grams of pure silver. Again, the woman must pay 2.5% of the amount in zakaat. For example, if a woman possesses 2000 grams of pure silver jewelry for one year, then she must pay 2000 X 2.5% or 50 grams of silver, either in kind or money.

The proof of the *nisaab* of gold comes from a narration on the authority of Ali that the Messenger of Allah (peace be upon him) said, "If you have a two hundred *dirham*s and a year passes (with it in your possession) then you must pay five *dirham*s. There is no (zakaat) upon gold until you reach twenty *dinaar*s. When you have twenty *dinaar*s (of gold) for a year, you must pay half a *dinaar*. If you have more (than twenty) reckon in like manner. And there is no zakaat on wealth until a year passes (with it in your possession)."[1]

Zakaat Given to the Wife's Husband

In the Quran, Allah states the recipients of the zakaat fund. The relevant verse reads,

---

[1] Recorded by Abu Daawood and al-Baihaqi. Al-Bukhari said it is *sahih* and ibn Hajr said it is *hasan*. Incidentally, *dinaar*s are always gold and *dirham*s are always silver.

إِنَّمَا الصَّدَقَاتُ لِلْفُقَرَاءِ وَالْمَسَاكِينِ وَالْعَامِلِينَ عَلَيْهَا وَالْمُؤَلَّفَةِ قُلُوبُهُمْ وَفِي الرِّقَابِ وَالْغَارِمِينَ وَفِي سَبِيلِ اللَّهِ وَابْنِ السَّبِيلِ

"The alms are only for the poor and the needy, and those who collect them, and those whose hearts are to be reconciled, and to free the slaves, and the debtors and for the cause of Allah and for the wayfarers" (al-Taubah 60). These different categories have been sufficiently described in the books of fiqh. There does appear an important question: Is it allowed for a woman to give zakaat to her poor or needy husband?

Abu Haneefah is of the opinion that it is not allowed for a woman to give her zakaat to her own husband, even if he is in great need. This does not seem to be the correct opinion.

The Prophet (peace be upon him) ordered the women to give charity (it is not clear from the hadith if it was obligatory or voluntary charity) and the wife of Abdullah ibn Masood asked him if it would suffice for her to give it to her own husband and he replied that she would receive two rewards, one for giving to relatives and the other for giving the charity.

Al-Shaukaani concludes that it is allowed for women to give their zakaat to their needy husbands based on the following two points: (1) There is no proof or evidence that it is not permissible. (2) In the hadith of the wife of Abdullah ibn Masood, the Prophet (peace be upon him) did not ask her whether she was referring to the voluntary or obligatory charity. Therefore, one can conclude that his statement applies to both.

This opinion that it is allowed to give the zakaat to one's needy husband is the opinion of al-Thauri, al-Shafi'ee, Abu Yoosuf and Muhammad (the students of Abu Haneefah), one narration from Maalik and Ahmad.

Zakaat and the Dowry

Is it obligatory for a woman to pay zakaat on what she has received as a dowry and, if so, what is the minimum amount over which she must pay the zakaat?

The Hanafis say that there is no zakaat on the dowry before the woman takes possession of it. After she takes possession of it, there is a zakaat upon it if it reaches the level of the relevant *nisaab*. They put the condition that it stays with the woman for a year's time after she take possession of the dowry. This is the case if she did not have other wealth that reached the level of *nisaab* without the dowry. If she previously had some wealth that reached the level of nisaab, then she is to add the value of the dowry to it and pay the zakaat on the entire amount if it passes one year in her possession.

The Shafi'ees are of the opinion that the woman must pay the zakaat on the dowry if it stays in her possession for a year. And she must pay zakaat on all of her wealth, the dowry included, at the end of the year. They are also of the opinion that there is no zakaat on one who lent money (like a dowry she has not yet received) unless he or she has use of what he or she has lent, in which case the person pays zakaat on the portion that he has the right to use.

The Malikis are of the opinion that there is no zakaat to be paid on a dowry that is yet to be given to the woman. From the day that she receives the dowry and then a year passes, she must pay the zakaat.

The Hanbalis say that the zakaat is to paid on the wealth after a year's time from the time that she actually receives the dowry. If she receives only part of the dowry, then the zakaat will only apply to the portion she receives.

Therefore, all of the four schools of thought are agreed that the woman must pay the zakaat on her dowry after she possesses the wealth for one entire lunar year and the amount of that wealth is above the *nisaab*.

If the dowry is of gold and/or silver, then the proper nisaab to use is that which was described earlier. Suppose the dowry is of banknotes or dollars, what then is the *nisaab*? Some say that if the amount of dollars one possesses reaches the equivalent of the value of the gold nisaab, then one must pay zakaat on the wealth. Others say that if the dollar amount reaches the equivalent of the *nisaab* weight of silver, then one must pay zakaat. Some argue for this latter opinion as this will lead to more zakaat and therefore it is more beneficial for the poor. The problem stems from the fact that in the Prophet's time a *dinaar* of gold was equal to ten *dirham*s of silver. But times have changed and this parity no longer exists. The value of gold has increased considerably, but the source of the measurement was originally the gold. Perhaps it is safest to use the method that will lead to the most amount of zakaat.

According to Khamees, it seems that one may pay zakaat on the basis of gold or silver. Perhaps, for more reward from Allah, the person should use the measure that gives the greatest amount of zakaat to be paid.

References

al-Albaani, Muhammad Naasir al-Deen. *Adaab al-Zafaaf*. Beirut: al-Maktab al-Islaami. 5th edition.

al-Ansaari, Ismaaeel ibn Muhammad. *Ibaahat al-Tahulli bi-l-Dhahab al-Muhallaq li-l-Nisaa wa al-Radd ala al-Albaani fi Tahreemihi*. Riyadh: Daar al-Ifta. 1984.

al-Basaarah, Nabeel. *Zakaat al-Hulli*. Kuwait: Daar al-Dawah. 1987.

Khamees, Muhammad Attiyah. *Fiqh al-Nisaa fi al-Zakaat wa al-Siyaam*. Cairo: Daar al-Ansaar. 1980.

ibn Rushd, Abu al-Waleed Muhammad. *Bidaayat al-Mujtaahid wa Nihaayat al-Muqtasid*. Cairo: Maktabah al-Kulliyat al-Azhaariyyah.

ibn Uthaimeen, Muhammad. *al-Mara al-Muslimah: Ahkaam Fiqhiyyah*. Riyadh: Daar Taibah. 1986.

al-Shaukaani, Muhammad ibn Ali. *Nail al-Autaar* Beirut: Daar al-Jeel. 1980.

al-Umari, Naadiyah. *al-Qiyaas fi al-Tashri al-Islaami*. n.c.: Hajr. 1987.

Questions and Answers: Comments on a Dialogue[1]

The Question Put to *Al-Basheer*

Question: In the videotape that I sent you on "Women in Islam," the speaker made the following comment: "There has been mention in the sayings of the Messenger of Allah and the most famous hadith that has been referred to is when the Prophet heard, and that is in al-Bukhari and al-Nasaai and other references also, that when he heard that the Persians chose a woman to be their leader, he commented by saying, 'A people will not succeed if they have a woman as their leader.' Now while that hadith appears in al-Bukhari, which is normally a reliable source, some scholars raised an issue that both in al-Bukhari and the other references that cited this hadith, there is Abu Bakra and they say that some scholars of biography have disqualified him as a trustworthy source of hadith. So there is some problem with the narrators of this hadith. Second, there is some problem with the *matn* or text of the hadith which is a legitimate source or criticism. Any text that is impossible has to be suspect and to say that no people who had a woman as a leader would get success—in worldly affairs or as a people—is contradictory to what we have witnessed in history. We have witnessed many queens and women presidents. The Prophet could not have said something like this that is contrary to established fact."

---

[1] This article appeared in *al-Basheer*, vol. 2, no. 4 (Nov.-Dec. 1988).

Could you please comment on this statement by the speaker.

O. Z., San Luis Obispo, CA

Introduction to the Reply

I shall reply to this question by discussing three points: (1) The speaker's discussion of the meaning of the hadith; (2) The speaker's comments about Abu Bakra; (3) Comments about other statements the speaker made on the tape.[1]

Perhaps it should be first mentioned that this hadith is *sahih* without any doubt. It is from the hadith in *Sahih al-Bukhari* that the whole *ummah* of Islam have accepted and the Prophet (peace be upon him) said that this nation would not agree on an error.

The Text of the Hadith

It is true that an examination of the text of the hadith is one of the means of hadith criticism. It also true that any statement that contradicts incontrovertible fact will be rejected as a fabricated hadith as it is not possible for the Prophet (peace be upon him), who was inspired by the Creator, to make a statement that would contradict reality. For example, there is a hadith that states that if one sneezes while speaking it means he is telling the truth. This hadith has been declared a forgery by the scholars of hadith because some people have spoken lies while sneezing and this proves this hadith to be a forgery. Although this is all true and well established, the speaker's use of this principle is incorrect.

---

[1] This question is being addressed in particular because this same speaker has made the same or similar comments on other occasions and the editor feels that his statements must be corrected.

One cannot make his own interpretation for a hadith and then say that the hadith could not possibly be true and, therefore, must be rejected. This is the way of the Mutazilah and of this speaker. He says that there have been woman queens and presidents whose people had "prospered" and, therefore, this contradicts this hadith.

What is a possible Islamic definition of *falaah* ("success") that may be applied to this hadith? Maudoodi writes,

> This question has been posed as a proof of the main theme of the *Soorah* [that is, *soorah al-Muminoon*]. It is meant to remove their misconception of "success", "welfare" and "prosperity", which the disbelievers had formed to delude themselves. According to them, the one who enjoyed the good things of life and wielded power and influence in the society, had attained "success". On the other hand, the one who was deprived of these things was a "failure". This misconception had involved them in another serious misunderstanding. They thought that the one who had attained "success" was in the right, and the beloved of Allah...As this misconception is one of the greatest deviations of the materialists, the Quran has stated it and refuted it in different ways and different places and made the reality plain... One should keep in view the following:... "Success" is a far higher thing than the material prosperity and the transitory success of an individual, community or nation.[1]

Hence, the *falaah* that is referred to in the hadith that this speaker rejected should not be understood as, "in worldly affairs or as a people." Given the proper Islamic interpretation

---

[1] Abul Ala Maudoodi, *The Meaning of the Quran* (Lahore: Islamic Publications, Ltd., 1979), vol. 8, p. 25.

of the word *falaah* or "success" found in this hadith, it cannot be argued that the text of the hadith contradicts actual fact—indeed, the real test of *falaah* is beyond the realm of human perception, so one could never claim "scientific fact" on this matter. Therefore, one may not reject this hadith on the basis that its text contradicts "what we have witnessed in history."

This example also points to the fact that in order to judge hadith, one has to be a *mujtahid* (which includes having an excellent knowledge of Arabic and hadith). Many times people reject hadith simply because they think that it goes against something they believe to be fact. If the person is not a scholar, he usually falls into two traps (as this speaker did). One, the manner in which he understands the hadith is not correct and, two, what he believes to be fact may not be fact at all. In conclusion, one must leave the accepting and rejecting of hadith to those scholars who are specialized in this field and not make judgments on hadith without any knowledge.

The Speaker's Comments about Abu Bakra

Probably most of the listeners did not realize that this speaker was referring to a Companion of the Prophet, Nufai' ibn al-Haarith, when the speaker said, "There is Abu Bakra and they say that some scholars of biography have disqualified him as a trustworthy source of hadith." Therefore, to reply to his statement, it would be proper to discuss the position of the Companions of the Prophet according to the scholars of hadith. After that, Abu Bakra himself will be discussed.

The Companions of the Prophet and their Hadith[1]

There is a general consensus among the Muslims that all of the people whom Allah selected to be the Prophet's Companions are *adl* (people of righteousness and acceptable character) *a priori*, meaning that there is no question that they would not fabricate hadith. Therefore, there is no need to do a great deal of research on their lives to confirm their being *adl*. One can see from the Quranic verses and hadith, to be mentioned, that the place of the Companions of the Prophet (peace be upon him) is really part of the creed of the Muslims. In al-Tahaawi's explanation of the Islamic creed, commonly referred to as *al-Aqeedah al-Tahaawiyyah*, the scholar wrote,

> We love the Companions of the Messenger (peace be upon him), we do not exaggerate our love for any one of them and we do not disassociate ourselves from any one of them. We are angered with anyone who is angry with them or who speaks anything but good about them. And we do not mention them except with good statements. Love for them is belief, faith and virtue while anger with them is disbelief, hypocrisy and transgression.[2]

In his commentary to al-Tahaawi's creed, ibn Abu al-Izz wrote,

> Here the teacher is referring to the Raafidhah and the Nasb. Allah and His Messenger praise the Companions, say they are pleased with them and

---

[1] This section is excerpted from Jamaal al-Din Zarabozo, "Abu Hurairah: The Preserver of the Sunnah," *Al-Basheer*, vol. 1, no. 1 (May 1987), pp. 13-15. That article is also included among this collection. Although the quote is virtually verbatim, for the sake of consistency, it was decided to leave the text here as well as in the other article, without deleting from either.

[2] See ibn Abu al-Izz al-Hanafi, *Sharh al-Aqeedah al-Tahaawiyyah* (Beirut: al-Maktab al-Islaami, 1983), p. 568.

promise them "the good." Allah says in the Quran, "And the first to lead the way, of the Emigrants and Helpers, and those who followed them in goodness—Allah is well pleased with them and they are well pleased with Him, and He has made ready for them gardens underneath which rivers flow, wherein they will abide forever. That is the supreme triumph" [al-Taubah 100]. "Muhammad is the Messenger of Allah. And those with him are hard against the disbelievers and merciful among themselves. You (Muhammad) see them bowing and falling prostrate [in worship], seeking bounties from Allah and His acceptance... Allah has promised unto such of them who believe and do good works forgiveness and immense rewards" [al-Fath 29]. "Allah was well-pleased with the believers when they swore allegiance unto you beneath the tree, and He knew what was in their hearts" [al-Fath 18].[1]

There also exists many hadith that point to the excellence of the Companions. The Prophet (peace be upon him) said,

يَأْتِي عَلَى النَّاسِ زَمَانٌ فَيَغْزُو فِئَامٌ مِنَ النَّاسِ فَيَقُولُونَ فِيكُمْ مَنْ صَاحَبَ رَسُولَ اللَّهِ صَلَّى اللَّهم عَلَيْهِ وَسَلَّمَ فَيَقُولُونَ نَعَمْ فَيُفْتَحُ لَهُمْ ثُمَّ يَأْتِي عَلَى النَّاسِ زَمَانٌ فَيَغْزُو فِئَامٌ مِنَ النَّاسِ فَيُقَالُ هَلْ فِيكُمْ مَنْ صَاحَبَ أَصْحَابَ رَسُولِ اللَّهِ صَلَّى اللَّهم

[1] Abu al-Izz, pp. 528-9. Abu al-Izz continues in that commentary to discuss the position of the Companions for three more pages. To save some space not all of the relevant Quranic verses will be quoted here but the interested reader should see al-Baqarah 173, ali-Imraan 110, al-Anfaal 72-75, al-Qamar 8-10 and al-Hadeed 10.

عَلَيْهِ وَسَلَّمَ فَيَقُولُونَ نَعَمْ فَيُفْتَحُ لَهُمْ ثُمَّ يَأْتِي عَلَى النَّاسِ زَمَانٌ

فَيَغْزُو فِئَامٌ مِنَ النَّاسِ فَيُقَالُ هَلْ فِيكُمْ مَنْ صَاحَبَ مَنْ

صَاحَبَ أَصْحَابَ رَسُولِ اللَّهِ صَلَّى اللَّهُم عَلَيْهِ وَسَلَّمَ فَيَقُولُونَ

نَعَمْ فَيُفْتَحُ لَهُمْ

"A time will come when a party of the people will go forth to
fight, and some will say, 'Is there among you anyone who has
kept company with the Apostle of Allah?' They will answer,
'Yes.' And they shall be victorious. Thereafter a time will
come when a party of the people will go forth to fight, and
someone will say, 'Is there among you anyone who has kept
company with the Companions of the Messenger of Allah?'
They will answer, 'Yes,' and they shall be victorious.
Thereafter a time will come when a party of the people will go
forth to fight, and someone will say, 'Is there among you
anyone who has kept company with a companion of the
Companions of the Messenger of Allah?' They will answer,
'Yes,' and they shall be victorious." (Recorded by al-Bukhari,
Muslim and others.)

The Messenger of Allah (peace be upon him) also said,

خَيْرُكُمْ قَرْنِي ثُمَّ الَّذِينَ يَلُونَهُمْ ثُمَّ الَّذِينَ يَلُونَهُمْ قَالَ عِمْرَانُ

لَا أَدْرِي أَذَكَرَ النَّبِيُّ صَلَّى اللَّهُم عَلَيْهِ وَسَلَّمَ بَعْدُ قَرْنَيْنِ أَوْ

ثَلَاثَةً قَالَ النَّبِيُّ صَلَّى اللَّهُم عَلَيْهِ وَسَلَّمَ إِنَّ بَعْدَكُمْ قَوْمًا

يَخُونُونَ وَلَا يُؤْتَمَنُونَ وَيَشْهَدُونَ وَلَا يُسْتَشْهَدُونَ وَيَنْذِرُونَ

وَلَا يَفُونَ وَيَظْهَرُ فِيهِمُ السِّمَنُ

"The best of you [my followers] is my generation, then those who will come after them, then those who come after them. [Imraan said, "And I do not know if he mentioned two or three generations after his own generation."] And behold, after you there will be people who will be betrayers and they cannot be trusted, who will testify without being asked to testify, who will make vows and will not fulfill them, and fatness will appear among them." (Recorded by al-Bukhari, Muslim and others with slightly different wordings.)

He (peace be upon him) also said,

$$\text{لَا تَسُبُّوا أَصْحَابِي فَلَوْ أَنَّ أَحَدَكُمْ أَنْفَقَ مِثْلَ أُحُدٍ ذَهَبًا مَا بَلَغَ مُدَّ أَحَدِهِمْ وَلَا نَصِيفَهُ}$$

"Do not revile my Companions. Do not revile my Companions. By him in whose hand is my life, if one among you would have spent as much gold as [the weight of] Uhud, it would not amount to as much as one *mudd* on behalf of one of them, or even half of that."[1]

As Muhammad al-Saawi pointed out, the status of the Companions of the Prophet is something that is "known by necessity" (Ar., *bi-l-dharoorah*), that is, it is so well established that even the commoner is not excused from knowing and believing it and there can be no doubt about it.[2]

---

[1] Recorded by Muslim and others. Uhud is a mountain near Madinah while a *mudd* is a measure that is equivalent to two handfuls when the hands are cupped together. For a more complete selection of hadith on the virtues of the Companions or of individual Companions or of specific groups of them, see ibn al-Atheer, *Jaami al-Usool min Ahaadeeth al-Rasool* (Beirut: Ihyaa al-Kutub al-Arabi, 1980), vol. 9, pp. 404-478 and vol. 10, pp. 1-142. It should be noted that all of the hadith which make statements like, "My Companions are like the stars and whichever one you follow will guide you..." are all fabricated as al-Albaani (*Silsilat...al-Dhaeefa*, vol. 1, pp. 72-3 and pp. 82-5) has shown.

[2] Muhammad Salaah al-Saawi, *Manzilat al-Sahaabah fi al-Quran* (Riyadh: Daar Taibah), p. 5.

Therefore, this speaker who said that Abu Bakra is not acceptable as a trustworthy transmitter of hadith is going against what Allah Himself has said about the Companions and also against the consensus of the scholars of the *ahl al-sunnah wa al-jamaah*. In fact, he should repent from this statement because what he said may be a type of *sabb* or reviling of a Companion which the Prophet (peace be upon him) warned about and which the scholars consider a grave sin.

This does not mean to imply that the Companions never committed any sins or mistakes. As al-Saawi wrote,

> The Quran bearing witness concerning the Companions of the Messenger of Allah of their true faith and giving them glad tidings of mercy and pleasure does not mean that they are protected from committing mistakes or from having flaws or slips as they are not angels or prophets. In fact, some of them did commit such things but they did not persist in such deeds but would quickly rush to ask for forgiveness and would repent. Therefore, this does not malign their truthfulness of their faith and does not affect what they have been given of tidings concerning forgiveness and mercy. The Quran itself records some of those instances and also records the repentance of Allah upon them and the promise of His mercy to them.[1]

This is enough to prove that they would not forge hadith of the Prophet.

Abu Bakra Nufai' ibn al-Haarith

The speaker said, "Some scholars of biography have disqualified him as a trustworthy source of hadith." This seems

---

[1] Al-Saawi, p. 43.

to be nothing more than a blatant falsehood. Abu Bakra's biography may be found in the following works—all essential reference works of biographies:

Ibn Saad, *Tabaqaat al-Kubra*, vol. 7, p. 15.

Ibn Abdul Barr, *al-Istiaab fi Asmaa al-Ashaab*, vol. 3, p. 567.

ibn Hajr, *al-Issabah fi Tamyeez al-Sahaabah*, vol. 3, p. 571.

ibn Katheer, *al-Bidaayah wa al-Nihaayah*, vol. 8, p. 57.

ibn Hajr, *Tahdheeb al-Tahdheeb*, vol. 10, p. 469.

ibn Hajr, *Taqreeb al-Tahdheeb*, vol. 2, p. 306.

ibn Abi Haatim, *al-Jarh wa al-Tadeel*, #2239.

al-Baaji, *al-Tadeel wa al-Tajreeh*, vol. 2, p. 778.

All of these works mention that Abu Bakra was one of the most virtuous of the Companions; in fact, he was a *maula* (freed slave) of the Prophet (peace be upon him). The only thing that occurred of note in Abu Bakra's life is that he and a group of others stated that they saw another commit adultery. However, at the last moment, one of the witnesses backed out saying that he had only seen something that was not right. Since the four witnesses were not presented, Abu Bakra was flogged for his claim. This incident was known and stated by the scholars of hadith and since it was concerning something that he had witnessed— and not simply someone slandering someone he had not claimed to witness— the scholars continued to accept his narrations after he willfully accepted the legal punishment and repented.

His hadith have been accepted by all of the major collectors of hadith, including al-Bukhari and Muslim. He was not even mentioned in the major works of weak or castigated narrators, such as al-Dhahabi's *Meezaan al-Itidaal* or ibn Adi's *al-Kamaal*.

Comments about Other Statements by the Speaker

It is amazing, but sadly far too common, that speakers, like the one under discussion here, open their talks by saying that everything one says about Islam must be based on the authentic teachings of Islam, the Quran and the authentic hadith of the Prophet (peace be upon him), and then they go on to quote a number of fabricated and weak hadith (and, in this case, to refute an authentic hadith). Below are just some examples of the rejected reports that this speaker used in his talk:

(1) The hadith: "The most hated act that God made permissible for you is divorce." Although this hadith is recorded in different forms by Abu Daawood, al-Baihaqi, ibn Maajah and others, it is well-known to be weak as ibn Hajr and al-Albaani clearly state.[1] But, as some scholars pointed out, there is a problem with the text of the hadith that further casts doubt upon its authenticity—a principle that this speaker seems to be well aware of. According to the principles of *usool al-fiqh* (Islamic legal theory), it is not possible that Allah dislikes any act that He permits. Al-Isnawi wrote,

> The majority of the scholars (Ar., *jamhoor*) are of the opinion that the permissible things (Ar., *mubaah*) are good. Some of the Mutazila say they are neither good or evil.... The Asharis say, "If the deed is prohibited by the lawgiver, the act is evil, regardless of whether it is forbidden (*haraam*) or disliked (*makrooh*)."[2]

---

[1] Cf., Ahmad ibn Ali ibn Hajr, *Talkhees al-Habeer bi Takhreej Ahaadeeth al-Raafi'ee al-Kabeer* (Madinah, 1964), p. 305; Muhammad Naasir al-Deen al-Albaani, *Irwa al-Ghaleel fi Takhreej Ahaadeeth Manaar al-Sabeel* (Beirut: Maktab al-Islaami, 1979), vol. 7, p. 106.

[2] Jamaal al-Deen al-Isnawi, *Al-Tamheed fi Takhreej al-Furoo ala al-Usool* (Beirut: Muasassat al-Risaalah, 1981), p. 61.

Al-Raazi even defines "the good" (*al-hasan*) as that which the performer knows is not prohibited by the law of Allah.[1] Therefore, based on the chain of this hadith itself, it is weak. But looking at the text of the hadith throws even more doubt on the acceptability of this hadith. In any case, it is not authentic and the speaker should not have used it—especially after his opening statement that whatever one says about Islam must be based on the authentic teachings of Islam.

(2) The hadith: "Some of my companions are equivalent in status to the Prophets of the Tribes of Israel." Here, it seems that the speaker did not even quote a fabricated hadith correctly.[2] The only hadith that is even similar to this speaker's statement is the following: "The scholars of my nation are like the prophets of the tribe of Israel." This hadith is not recorded in any of the known or acceptable books of hadith and is rejected (and most likely fabricated).[3]

(3) The speaker said that Umar was presenting a bill for legislation (?) that would limit the dowry paid to women and a woman came and told Umar that he was mistaken and Umar admitted his mistake. This report was recorded by al-Baihaqi who said, "Its chain is broken." Furthermore, it is narrated by Mujaalid ibn Saeed who is not a strong narrator. Abdul Razzaaq also narrated it with a different chain in his *al-Musannaf* but its chain has two problems: First, the chain is broken. Second, Qais ibn al-Rabeeah, one of the narrators, has a poor memory.[4]

---

[1] Fakhr al-Deen al-Raazi, *al-Mahsool fi Ilm Usool al-Fiqh* (Riyadh: Muhammad ibn Saud University, 1979), Vol. 1, Part 1, p. 137.

[2] This author will not bother to discuss what he was trying to prove when he quoted this hadith.

[3] Cf., Muhammad ibn Ali al-Shaukaani, *Al-Fawaaid al-Majmooat fi al-Ahaadeeth al-Maudhooah* (Beirut: al-Maktab al-Islaami, 1982), p. 286; Shaams al-Deen al-Sakhaawi, *Al-Maqaasid al-Hasanah* (Makkah: Daar al-Baaz, 1979), p. 286; Muhammad Naasir al-Deen al-Albaani, *Silsilat al-Ahaadeeth al-Dhaeefah* (Beirut: al-Maktab al-Islaami, 1978), p. 480.

[4] Cf., al-Albaani, *Irwa al-Ghaleel*, vol. 6, pp. 247-8.

(4) The report that Umar appointed Umm Shifa (actually her name was Shifa bint Abdullah and she was a very early Companion of the Prophet) as an inspector in the market place, although well-known, seems to be weak. Ibn al-Arabi (in *Ahkaam al-Quran*, vol. 3, p. 1445) states that this narration is weak. In fact, it is mentioned in a number of places but always without a chain of narrators (for example, ibn Hazm's *al-Muhalla*, vol. 9, p. 429). In *al-Istiaab fi Asmaa al-Ashaab*, ibn Abdul Barr mentions it with a *seeghat al-tamreedh* (in other words, he mentions it in such a way that points to it as being a weak narration). Furthermore, ibn Hajr, in both *al-Isaaba fi Tamyeez al-Sahaabah* (vol. 4, p. 341) and *Tahdheeb al-Tahdheeb* (vol. 12, p. 428), states, concerning this report, "perhaps Umar appointed her to some position in the marketplace." Umar Ridha Kahhala, (*Ilaam al-Nisaa*, vol. 2, p. 300) probably following ibn Hajr, also states that Umar "may have appointed her..."[1]

Conclusion

Unfortunately, the comments that this person made were made during a dialogue concerning Women in Islam and Christianity. *Dawah* and the passing on of knowledge is one of the greatest trusts that Muslims must fulfill and must fulfill honestly and sincerely. The only way this can be done is by going to the guidance of the Quran and authentic hadith and not letting one's ideas become too influenced by the environment around him. Everyone wants to see non-Muslims embrace Islam but their guidance is in the hand of Allah. It is only the Muslim's duty to follow the path of *dawah* as laid down by the Prophet (peace be upon him) and leave the rest to Allah.

---

[1] For a discussion of the meaning of this report and whether it is consistent with Umar's overall fiqh positions, see Abdul Hameed al-Ansaari, *Al-Shoora wa Atharuhaa fi al-Deemaqratiyya* (Beirut: al-Maktabah al-Asriyyah), p. 298.

Selected References

al-Albaani, Muhammad Naasir al-Deen. *Irwa al-Ghaleel fi Takhreej Ahaadeeth Manaar al-Sabeel*. Beirut: Maktab al-Islaami. 1979.

al-Ansaari, Abdul Hameed. *Al-Shoora wa Atharuhaa fi al-Deemaqratiyya*. Beirut: al-Maktabah al-Asriyya.

al-Baaji, Abu al-Waleed. *al-Tadeel wa al-Tajreeh*. Daar al-Lawa. 1987.

ibn Abdul Barr, *al-Istiaab fi Asmaa al-Ashaab*. On the margin of Ahmad ibn Hajr, *al-Isaabah*.

ibn Abu al-Izz al-Hanafi. *Sharh al-Aqeedah al-Tahaawiyyah*. al-Maktab al-Islaami. Beirut. 1983.

ibn al-Arabi, Abu Bakr. *Ahkaam al-Quran*. Cairo: Isa al-Babi al-Halbi. 1958.

ibn Hajr, Ahmad ibn Ali. *al-Isaabah fi Tamyeez al-Sahaabah*. al-Riyadh: Maktabah al-Riyadh al-Hadeethah. 1978.

-----*Tahdheeb al-Tahdheeb*. Hyderabad. Majlis Daairat al-Maarif.

-----*Talkhees al-Habeer bi Takhreej Ahaadeeth al-Raafi'ee al-Kabeer*. Madinah. 1964.

ibn Hazm, Ali ibn Ahmad. *al-Muhalla*. Beirut: The Trading Office.

al-Isnawi, Jamaal al-Deen. *Al-Tamheed fi Takhreej al-Furoo ala al-Usool*. Beirut: Muasassah al-Risaalah. 1981.

Kahhala, Umar Ridha. *Ilaam al-Nisaa*. Beirut: Muasassah al-Risaalah.

Maudoodi, Abul Ala. *The Meaning of the Quran*. Lahore: Islamic Publications, Ltd. 1979.

al-Raazi, Fakhr al-Deen. *al-Mahsool fi Ilm Usool al-Fiqh*. Riyadh: Muhammad ibn Saud University. 1979.

al-Saawi, Muhammad Salaah. *Manzilat al-Sahaabah fi al-Quran*. Riyadh: Daar Taibah.

Book Review:
Azami's *On Schacht's Origins of Muhammadan Jurisprudence*

Muhammad Mustafa al-Azami. On Schacht's Origins of Muhammadan Jurisprudence. (New York: John Wiley and Sons, Inc. 1985). Approximately $35.

About the Author

Muhammad Mustafa al-Azami should be no stranger to the American audience. He is originally from India and studied at Daar al-Ulum in India. He also studied at al-Azhar University in Cairo, Egypt. He completed his doctorate in Islamic Studies in 1967 at the University of Cambridge, England. His doctoral research was about the early writings of hadith and has been published under the title, *Studies in Early Hadith Literature* (American Trust Publications). He has received the King Faisal Award for his research in Islamic topics. He is currently a Professor at King Saud University in Riyadh, Saudi Arabia. At the present time, he is on sabbatical leave and residing in Boulder, CO. For the past several years he has been working on an extensive project dealing with the computer transcribing of hadith literature.

His many publications include the above referred to *Studies in Early Hadith Literature, Studies in Hadith Methodology* (also published by American Trust Publications) and the book under review here, *On Schacht's Origins of Muhammadan Jurisprudence*. He also has many publications

---

[1] This article appeared in *al-Basheer*, vol. 2, no. 5 (Jan.-Feb. 1989).

in Arabic, including an edition of *Sunan ibn Maajah*, an edition of *Sahih ibn Khuzaimah* and *Minhaj al-Naqd Ind al-Muhaditheen*.

About Schacht

Joseph Schacht was originally from Holland but later became an English citizen. He studied Near Eastern Languages and specialized in Arabic. He completed a Ph.D. in Philosophy in 1923 and taught Near Eastern Languages at the University of Freiburg from 1927 until 1932 at which time he moved to the University of Koenigberg. In 1934, he was granted a Professorship at the University of Egypt. He was a member of the *Majma al-Ilmy al-Araby* in Damascus. He later taught at Oxford and Leiden and, finally, at Columbia University, New York.[1]

He edited and published a number of Arabic manuscripts and also wrote on a number of Islamic topics. His most important works are probably *An Introduction to Islamic Law* and *The Origins of Muhammadan Jurisprudence*. He greatly enhanced and improved upon the theories of Ignazer Goldziher.

His writings have greatly affected other Orientalists. In 1951, H. A. R. Gibb wrote about *Origins of Muhammadan Jurisprudence*, "it will become the foundation for all future study of Islamic civilization and law, at least in the West."[2]

When this reviewer was a student at the University of California at Berkeley, Schacht's theories were still referred to as the major and most important theories concerning the history of Islamic jurisprudence. Thus, to this day, he still has his influence in the world of the Orientalists. Hence, the

---

[1] See Khair al-Deen al-Zirikly, *al-Ilaam* (Beirut: Daar al-Ilm al-Malayeen, 1980), vol. 8, p. 234.
[2] Quoted in al-Azami, p. 1.

importance of this book by Dr. al-Azami should not be underestimated.

Schacht's Basic Theories

Schacht's basic theories concerning Islamic law can be summarized in the following points:[1]

(1) Law fell outside the realm of religion and the Prophet (peace be upon him) did not actually have any legal authority among the Muslims but he was simply, what Westerners today would call, "a religious leader".

(2) The ancient schools of law developed in the early decades of the second century and their idea of sunnah was not as it is understood today by the Muslims but it simply referred to the "common practice of the community" in which the school of thought was born. Hence, this concept was not related to the sayings of the Prophet (peace be upon him); at least, not until al-Shafi'ee related it back to the Prophet (peace be upon him).

(3) These ancient schools of law were opposed by a religious party that falsely produced statements of the Prophet (peace be upon him) in order to support or to give an authority to their opinions.

(4) The latter group had to respond to this movement by starting to fabricate their own hadith and ascribe them to the Prophet (peace be upon him) in favor of their own views.

(5) This dispute led to both groups, during the second and third centuries, having the habit of projecting their own statements into the mouth of the Prophet (peace be upon him).

(6) Therefore, hardly any legal Prophetic hadith can be considered authentic.

---

[1] These are summarized on pages 1-2 of Azami's book.

(7) The system of *isnaad*[1], therefore, has no historical value. In fact, at most, it can only be used to date forgeries.

Al-Azami's Approach

In al-Azami's doctoral dissertation, he has demonstrated that he is an excellent researcher. He leaves no stones unturned to discover the minutest details about any particular research question. He is willing to go through numerous manuscripts in order to find the truth on any question.

This particular work of al-Azami's is no exception. He has carefully scrutinized all of Schacht's references and way of reasoning and has dealt with all of the above theories and refuted them one by one.[2]

Schacht's First Point

The first thesis of Schacht mentioned above is: (1) Law fell outside the realm of religion and the Prophet (peace be upon him) did not actually have any legal authority among the Muslims but he was simply, what Westerners today would call, "a religious leader".

Schacht wrote in *Introduction to Islamic Law*,

> As had been the case in the time of the Prophet, law as such fell outside the sphere of religion, and as far as there were no religious or moral objections to specific transactions or modes of behavior, the

---

[1] The *isnaad* is the chain of the authorities from the narrator back to the Prophet (peace be upon him).

[2] Of course, the review here will be quite brief but, it is hoped, the reader will be able to get some idea of how poorly Schacht reasoned and how al-Azami was able to refute Schacht's claims.

technical aspects of law were a matter of indifference to the Muslims.[1]

This claim of Schacht's is rather absurd and simple to refute. Professor al-Azami quotes verses from the Quran to show that the Prophet (peace be upon him) was the expounder of the Quran, a legislator, a person to be obeyed and a model for Muslim behavior.[2] These were discussed in detail in an earlier edition of *al-Basheer*.[3]

After quoting the relevant Quranic verses, al-Azami concludes,

> Law was an integral part of Islam. There was no aspect of behavior that was not intended to be covered by the revealed law and this law was to be binding on all Muslims; none had authority to alter it.
>
> It was intended by Allah that His Prophet's whole life, decisions, judgments, and commands should have the force of law. The authority of the Prophet does not rest on the acceptance of the community or on lawyers and scholars, but on the will of Allah Himself.

Schacht's Second Point

Schacht's second point is: (2) The ancient schools of law developed in the early decades of the second century and their idea of sunnah was not as it is understood today by the

---

[1] Quoted in Azami, p. 16.

[2] A similar discussion may be found in M. M. Azami, *Studies in Hadith Methodology and Literature* (Indianapolis: American Trust Publications, 1977), pp. 5-6.

[3] See Jamaal al-Din Zarabozo, "The Importance of the Sunnah and Hadith in Islam", *Al-Basheer* (Mar.-Apr. 1988, vol. 1, No. 6), pp. 19-23. Note: That article is also part of this present collection.

Muslims but it simply referred to the "common practice of the community" in which the school of thought was born. Hence, this concept was not related to the sayings of the Prophet (peace be upon him); at least, not until al-Shafi'ee related it back to the Prophet (peace be upon him).

Here Schacht contends that the early concept of sunnah was merely a reference to what he calls "living tradition". The concept of the sunnah of the Prophet (peace be upon him) was of relatively late origin—coined by the Iraqis some time in the second century. Finally, he argues that the use of the term "sunnah of the Prophet" was simply referring to the living tradition projected back into the mouth of the Prophet (peace be upon him).

Much of this is based on Margoliouth and one statement from ibn al-Muqaffa. Al-Azami (pp. 37-43) has gone through each of the proofs used by Margoliouth to show that Margoliouth has presented some evidence that proves one thing, and then he concludes something completely different than what the evidence points to.

Besides that, al-Azami also note (p. 40):

> What is perhaps most damning, as far as Schacht's reliance on Margoliouth goes, is that most of Margoliouth's references are dated from the first half of the first century. If Schacht accepted these references as authentic, he would also have to accept the fact that the expression "sunna of the Prophet" was widely used a hundred years before he contended it was.

This is one of the most remarkable aspects of al-Azami's work. He uses Schacht's own references and reasoning to show the fallacy of Schacht's theories.

Schacht's Third Point

Schacht's third point is: (3) These ancient schools of law were opposed by a religious party (which he calls traditionists) that falsely produced statements of the Prophet (peace be upon him) in order to support or to give an authority to their opinions.

Schacht wrote (quoted in al-Azami, p. 73):

> The movement of the Traditionists... in the second century of the *hijra*, was the natural outcome and continuation of a movement of religiously and ethically inspired opposition to the ancient schools of law... The main thesis of the Traditionists, as opposed to the ancient schools of law, was that formal "traditions"... deriving from the Prophet superseded the living tradition of the school... The Traditionists produced detailed statements or "traditions" which claimed to be the reports of ear- or eye-witnesses of the words or acts of the Prophet, handed down orally[1] by an uninterrupted chain (*isnaad*) of trustworthy persons. Hardly any of these traditions, as far as matters of religious law are concerned, can be considered authentic; they were put into circulation, no doubt from the loftiest of motives[2], by the Traditionists themselves from the first half of the second century onwards.

Al-Azami (pp. 76-79) shows many weaknesses in Schacht's theory. First, there is an arbitrary use of source

---

[1] In al-Azami's doctoral dissertation, he proves that these hadith were not, in fact, just passed on orally.

[2] Schacht does not deal with the paradoxical theory that he is purporting here. If these people were both "religiously and ethically inspired" and had "the loftiest of motives", why were they so willing to fabricate statements of the Prophet (peace be upon him) and to claim that these were related from the Prophet (peace be upon him) when they knew full well that they did not originate with the Prophet?

material. Most of Schacht's theories are based on "Schacht's own deductions from those writings [that is, the writings of al-Shafi'ee] or the accusations of Shafi'ee against his opponents." But elsewhere Schacht himself makes the following comments about Shafi'ee—Schacht's own source for his conclusions: "He [Shafi'ee] often misrepresents the Iraqian doctrine", "Shafi'ee often misrepresents the Medinese doctrine" and he presents a few dozen examples to substantiate his claim. Then how can Schacht rely on Shafi'ee's writings as source material in dealing with the history of the Sunna in the views of the Medinese and Iraqis?

Second, Schacht has a tendency to overgeneralize. For example, he takes the Hanafi school as representative of all of Iraq while he himself wrote, "it would be a mistake to generalize, even within the circle of the Kufans, the uniformity of doctrine" (quoted in al-Azami, p. 77).

Third, there are many internal inconsistencies in his theories. For example, take the following two statements that form the bulk of many of his conclusions:

"Traditions from the Prophet had to overcome a strong opposition on the part of the ancient schools of law, let alone the *ahl al-kalam*, before they gained general acceptance" (from p. 57 of *Origins*).

"The best way of proving that a tradition did not exist at a certain time is to show that it was not used as a legal argument in a discussion which would have made reference to it imperative, if it had existed" (from p. 140 of *Origins*).

The contradiction here should be evident. Either hadith were used as evidence by the ancient schools of law (which the second quote assumes) or there were not (which the first quote assumes), but Schacht cannot have it both ways.

Al-Azami goes on to show (pp. 78-95) that the ancient schools of Maalik, Abu Haneefah and Auzaaee evidenced strong adherence to the hadith of the Prophet (peace be upon him). Thus, refuting Schacht's third point.

Schacht's Fourth and Fifth Points

Schacht's fourth point is: (4) The latter group had to respond to this movement by starting to fabricate their own hadith and ascribe them to the Prophet (peace be upon him) in favor of their own views. Schacht's fifth point is: (5) This dispute led to both groups, during the second and third centuries, having the habit of projecting their own statements into the mouth of the Prophet (peace be upon him).

Al-Azami discusses this claim with respect to particular scholars that Schacht refers to, such as al-Auzaaee, Abu Yoosuf, Muhammad al-Shaibaani.

With respect to al-Auzaaee, for example, Schacht wrote, "he is inclined to project the whole 'living tradition', the continuous practice of the Muslims, as he finds it, back to the Prophet and to give it the Prophet's authority, whether he can adduce a precedent established by the Prophet or not. He has this feature in common with the Iraqians."[1] Al-Azami goes to the same references referred to by Schacht and makes the following points (p. 106):

> In fact, Auzai refers to the practice of the Prophet and the Muslims in only nine cases out of 50. In six cases, he refers to the practice of the Muslims but does not refer to the practice of the Prophet. In five cases, he refers to authorities such as Abu Bakr, Umar, and so on and not to the Prophet. Thus, Schacht's statement that he projects back "the whole living tradition" to the Prophet does not tally with the real references of Auzai.

He points out that Auzai and his opponent Abu Yoosuf agreed on the authenticity of many hadith from the Prophet although the two disagree on their interpretation. Al-Azami points out (p. 106),

---

[1] Quoted in al-Azami, p. 106.

Had the two been in agreement on the interpretations, it might have been possible to say that their "living tradition" was similar and that they had projected their traditions back to the Prophet and accidentally tallied with each other... Their agreement on the authenticity of the traditions while differing about their implications means that those traditions originally belonged to a common stock far from the inventions of the schools. That common stock is the personality of the Prophet.

Schacht's Sixth Point

Schacht's sixth point is: (6) Hardly any legal Prophetic hadith can be considered authentic.

Schacht wrote,

We shall find that the bulk of legal traditions from the Prophet known to Maalik originated in the generation preceding him, that is in the second quarter of the second century A.H., and we shall not meet any legal tradition from the Prophet which can be considered authentic.[1]

This thesis of Schacht, as he himself mentions, is based on the *e silentio* principle— that is, if a hadith is related to a certain topic and an early scholar did not quote that hadith while discussing that topic, then it must be the case that that hadith did not exist at the time of that scholar. Schacht extends it also to apply to hadith with incomplete chains that later are found with complete chains; these latter chains, therefore, must have been improved upon in later years. Commenting on this reasoning in general, al-Azami states (p. 116), "In a *reductio ad absurdum*, this argument would mean that if one

---

[1] Quoted in al-Azami, p. 115.

writer in the Middle East failed to mention London as one of the major cities in the world, then all other writers who mentioned it later would be guilty of collusion in creating a fictional city."

Al-Azami scrutinizes Schacht's examples very carefully. With respect to this point alone, in this book, pp. 117-153, al-Azami painstakingly goes through twenty-four of the forty-seven examples referred to by Schacht. In this research, he reveals "inconsistencies both within the theory itself and in the use of source material, unwarranted assumptions and unscientific method of research, mistakes of fact, ignorance of the political and geographical realities of the time, and misinterpretation of the meaning of the texts quoted, and misunderstanding of the method of quotation of early scholars."[1]

Schacht's Seventh Point

Schacht's seventh point is: (7) The system of *isnaad*, therefore, has no historical value. In fact, at most, it can only be used to date forgeries.

Al-Azami writes (p. 167),

> His [Schacht's] denial of the early existence of *isnad* is a natural outcome of his theory regarding the *hadith* of the Prophet. As there were no *ahadith* of the Prophet in the first century, according to Schacht, naturally there could be no *isnad*. The necessity for Schacht not to find first-century *isnad*s blinds him to any contrary evidence.

Al-Azami discusses Schacht's theory that *isnaad*s were put together in a careless and arbitrary fashion. He comments (p. 177),

---

[1] Due to space limitations, no particular examples will be discussed in detail here.

In fact, if we adopt Schacht's view that *isnad*s were fabricated in the second century, we may find ourselves surprised that scholars widely scattered throughout the Islamic world were able to reach so much agreement on the *isnad*s they created. Without modern methods of communication, this would seem improbable, if not impossible.

Al-Azami also comments that Schacht was using the wrong types of sources to discover the beginnings of the usage of *isnaad*s. He says that Orientalists tend to rely on *sirah* and *hadith-fiqh* literature instead of pure hadith literature. This is an important point because the mentioning of the *isnaad* was not considered as important for the former books as it was for the latter works.

In Schacht's work, he gives six examples of the gradual improvement of *isnaad*s over time. Commenting on these examples, after scrutinizing them carefully, al-Azami wrote (p. 188), "We find four cases of full *isnad*s being recorded before the partial or incomplete version he quotes."

General Comments about the Book

Definitely this book is not meant for a layman. As in al-Azami's other works, he spares no efforts in discussing a question. A novice, or one not completely interested in the work, may get bogged down in the tedious details that al-Azami goes through in this book. Yet, at the same time, the reader must realize that this type of detail is what is needed to clearly and finally put to rest the claims of many of the Orientalists, including their masters Goldziher and Schacht.

Perhaps it would not be an understatement to say that this book is a must for anyone studying Islam in the colleges and universities of the United States. Although some people may state otherwise, Schacht and his works are still very much praised among the non-Muslim academic circles. No Orientalist that this reviewer knows of accepts the Muslim version of the history of hadith— and it seems that they have all been influenced by Schacht and Goldziher on this point. This book provides the student with the knowledge that he needs to refute the theories of Schacht and other Orientalists concerning the hadith of the Prophet (peace be upon him).

Comments on Fazlur Rahman's Review of the Book

In an in-house journal from the Research Archives at the Oriental Institute of the University of Chicago, Fazlur Rahman[1] also reviewed this book by Mustafa al-Azami. This reviewer feels compelled to comment on a few of Fazlur Rahman's comments.

Rahman wrote, "Azami tends to bring forth only that part of the evidence that seems to support his views and rejects that which tends to detract from his thesis." This is a rather bold statement from Rahman (and it is easy to make such a statement when one does not bother to justify it). First, he used the word "tends" which implies that Azami does this often in his work yet he just presents one inconsequential example concerning a quote from Ibn al-Muqaffa. Rereading the passage from al-Azami's work, one finds that it is Rahman who is misinterpreting the importance of ibn al-Muqaffa's statement. Furthermore, al-Azami began his discussion by correctly stating (p. 41), "Leaving aside the fact that ibn al-Muqaffa was neither a lawyer nor a theologian but an anti-Umayyad, indeed, charged with heresy..." These facts alone are actually sufficient to justify not using ibn al-Muqaffa as a source of early Islamic legal thought.

---

[1] Fazlur Rahman is probably familiar to many readers. He has written, among other works, *Major Themes of the Quran* and *Islam*.

Rahman, writing about himself, said, "I voice a general skepticism of legal hadith, not by referring to Schacht but by referring to the Prophet himself who was certainly not an enunciator of the minutiae of law, as the legal literature of Islam makes him out to be." This is a very unfortunate statement from Rahman. He has a doubt about hadith that have been accepted by the *ummah* of Islam simply because *he does not feel* that the Prophet (peace be upon him) laid down as many laws as the scholars have said. It also seems that Rahman did not read Part One of al-Azami's work in which he shows that "the revealed principles of law cover all facets of human activity". And, as was written earlier in *al-Basheer*,

> Allah says in the Quran, "For he [the Prophet] commands them what is just and forbids them what is evil; He allows them as lawful what is good and pure and prohibits them from what is bad and impure. He releases them from their heavy burdens and from the yokes that are upon them" (*al-Araaf* 157). This verse is a description of the Messenger of Allah (peace be upon him). In this verse Allah describes the Messenger of Allah as being the one who "allows them as lawful..." This is because the Messenger of Allah (peace be upon him) himself has been commissioned by Allah to give commandments and issue regulations. In this manner, what the Messenger of Allah (peace be upon him) ordered is similar to what Allah has ordered."[1]

Finally, Rahman states, "In my view, the harm done to Islam by its apologetic 'defenders' [like al-Azami] can far outweigh any that may be done by prejudiced Western scholarship." This is a strange statement from Rahman because

---

[1] Jamaal al-Deen Zarabozo, "The Importance of the Sunnah and Hadith in Islam," *Al-Basheer* (Vol. 1, No. 6, Mar.-Apr. 1988), p. 20. Appearing later in this collection.

his own writings, especially his earlier works, it can be argued, are filled with apologetic theories that are not based on facts but on supposition. Al-Azami, on the other hand, has clearly shown, in this work and others, an objective and scientific approach to the topics he covers.

Comments on Orientalists' Works

In general, one should be wary of the works that come from the Orientalists. In fact, this can probably be taken as a general rule. This is especially true if the reader is new to Islam or not that well-grounded in the Islamic sciences. The Orientalists are very deceptive in their writings although it is usually possible to spot their mistakes or deceptions.

Some time ago, a Muslim book distributor ran an advertisement concerning G. H. A. Juynboll's *Muslim Tradition* and stated that this book is a must for any student of hadith. Unfamiliar with Juynboll, this reviewer was duped into buying it although its price was a forbidding $54.50. Although published in 1983, this book, with respect to its methodology, mistakes and deceptions, is not much different from Schacht's work that al-Azami critiqued. Below are some examples that will demonstrate the nature of this book:

As with many other Orientalists, Juynboll tries to demonstrate that the sunnah of the Prophet (peace be upon him) was not a very important concept until many years after the death of the Prophet (peace be upon him).[1] They are always trying to attack the sunnah or to show that it is not important in order to tear the Muslims away from the sunnah. They know that if the Muslims abandon the sunnah, they are abandoning one-half of Islam and it will not be difficult for them to make the Muslims abandon Islam entirely. There is an incident narrated concerning Ali and ibn Abbaas who was going to

---

[1] Note the apparent influence of Schacht's conclusions on Juynboll.

debate the Khawarij. Ali told ibn Abbaas "to avoid confining the argument with the Khawarij to the Quran alone inasmuch as the Quran was capable of various possible interpretations until reference was made to the Sunnah, which would put them into a tight corner."[1]

Therefore, Juynboll (pp. 30-39) goes through the steps to prove that the sunnah was not important in the early history of Islam and, in general, hadith were never quoted in these early years. This presents an example of Juynboll's mistakes in methodology. Juynboll makes the classic contradiction that so many Orientalists make. On page 74, he writes, "Fabrication or forgery... had begun probably almost immediately after the prophet's death, if not on a small scale even already during his lifetime." But one cannot have his cake and eat it too. Which one is it: Nobody was relating hadith since hadith were not important or hadith had such an authority that it even led people to fabricate hadith? If nobody is quoting hadith in the early years or if the hadith are not important in the early years, why are people forging hadith? There must have been some call for the people to forge hadith in these early years and that was the importance of the sunnah of the Prophet (peace be upon him) in those early years.[2]

An example of the types of mistakes that Juynboll made can be found on p. 72. He writes, "Historical sources can sometimes be called upon to date a certain precept more accurately[3] as in the case of, for example, the fast of Ramadhan which was for the first time made obligatory under Umar b. al-Khattab's caliphate." Does this require any comment? It is Allah who says in the Quran, *"Kutiba alaikum al-siyaam"* or "Fasting is prescribed for you..."

---

[1] Quoted in S. M. Yusuf, *An Essay on the Sunnah* (Lahore: Institute of Islamic Culture, 1966), p. 34.

[2] Of course, this does not mean to imply that the forging of hadith did begin in those early years. (Juynboll states that without offering any historical evidence for it.)

[3] Notice the influence of Schacht on Juynbol in this passage.

An example of the type of deceptions that he tries to perform can be found on page 143. In this passage he is trying to prove that many of the early referred to narrators were actually fictitious characters; in other words, they never existed. He writes, "In the *Jarh* [of ibn Abi Haatim] the number of Shubas was nine, but in the *Tahdheeb* and the *Lisan* [both from ibn Hajr] together we find only seven Shubas." Unless Juynboll is completely ignorant of the nature of these different works, this statement makes no sense whatsoever. Before discussing the Shubas, a discussion of the referred to works are in order.

Kitaab al-Jarh wa al-Tadeel is by ibn Abi Haatim al-Raazi. Ibn Abu Haatim died in 327. This work is basically a collection of narrators that ibn Abi Haatim's father, and other scholars such as Abu Zura, had discussed. It was not confined to the narrators of any particular books nor did it contain only weak narrators.

Tahdheeb al-Tahdheeb by ibn Hajr is basically the collection of only those narrators whose hadith may be found in the "six books," that is, *Sahih al-Bukhari, Sahih Muslim, Sunan Abi Daawood, Sunan al-Nasaai, Sunan al-Tirmidhi* and *Sunan ibn Maajah*. In general, any narrator not found in those books will not be found in *Tahdheeb al-Tahdheeb* regardless of whether he is well-known or obscure, trustworthy or weak.

Lisaan al-Meezaan by ibn Hajr is based on al-Dhahabi's *Meezaan al-Itidaal*. It is a collection of narrators who have been criticized by at least one scholar. That is, if a narrator is known and proven to be trustworthy but he has been criticized, he may still be recorded in *Lisaan*. (Of course, it is hardly possible for all weak narrators to be included in one book.)

What this means is that the purpose and nature of the three books are completely different. Therefore, it is not surprising that ibn Abi Haatim's book may have many narrators that are not found in the other books.

From that introduction, the Shubas found in ibn Abi Haatim's book may be discussed. He includes nine narrators with the name Shuba.

(1) Shuba, the *maula* of ibn Abbaas: Most scholars consider him strong although Maalik said he is not trustworthy. Therefore, he should be found in al-Dhahabi's *Meezaan* and he is.[1] His hadith have been recorded by Abu Daawood so his biography is mentioned in *Tahdheeb*.

(2) Shuba al-Dhabi: Ibn Abu Haatim does not state if he is a weak or strong narrator. Since no disparaging remarks are known about him and since his hadith are not to be found in any of the "six books", it is not necessary to find him in either *Meezaan* or *al-Tahdheeb*. In fact, he is in neither of these two books.

(3) Shuba ibn Deenaar al-Kufi: Ibn Abu Haatim only records praise for him without any disparaging remarks. Therefore, there is no call for al-Dhahabi to mention him in *Meezaan*. His hadith are recorded by al-Nasaai, so his biography is found in *Tahdheeb*.

(4) Shuba ibn Amr Basri: Ibn Abu Haatim records that his father stated that he is unknown (Ar., *majhool*[2]) and he narrated hadith that are rejected or not known. Therefore, he is weak. And, therefore, al-Dhahabi mentioned him in *Meezaan*.

(5) Shuba ibn Abdul Rahmaan Madeeni: Ibn Abu Haatim does not state if he is a weak or strong narrator. Again, since no disparaging remarks are known about him and since his hadith are not to be found in any of the "six books", it is not necessary to find him in either *Meezaan* or *Tahdheeb*. In fact, he is in neither of these two books.

---

[1] Note that at the time of this writing ibn Hajr's *Lisaan* is not available to this reviewer, so use will be made of Ibn Hajr's source work, al-Dhahabi's *Meezaan* in this discussion.

[2] If a narrator is unknown, he is considered unacceptable. That is, in narration, in general, a narrator is considered unacceptable until he is proven to be trustworthy.

(6) Shuba ibn al-Hajjaaj: He was one of the greatest scholars of hadith and ibn Abi Haatim does not record anything but praise for him. His hadith are in all of the "six books" and therefore his biography is found in *Tahdheeb*.

(7) Shuba ibn Ajlaan: Ibn Abu Haatim recorded that his father stated him to be unknown (Ar., *majhool*). Since he was unknown, it is likely that al-Dhahabi mentioned him in *Meezaan*; and that, in fact, is the case.

(8) Shuba ibn Yazeed: Ibn Abu Haatim does not state if he is a weak or strong narrator. Once again, since no disparaging remarks are known about him and since his hadith are not to be found in any of the "six books", it is not necessary to find him in either *Meezaan* or *Tahdheeb*. In fact, he is in neither of these two books.

(9) Shuba who narrated from Kuraib: Ibn Abu Haatim recorded that his father stated him to be unknown. Al-Dhahabi also mentions him and also calls him unknown.

Juynboll fails (intentionally or unintentionally) to mention that al-Dhahabi also records a Shuba ibn Iyyaash and a Shuba ibn Buraida who are not mentioned by ibn Abi Haatim.

To reiterate, Juynboll is either ignorant of the nature of these three different books or he is trying to deceive the reader. Of the above nine Shubas mentioned by ibn Abi Haatim, those that should have been mentioned by ibn Hajr in *Tahdheeb* or by al-Dhahabi in *Meezaan* are, in fact, mentioned in those works. Thus, Juynboll has offered no evidence for his theory that there were many fictitious narrators that many people used to refer to.[1]

---

[1] The same type of analysis can be made for the other examples he gives.

Guillaume's Life of Muhammad

One more book ought to be mentioned here and that is Alfred Guillaume's *Life of Muhammad*.[1] The saddest aspect concerning this book is that he subtitles it, *A Translation of ibn Ishaq's Sirat Rasul Allah*. This may deceive many readers. Actually, it is not a true translation of ibn Ishaaq's work but it is a translation (and a poor one at that) of something that Guillaume himself, an Anglican clergyman, constructed that he calls Ibn Ishaaq's *Sira*.

This book was reviewed in detail by A. L. Tibawi.[2] For the sake of brevity, just a few of Tibawi's remarks will be quoted here.

Concerning the new construction of ibn Ishaaq, Tibawi wrote (pp. 29-30),

> In the process of separating Ibn Ishaq's supposed text from that of ibn Hishaam, and the accompanying process of rearrangement, omission, abbreviations, and additions, the style has also been changed. Thus the dialogue was much shortened in many cases, direct speech was often changed into indirect, and change of person is very frequent. As a result, the English translation has many instances of confusion, obscurity, and misunderstanding. This is aggravated by the ill effects of certain subtle twists of vital matters in the life of Muhammad. [This work amounts to] destruction, not reconstruction.

Tibawi points out a number of mistakes in the translation. He states (p. 37), "Inaccuracies are to be found almost on every page in this translation." After reviewing a number of mistakes, he states (p. 41),

---

[1] Alfred Guillaume, *Life of Muhammad* (Oxford: Oxford University Press, 1978).
[2] See A. L. Tibawi, *Arabic and Islamic Themes: Historical, Educational and Literary Studies* (London: Luzac & Company, Ltd., 1976), pp. 25-52.

This is then the value of Professor Guillaume's translation as it emerges from the consideration of only some 40 pages out of his 800. If so many inaccuracies, mistakes, omissions, and twists of the text could be noted in such a small part of the translation, how much could be found in the whole?... Another conclusion is that students wishing to quote ibn Ishaaq or ibn Hishaam will be well advised to go back to the Arabic; the English translation cannot be safely used on its own.

Concerning Guillaume's notes, Tibawi had this to say (p. 47), "But the most disturbing thing about Professor Guillaume's Notes is their unreliability..." Tibawi even points out examples where Guillaume misquoted his own writings.

Tibawi's last words on this book (p. 52) are: "As it stands, Professor Guillaume's translation cannot be accepted as a reliable reproduction of the received Arabic text of the Sira."

Final Words

Finally, after reviewing these three books, it is clear that the purpose of many of the Orientalists is not to find the truth but simply to deceive and mislead those people who read their books—or, it seems, they are simply not qualified to write about Islam. Therefore, it is recommended for Muslims to read those books that they know are trustworthy first before reading books like these that will only confuse them.

Feature Article:
Abu Hurairah—A Preserver of the Sunnah[1]

Abu Hurairah was one of the most famous and most knowledgeable of the Companions of the Prophet (peace be upon him). He can rightly be called one of the saviors of the Sunnah of the Prophet (peace be upon him). Although his reputation as a scholar of the Prophet's hadith cannot be questioned, many people have accused Abu Hurairah of some improper acts. In this article we wish to discuss the accusations against Abu Hurairah. The discussion will be broken down into the following topics: (A) The Position of the Companions according to the *Ahl al-Sunnah wa al-Jamaah*. (B) The Life of Abu Hurairah. (C) Statements Concerning Abu Hurairah from the Prophet (peace be upon him) Himself and from Other Companions. (D) The Accusations against Abu Hurairah.

(A) The Position of the Companions According to the *Ahl al-Sunnah wa al-Jamaah*

There is a general consensus among the Muslims that all of the people whom Allah selected to be the Prophet's Companions are *adl* (righteous, just, acceptable) *a priori*, meaning that there is no question that they are honest people who performed the obligatory acts of Islam and abstained from the major sins and who would not fabricate hadith. One can see from the Quranic verses and hadith, to be mentioned, that

---

[1] This article orginally appeared in *al-Basheer*, vol. 1, no. 1 (May 1987).

the place of the Companions of the Prophet (peace be upon him) is really part of the creed of the Muslims. In al-Tahaawi's explanation of the Islamic creed, commonly referred to as *al-Aqeedah al-Tahaawiyyah*, the scholar wrote,

> We love the Companions of the Messenger (peace be upon him), we do not exaggerate our love for any one of them and we do not disassociate ourselves from any one of them. We are angered with anyone who is angry with them or who speaks anything but good about them. And we do not mention them except with good statements about them. Love for them is belief, faith and good deeds while anger with them is disbelief, hypocrisy and transgression.[1]

In his commentary to al-Tahaawi's creed, ibn Abu al-Izz wrote,

> Here the teacher is referring to the Raafidhah and the Nasb. Allah and His Messenger praise the Companions, say they are pleased with them and promise them "the good." Allah says in the Quran, "And the first to lead the way, of the Emigrants and Helpers, and those who followed them in goodness—Allah is well pleased with them and they are well pleased with Him, and He has made ready for them gardens underneath which rivers flow, wherein they will abide forever. That is the supreme triumph" [*al-Taubah* 100]. "Muhammad is the Messenger of Allah. And those with him are hard against the disbelievers and merciful among themselves. You (Muhammad) see them bowing and falling prostrate [in worship], seeking bounties from Allah and His acceptance... Allah has promised unto such of them who believe and do good works

---

[1] See ibn Abi al-Izz al-Hanafi, *Sharh al-Aqeedah al-Tahaawiyyah* (Beirut: al-Maktab al-Islaami, 1983), p. 568.

forgiveness and immense rewards" [*al-Fath* 29].
"Allah was well-pleased with the believers when they
swore allegiance unto you beneath the tree, and He
knew what was in their hearts" [*al-Fath* 18].[1]

There also exist many hadith that point to the
excellence of the Companions. The Prophet (peace be upon
him) said,

يَأْتِي عَلَى النَّاسِ زَمَانٌ فَيَغْزُو فِئَامٌ مِنَ النَّاسِ فَيَقُولُونَ فِيكُمْ مَنْ

صَاحَبَ رَسُولَ اللَّهِ صَلَّى اللَّهم عَلَيْهِ وَسَلَّمَ فَيَقُولُونَ نَعَمْ

فَيُفْتَحُ لَهُمْ ثُمَّ يَأْتِي عَلَى النَّاسِ زَمَانٌ فَيَغْزُو فِئَامٌ مِنَ النَّاسِ

فَيُقَالُ هَلْ فِيكُمْ مَنْ صَاحَبَ أَصْحَابَ رَسُولِ اللَّهِ صَلَّى اللَّهم

عَلَيْهِ وَسَلَّمَ فَيَقُولُونَ نَعَمْ فَيُفْتَحُ لَهُمْ ثُمَّ يَأْتِي عَلَى النَّاسِ زَمَانٌ

فَيَغْزُو فِئَامٌ مِنَ النَّاسِ فَيُقَالُ هَلْ فِيكُمْ مَنْ صَاحَبَ مَنْ

صَاحَبَ أَصْحَابَ رَسُولِ اللَّهِ صَلَّى اللَّهم عَلَيْهِ وَسَلَّمَ فَيَقُولُونَ

نَعَمْ فَيُفْتَحُ لَهُمْ

"A time will come when a party of the people will go forth to
fight, and some will say, 'Is there among you anyone who has
kept company with the Apostle of Allah?' They will answer,
'Yes.' And they shall be victorious. Thereafter a time will
come when a party of the people will go forth to fight, and
someone will say, 'Is there among you anyone who has kept

---

[1] Ibn Abi al-Izz, pp. 528-9. The Quranic passages he quoted were *al-Taubah* 100,
48:29 and 48:18. As noted earlier, ibn Abi al-Izz continues in his commentary to
discuss the position of the Companions for three more pages. To save some
space not all of the relevant Quranic verses will be quoted here but the interested
reader should see *al-Baqarah* 173, *ali-Imraan* 110, *al-Anfaal* 72-75, *al-Qamar*
8-10 and *al-Hadeed* 10.

company with the Companions of the Messenger of Allah?' They will answer, 'Yes,' and they shall be victorious. Thereafter a time will come when a party of the people will go forth to fight, and someone will say, 'Is there among you anyone who has kept company with a companion of the Companions of the Messenger of Allah?' They will answer, 'Yes,' and they shall be victorious." (Recorded by al-Bukhari, Muslim and others.)

The Messenger of Allah (peace be upon him) also said,

خَيْرُكُمْ قَرْنِي ثُمَّ الَّذِينَ يَلُونَهُمْ ثُمَّ الَّذِينَ يَلُونَهُمْ قَالَ عِمْرَانُ
لا أَدْرِي أَذَكَرَ النَّبِيُّ صَلَّى اللَّهم عَلَيْهِ وَسَلَّمَ بَعْدُ قَرْنَيْنِ أَوْ
ثَلاثَةً قَالَ النَّبِيُّ صَلَّى اللَّهم عَلَيْهِ وَسَلَّمَ إِنَّ بَعْدَكُمْ قَوْمًا
يَخُونُونَ وَلا يُؤْتَمَنُونَ وَيَشْهَدُونَ وَلا يُسْتَشْهَدُونَ وَيَنْذِرُونَ
وَلا يَفُونَ وَيَظْهَرُ فِيهِمُ السِّمَنُ

"The best of you [my followers] is my generation, then those who will come after them, then those who come after them. [Imraan said, "And I do not know if he mentioned two or three generations after his own generation."] And behold, after you there will be people who will be betrayers and they cannot be trusted, who will testify without being asked to testify, who will make vows and will not fulfill them, and fatness will appear among them." (Recorded by al-Bukhari, Muslim and others with slightly different wordings.)

He (peace be upon him) also said,

لا تَسُبُّوا أَصْحَابِي فَلَوْ أَنَّ أَحَدَكُمْ أَنْفَقَ مِثْلَ أُحُدٍ ذَهَبًا مَا بَلَغَ
مُدَّ أَحَدِهِمْ وَلا نَصِيفَهُ

"Do not revile my Companions. Do not revile my Companions. By him in whose hand is my life, if one among you would have spent as much gold as [the weight of] Uhud, it would not amount to as much as one *mudd* on behalf of one of them, or even half of that." (Recorded by Muslim and others.) Uhud is a mountain near Madinah while a *mudd* is a measure that is equivalent to two handfuls when the hands are cupped together.

Although the Quran and the hadith are clear on the status of the Companions there have existed some people who have held divergent views concerning them. For example, some Shiah say that after the Messenger of Allah died most of the Companions reverted to disbelief. In one of the books that they base their religion on, Rijaal al-Kashi, the following statement is attributed to Abu Jafar, "The people were apostates after the death of the Prophet except for three of them." He was asked, "Who were they?" He answered, "Al-Miqdaad ibn al-Aswad, Abu Dharr al-Ghafaari and Salmaan al-Farsi."[1] This report goes against how Allah describes the Companions in the Quran and in the hadith of the Prophet (peace be upon him). In fact, even the Shiahs should reject such a report as, according to this report, even Ali, Faatimah, al-Husain and al-Hasan were apostates. Some of the Khawaarij say that after the Civil War between Ali and Muawiya, the Companions were no longer to be considered just and trustworthy (Ar., *adl*). This opinion also is not acceptable as one cannot declare a person to be unjust based on an incorrect personal judgment or *ijtihaad*. Again, the position of the group known as "The People of the Sunnah and the Community," say that all of the Companions were adl and they were so for all of their lives and that Allah is pleased with them as He states so in the Quran.[2]

---

[1] See Ihsaan Ilaahi Dhaheer, *Al-Shia wa al-Sunnah* (Lahore: Idaarah Tarjumaan al-Sunnah, 1983), p. 49.

[2] For a more complete selection of hadith on the virtues of the Companions or of individual Companions or of specific groups of them, see ibn al-Atheer, *Jaami*

(B) The Life of Abu Hurairah

Abu Hurairah was so well-known by his nickname, given to him by the Prophet (peace be upon him), that it is not certain what his actual name was. The strongest opinion is that it was Abdul Rahmaan ibn Sakhr al-Dausi. He was from Yemen and embraced Islam at the hand of al-Tufail ibn Amr al-Dausi when the latter had returned from Madinah to Yemen.[1] In 7 A. H., he left Yemen to join the Messenger of Allah (peace be upon him) in Madinah. He was a poor man and he devoted all of his time to serving the Prophet (peace be upon him) and learning about the religion. He was from the *ahl al-Suffah* who lived in the mosque of the Prophet (peace be upon him) at Madinah. The Prophet (peace be upon him) admired his devotion and knowledge and sent him with al-Ala al-Hadhrami to Bahrain (present-day al-Hasa) to teach the people about the religion of Islam. Also Umar, when he was the caliph, appointed him the Governor of Bahrain for a couple of years. Later, Umar again asked him to be a governor but he refused. He was in the house of Uthmaan on the day that Uthmaan was killed and tried to prevent the confederates from murdering him. After the martyrdom of Uthmaan and the beginning of the Civil War, he completely avoided the political problems of his time, as did Ibn Umar. Muawiya later appointed Abu Hurairah the governor of Madinah but he became upset with him and replaced him with Marwaan. Abu Hurairah died, according to the strongest opinion, in 59 A. H.

---

al-Usool min Ahaadeeth al-Rasool (Beirut: Ihyaa al-Kutub al-Arabi, 1980), vol. 9, pp. 404-478 and vol. 10, pp. 1-142.
[1] See Ahmad ibn Hajr, *Al-Isaabah fi Tamyeez al-Sahaabah*, under the heading al-Tufail.

(C) Statements Concerning Abu Hurairah from the Prophet (peace be upon him) Himself and from Other Companions.

Abu Hurairah's mother was a polytheist and he had asked the Prophet (peace be upon him) to pray for her guidance and she afterwards accepted Islam. Abu Hurairah returned to the Prophet (peace be upon him) to tell him the good news and then said, "Allah's Messenger, pray to Allah that He may instill love for me and for my mother in the believing servants and let our hearts be filled with their love." The Prophet (peace be upon him) then said, "O Allah, let their be love for these two servants of yours in the hearts of the believers and let their hearts be filled with love for your believing servants." Later, Abu Hurairah said, "This prayer was so answered by Allah that no believer was ever born who heard of me and who saw me except that he had love for me."[1] This incident shows that the true believer will have love in his heart for Abu Hurairah. How could this not be the case when he was the one who preserved and passed on so many hadith of the Prophet (peace be upon him)?

His knowledge was well-known among the Companions. He used to lecture in the Prophet's mosque in the presence of older Companions. Talha and ibn Umar both stated that he was the most knowledgeable of the Companions. Some Followers (the generation after that of the Companions) found it strange that he knew so many hadith of the Prophet. He replied to them by saying, "You people say, 'Abu Hurairah relates too many hadith on the authority of the Prophet,' and you say, 'How come the Emigrants do not relate such hadith?' My Companions from among the Emigrants were busy taking

---

[1] This incident may be found in *Sahih Muslim* (A. H. Siddiqi, trans.,Lahore: Muhammad Ashraf, 1975), vol. 4, p. 1329.

care of their business while I was poor and I stayed with the Messenger of Allah and was satisfied with whatever filled my stomach. I was in more gatherings with the Messenger of Allah and I was present when they were absent and I remembered when they forgot."[1] Umar, who was very careful about spreading too many hadith as he feared that the people may not be careful in replicating the exact words of the Prophet, considered preventing Abu Hurairah from narrating so many hadith but when he found him to be proficient and exact he allowed him to continue.

(D) The Accusations against Abu Hurairah

Even though Abu Hurairah's knowledge and proficiency was praised and respected by all of the Companions, Followers and great scholars of Islam, this did not prevent him from coming under attack by some people. In general, one can group the people who attacked or attack Abu Hurairah into the following categories: (a) Mutazilis, (b) Orientalists, (c) Muslims blinded or deceived by the Orientalists and (d) Shiahs.

It seems that the first people to attack Abu Hurairah were some of the Mutazila, in particular al-Nidhaam.[2] Many aspects of the sunnah disagree with al-Nidhaam's reasoning so he tried to attack Abu Hurairah and, thereby, the entire sunnah. The Shiah were the next to attack him as the authentic and well-established hadith show their creed to be entirely baseless; so they tried to attack the superstructure of hadith by attacking one of its more important original sources, Abu Hurairah. The Orientalists then attacked him as they know that

---

[1] See Ahmad ibn Hajr, *Fath al-Baari bi-Sharh Saheeh al-Bukhaari* (Riyadh: Daar al-Ifta), vol. 1, p. 217; and *Sahih Muslim*, vol. 4, p. 1330.

[2] Abdul Qaahir al-Baghdaadi wrote that the other Mutazilah consider al-Nidhaam and his followers to be unbelievers. See al-Baghdaadi, *al-Farq bain al-Firaq*, p. 126.

if the Muslims can be divorced from the Sunnah of the Prophet (peace be upon him) they will be, in essence, divorced from Islam. Ahmad Amin, a copious student of the Orientalists, tried to extend their arguments in his book *Fajr al-Islaam*. Two recent Shiahs have also attacked Abu Hurairah again. They are Abdul Husain Sharf al-Deen al-Amali, who authored *Abu Hurairah*, and his student Mahmood Abu Rayyah, the author of *Adhwa ala al-Sunnah al-Muhammadiyyah*. The claims against Abu Hurairah have been refuted by Muhammad Abdul Razzaaq Hamza, Abdul Rahmaan al-Mualamy al-Yamany, Muhammad Ijaaj al-Khateeb and Mustafa al-Sabai.[1]

Actually, most of their claims against Abu Hurairah are nothing but lies or deceptions. For example, Ibn Qutaiba, in his famous work *Taweel Mukhtalaf al-Hadith*, quoted the views of the Mutazilah and then proceeded to refute them. What did Abu Rayyah do? He quoted the portion where Ibn Qutaiba quoted the Mutazila (leaving out ibn Qutaiba's refutations) and then he had the audacity to claim that this passage contained the views of the great Sunni scholar ibn Qutaiba. Mustafa al-Sibaa'ee wrote,

> This man [Abu Rayyah] is not trustworthy in what he has recorded. Many times he would add something to a quote that would completely change its meaning. And he interprets the texts in the manner that he wishes and not according to what the person quoted

---

[1] See the following works: Muhammad Abdul Razzaaq Hamza, *Dhulumaat Abu Rayyah Amaam Adhwa al-Sunnah al-Muhammadiyyah* (Madeenah: Daar al-Salafiyyah, 1379 A.H.); Abdul Rahmaan al-Mualami al-Yamani, *Al-Anwaar al-Kaashifah lima fi Kitaab Adhwa al-Sunnah min al-Zalaal wa al-Tadhleel wa al-Mujaazifah* (Madeenah: Daar al-Salafiyyah, 1378 A.H.); Muhammad Ijaaj al-Khateeb, *Al-Sunnah Qabl al-Tadween* (Cairo: Maktabah Wuhaibah, 1963). All of them basically deal with Abu Rayyah and al-Amaly while Mustafa al-Sibaai, *Al-Sunnah wa Makaanatuhaa fi al-Tashree al-Islaami* (no publication information given) also refuted the views of Ahmad Amin and those of the Orientalists.

meant. Many times he would ascribe a statement to someone who never made such a statement just for the sake of deception.[1]

Throughout his book, Abu Rayyah claims that his is a scientific study, the likes of which has never been produced before. He also states in his work, "May the curse of Allah be on the liars, those who do so intentionally or unintentionally!"[2] It seems that he is, in reality, cursing himself.

We shall begin our detailed refutation of their claims against Abu Hurairah with a discussion of the claims of the Shiahs. This is basically because to this day the Shiahs in the United States are still repeating their blasphemous claims against this noble Companion of the Prophet (peace be upon him). The author of this article is a convert to Islam and he heard many of these claims coming from the Shiahs in the United States after he embraced Islam.

Khomeini, today's leader of the Shiah, has written on p. 43 of his book *Islam and Revolution* (translated by Hamid Alger), "Abu Hurayra was one of the *fuqaha*, but God knows what judgments he falsified for Muawiya and others like him, and what damage he inflicted upon Islam."[3] Abdul Husain Sharf al-Deen al-Amaly, referred to above, has declared Abu Hurairah to be an unbeliever. Here is a discussion of some of their claims on a point by point basis.

Claim #1. Al-Amaly (pp. 14-15) and Abu Rayyah (pp. 192-3) claim that Abu Hurairah stole 10,000 *dinar*s while he was the governor of Bahrain during the caliphate of Umar and, therefore, Umar punished him. This incident has not been

---

[1] Al-Sibaai, p. 363. Al-Sibaai goes on to present many examples that support the contention he made in this passage.

[2] This is not an uncommon ploy in an attempt to deceive others. Deceivers like to use catchy phrases and so forth to make it seem like it is not possible that they could be lying.

[3] Khomeini, *Islam and Revolution* (Berkeley: Mizan Press, 1981), p. 143. One may see p. 71 for disparaging remarks about another Companion, Samurah ibn Jundub.

recorded in any of the trustworthy books of history. It can only be found in *Al-Aqd al-Fareed* by ibn Abd Rabbih which is a book of literature and not a history book that may be relied upon for historical facts. Abu Rayyah, probably noticing this fact, did not even bother to mention the source of this story although his teacher, al-Amaly, did. The fact of the matter is that Abu Hurairah stole nothing and no authentic reports state that he did. Umar treated him and distributed the wealth of his area in the same way that he treated all of his other governors, including Abu Moosa al-Ashari.[1] In fact, later in his life Umar asked Abu Hurairah to act as a governor again. Would this have been possible if Abu Hurairah had previously stolen 10,000 *dinar*s?

Claim #2. Al-Amaly (pp. 26-31) and Abu Rayyah (185-190) say that Abu Hurairah supported the Umayyad rulers and forged hadith in their favor. Nothing could be further from the truth. A study of the history of that time will show that there were many times in which he opposed the Umayyad rulers and, furthermore, his love for the family of the Prophet (peace be upon him) was well-known. The stories of his opposition to Marwaan can be found in *Al-Bidaayah wa al-Nihaayah* (vol. 8, pp. 108f). If one goes today to the well-known collections of hadith, one can find many hadith narrated by Abu Hurairah that state the virtues of the family of the Prophet (peace be upon him). In fact, it was Abu Hurairah who reported the hadith that during the battle of Khaibar the Prophet (peace be upon him) said,

$$\text{لَأُعْطِيَنَّ هَذِهِ الرَّايَةَ رَجُلاً يُحِبُّ اللَّهَ وَرَسُولَهُ يَفْتَحُ اللَّهُ عَلَى يَدَيْهِ}$$

"I certainly shall give the banner to one who loves Allah and His Messenger, and Allah shall conquer them by his hand,"

---

[1] See *Tabaqaat ibn Saad*, vol. 4, pp. 60f.

and then he gave the banner to Ali ibn Abu Taalib. (Recorded by Muslim.)

Concerning Abu Hurairah's forging of hadith, al-Amaly and Abu Rayyah quote two stories that are fabricated or that have no source. In these stories Abu Hurairah is supposed to have forged hadith for Muawiya or Marwaan. Ibn Abu al-Hadeed (a Shiah) in *Sharh Nahj al-Balaaghah* (vol. 1, p. 467) quotes these stories. The only one who narrated them was ibn Abu al-Hadeed's teacher Abu Jafar al-Iskaafi (d. 240, a Shiah Mutazili) and he did not even give the chain of authorities for the story although he lived some one hundred years after the death of Abu Hurairah.[1] Concerning this Abu Jafar al-Iskaafi, his student ibn Abu al-Hadeed said that he was the staunchest and most extreme of the people of Baghdad in his Shia and Mutazili views. The hatred between the Mutazilis and the scholars of hadith is a well-known fact of history that need not be recounted here.[2]

Claim #3. Al-Amaly (pp. 45f) and Abu Rayyah (pp. 162f) claim that Abu Hurairah narrated too many hadith; although he accepted Islam relatively late, he still related more hadith than any other Companion. That is all true. But that does not, by any means, imply that he forged hadith as the Shiahs claim. The reasons he narrated, relatively speaking, so many hadith were: (1) He was of the *ahl al-Suffah* and he spent all of his time with the Messenger of Allah (peace be upon him) while the other Companions were busy with their business, farming, and families. This allowed him to hear more hadith than many others. (2) The Messenger of Allah (peace be upon him) made a supplication for him which allowed him not

---

[1] For other reasons why this story is to be rejected, see ibn al-Arabi, *al-Awaasim min al-Qawaasim*, pp. 177-184.

[2] For a discussion of the problems between the Mutazilis and the scholars of hadith, see Abdul Majeed Abdul Majeed, *al-Ittijihaat al-Fiqhiyyah ind Ashaab al-Hadeeth* (1979), pp. 93-105.

to forget any of the hadith he heard.[1] (3) He outlived many other Companions and, therefore, many newcomers came to him to ask him about the religion and he answered them by relating hadith. (4) He lived most of his life in Madinah, the city where most of the people traveled to in order to hear hadith (as opposed to Abdullah ibn Amr, for example, who lived in Egypt). (5) He himself stated that because the Quran warns against concealing knowledge, he did his best to transmit all of the hadith that he knew.

Furthermore, the Shiahs have no room for argument on this point as they claim to have many narrators who heard many more hadith than this from their Imams. For example, they claim that Muhammad ibn Muslim ibn Ribaah heard 30,000 hadith from al-Baaqir and another 16,000 from Jafar al-Saadiq. They credit Jaabir ibn Yazeed al-Jufy with narrating 70,000 hadith from al-Baaqir (Jafar's father) and 140,000 hadith from the other Imams. While in their own books of narrators they record that Jafar stated that he knew of Jaabir meeting his father on only one occasion and that Jaabir had never met with Jafar. From where then did he receive those thousands of hadith and why do Shia authors like Abdul Husain (author of *al-Muraajiaat*) consider him a trustworthy narrator?[2]

Claim #4. Al-Amaly (pp. 262f) and Abu Rayyah (pp. 166f) claim that the other Companions stated that Abu Hurairah was a liar. All of their sources for this point are either fabricated (as are the narrations from Umar, Uthmaan and Ali) or simply mean that Abu Hurairah was mistaken (as in the narration from Aishah), which is another meaning of the word

---

[1] Al-Amaly (p. 197) claims that Abu Hurairah was the only Companion to narrate the hadith concerning the Prophet's supplication for his memory. Al-Zariy has shown this claim to be false. See Abdul Rahmaan al-Zariy, *Abu Hurairah wa Aqlaam al-Haaqideen* (Kuwait: Daar al-Arqam, 1985), pp. 73f.

[2] See Abdul Rahmaan al-Zariy, *Rijaal al-Sheeah fi al-Meezaan* (Kuwait: Daar al-Arqam, 1983), pp. 72-77; al-Zariy, *Abu Hurairah*, p. 3.

kidhb in Hijazi Arabic.[1] They record that Umar called him a liar. This narration is a fabrication. How could it be that Umar would ask him to be governor when he called him a liar? The narration from Ali comes, again, from Abu Jafar al-Iskaafi and is worthless.[2]

Claim #5. Al-Amaly (p. 163) and Abu Rayyah (p. 268) claim that Umar had Abu Hurairah beaten because he narrated too many hadith. This is, again, based on a narration by Abu Jafar al-Iskaafi whom even some Shiahs reject as a narrator. It is true that Umar advised Abu Hurairah not to relate so many hadith as Umar was very much worried about people making mistakes in hadith narrations but after he found out that Abu Hurairah was not prone to making mistakes, he permitted him to narrate as many hadith as he wished.[3]

Finally, as al-Zariy points out, the hadith that these Shiah authors point to as being fabricated by Abu Hurairah may also be found in the most authentic Shiah collections of hadith of the Prophet or of their Imams. For the sake of brevity, I shall discuss only one such hadith here. The Shiahs claim that the Prophetic hadith that state that the Prophets do not leave any inheritance have been fabricated by the Sunnis to rob the Prophet's daughter, Faatimah, from her rightful inheritance. Al-Amaly (p. 137) claims that Abu Hurairah fabricated these hadith. In the Shiahs most important collection of hadith, *Al-Usool al-Kaafi*, one may find the following narration, "Abu Abdullah (peace be upon him) said, 'Verily, the scholars are the heirs of the prophets because the prophets do not leave for inheritance *dirham*s or *dinar*s but they leave only their statements...'"[4]

---

[1] See this author's footnote concerning this term in al-Sayyid Sabiq, *Fiqh al-Sunnah* (Indianapolis, IN: American Trust Publications, 1985), vol. 1, p. 81, fn. 8.

[2] See al-Khateeb, *Al-Sunnah Qabl al-Tadween*, pp. 394ff.

[3] See ibn Katheer, *Al-Bidaayah wa al-Nihaayah*, vol. 8, p. 107.

[4] See al-Kulaini, *Usool al-Kaafi* (Intisharaat Ilmiyyah Islaamiyyah, Bazar Sheeraazi), vol. 1, p. 39.

One should not be surprised by the Shiah's attitude towards Abu Hurairah. According to them almost all of the Companions of the Prophet (peace be upon him) were unbelievers. As quoted earlier, they claim that Abu Jafar said, "The people became apostates after the Prophet except for three: al-Miqdaad ibn al-Aswad, Abu Dharr al-Ghafaari and Salmaan al-Faarisi." Another narration, in the same book, from Moosa ibn Jafar, their seventh Imam, states, "On the Day of Judgment a caller will proclaim, 'Where are the helpers of Muhammad ibn Abdullah, the Messenger, who did not turn on him?' Salmaan, al-Miqdaad and Abu Dharr will then stand." Khomeini also holds similar views. In *Kashf al-Asraar*, he wrote, "These persons (the companions) had nothing to do with Islam and the Quran save to utilize these as the means for their worldly gains and holding the helm."[1]

Now we may move along to the claims of Ahmad Amin in his book *Fajr al-Islam*. His claims have been adequately refuted by Mustafa al-Sibaa'ee and it will be his presentation that will be followed here. Amin's arguments may be summarized in the following six points: (1) Some of the other Companions rejected some of Abu Hurairah's hadith and called him a liar. (2) Abu Hurairah did not record hadith and would always relate the hadith from his memory. (3) Abu Hurairah would not relate only what he heard directly from the Prophet (peace be upon him) but he would also narrate what he heard from others. (4) Some of the Companions strongly criticized him and doubted his sincerity. (5) The Hanafis would reject his narration if it opposed the principles of analogy and they would state that Abu Hurairah was not a *faqeeh* or jurist. (6) People who fabricated hadith fabricated

---

[1] Quoted in Abul Hasan Ali Nadwi, *Islam and the Earliest Muslims: Two Conflicting Portraits* (Lucknow, India: Academy of Research and Publications), p. 33. For more on this point, see Ihsan Ilahi Zaheer, *Shias & Shiaism: Their Genesis and Evolution* (Lahore, Pakistan: Idaarah Tarjumaan al-Sunnah, 1986), pp. 470-481.

many hadith on his authority. Since this article is already somewhat lengthy, these points shall be dealt with briefly.

Concerning (1), some of the other Companions rejected some of Abu Hurairah's hadith and called him a liar: Amin quotes ibn Abbaas and Aishah not accepting the hadith that Abu Hurairah had reported. Dr. Abdul Majeed Abdul Majeed has shown that they did not accept the literal interpretation of what Abu Hurairah reported based on their own understanding of the Quran and other hadith but they did not accuse the noble Companion Abu Hurairah of fabricating such hadith.[1] Furthermore, the hadith that Amin refers to were also narrated by other Companions besides Abu Hurairah.

With respect to (2), Abu Hurairah did not record hadith and would always relate the hadith from his memory: this is not valid as a particular attack on Abu Hurairah as it was the practice of most, if not all, of the Companions to narrate from their memories (although a large number of them aided their memories by also recording the hadith they knew). The Prophet (peace be upon him) himself prayed that Abu Hurairah may be safe from forgetting hadith and Abu Hurairah said that after that supplication he never forgot any of the hadith he heard. All of the Companions praised his outstanding memory and would go to him to ask him about hadith of the Prophet (peace be upon him).

Amin also states that Abu Hurairah would not relate only what he heard directly from the Prophet (peace be upon him) but he would also narrate what he heard from others. This was a common practice of many of the Companions, especially the younger ones. This is called the *mursal* reports of the Companions. It is considered acceptable according to all of the scholars of hadith and there is absolutely nothing wrong with it. Many times the Companions used to distinguish, in their narrations, what they heard directly from the Prophet (peace be

---

[1] Abdul Majeed, pp. 160-176.

upon him) from what they had heard through intermediary sources.

One last point concerning what Amin has written on this topic. What actually happened was that Abu Hurairah stated that one who wakes while sexually defiled during the day of Ramadhaan is not to fast that day. Aishah stated that the Prophet (peace be upon him) would wake in such a state and would still fast the day. Abu Hurairah then reversed his decision and stated that he had heard that statement from al-Fadhl ibn Abbaas and not from the Prophet (peace be upon him). The important point to note is that Abu Hurairah never narrated the first statement as a hadith of the Prophet (peace be upon him) but it was his own personal statement while Ahmad Amin wrote that Abu Hurairah narrated it as a Prophetic hadith and then when Aishah corrected him he said that he had heard it from al-Fadhl and not from the Prophet (peace be upon him). The way Ahmad Amin records it, it looks like Abu Hurairah was a liar but that is due to the fact that Amin records it incorrectly.

Amin also states that some of the Companions strongly criticized him and doubted his sincerity. This statement by Amin is based on what Goldziher wrote, although Goldziher referred it to some of the Followers (the generation after the Companions) while Amin referred it to some of the Companions. This claim has already been discussed under claim number 4 from al-Amaly and Abu Rayyah. Concerning the Followers, they simply stated that Abu Hurairah seems to narrate too many hadith when compared to the other Companions. The reasons he narrated so many hadith have also been discussed earlier.

Concerning (5), the Hanafis would reject his narration if it opposed the principles of analogy and they would state that Abu Hurairah was not a *faqeeh* or jurist: al-Sibaa'ee says that this argument points to three conclusions: (a) The Hanafis put analogy before reports if there is some contradiction. (b) They especially did that with respect to reports from Abu

Haneefah. (c) They did not consider Abu Hurairah to be a jurist.[1] This is not the proper place to discuss (a) in detail. Perhaps it will be sufficient to quote a few statements from Abu Haneefah. He said, "If the hadith is authentic, it is my *madhhab* [or opinion]." He also said, "If I proclaim something that differs from the Book of Allah and the statements of the Messenger of Allah, discard my pronouncement."[2] With respect to (b), it is true that the Hanafis will reject someone's narration if it is directly opposed to what they consider clear or direct analogies of verses of the Quran or well-established hadith. But that is true for almost all narrators and not only Abu Hurairah. Finally, concerning (c), al-Sibaa'ee says that this is only true for a very small number of Hanafis and it is not true for the majority of the Hanafi scholars.[3]

Amin then points out that people who fabricated hadith fabricated many hadith on his authority. This is no argument whatsoever. Why didn't he just say, "Many hadith have been fabricated on the authority of the Prophet (peace be upon him) and therefore we should not accept any narration from the Prophet (peace be upon him)." The scholars of hadith, from the time of the Companions until the present day, have labored endlessly to ensure that all of the fabricators are spotted and their hadith discarded.[4]

We stated earlier that the main reason for the attacks on Abu Hurairah by the Shiahs, Orientalists and those who follow the Orientalists is that they wish to take the Muslims away from the sunnah of the Prophet (peace be upon him) and, unfortunately, they have been able to affect many Muslims,

---

[1] See al-Sibaai, pp. 324f.
[2] Quoted in Muhammad Naasir al-Deen al-Albaani, *Sifat Salaat al-Nabi* (Beirut: al-Maktab al-Islaami, 1983), pp. 24 and 26.
[3] Al-Sibaai, pp. 316ff.
[4] About a quarter of al-Sibaai's book is devoted to showing how the Muslim scholars preserved the hadith literature from being infiltrated by fabricated hadith.

especially in this country, although Allah says about the Prophet (peace be upon him),

لَقَدْ كَانَ لَكُمْ فِي رَسُولِ اللَّهِ أُسْوَةٌ حَسَنَةٌ لِمَنْ كَانَ يَرْجُو
اللَّهَ وَالْيَوْمَ الآخِرَ وَذَكَرَ اللَّهَ كَثِيرًا

"Verily you have in the Messenger of Allah a perfect example for whosoever is looking towards Allah and the Day of Resurrection and whosoever remembers Allah often" (*al-Ahzaab* 21). It is hoped that this brief discussion of the claims against Abu Hurairah will make Abu Hurairah's position very clear for those who are sincerely seeking the truth.

All praise is due to Allah.

Selected References

Shiah Sources:

Abu Rayyah, Mahmood. *Adwa ala al-Sunnah al-Muhammadiyyah*. Daar Taleef. Cairo. 1958.

al-Amaly, Abdul Husain Sharf al-Deen. *Abu Hurairah*. First edition. Said.

Ibn Abu al-Hadeed. *Sharh Nahj al-Balaaghah*. Beirut: Daar al-Fikr.

Khomeini. *Islam and Revolution*. Berkeley: Mizan Press. 1981.

Al-Kulainy al-Raazi, Abu Jafar Muhammad ibn Yaqoob. *Usool Kaafi*. Intishaarat Ilmiyyah Islaamiyyah. Bazar Sheeraazi.

Sunni sources:

Abdul Majeed, Abdul Majeed. *Al-Ittijihaat al-Fiqhiyyah Ind Ashaab al-Hadeeth*. 1979.

Al-Albaani, Muhammad Naasir al-Deen. *Sifat Salaat al-Nabi*. Beirut: Al-Maktab al-Islaami. 1983.

-----*Silsilat al-Ahaadeeth al-Dhaeefah*. Beirut: Maktab al-Islaami. 1978. Vol. 1.

Dhaheer, Ihsan Ilahi. *Al-Sheeah wa al-Sunnah*. Lahore, Pakistan: Idaarah Tarjumaan al-Sunnah. 1983.

-----*Shias & Shiaism: Their Genesis and Evolution*. Lahore, Pakistan: Idaarah Tarjumaan al-Sunnah. 1986.

Ibn Abu al-Izz al-Hanafi. *Sharh al-Aqeedah al-Tahaawiyyah*. Beirut: Al-Maktab al-Islaami. 1983.

ibn al-Atheer. *Jaami al-Usool min Ahaadeeth al-Rasool*. Beirut: Ihya al-Kutub al-Arabi. 1980.

Ibn al-Arabi, Abu Bakr. *Al-Awaasim min al-Qawaasim*. Beirut: Al-Maktabah al-lmiyyah. 1985.

Ibn Katheer, Imaad al-Deen. *Al-Bidaayah wa al-Nihaayah*. Cairo: Matbaa al-Saada. 1932.

al-Khateeb, Muhammad Ijaaj. *Al-Sunnah Qabl al-Tadween*. Cairo: Maktab Wahba. 1963.

Nadwi, Abul Hasan Ali. *Islam and the Earliest Muslims: Two Conflicting Portraits*. Lucknow, India: Academy of Islamic Research and Publications.

Sabiq, As-Sayyid. *Fiqh us-Sunnah*. Indianapolis, IN: American Trust Publications. 1985.

Al-Sibaa'ee, Mustafa. *Al-Sunnah wa Makaanatuhu fi al-Tashri al-Islaami*. No publication information given.

Siddiqi, A. H., trans. *Sahih Muslim*. Lahore, Paksitan: Muhammad Ashraf. 1975.

al-Zariy, Abdul Rahmaan. *Abu Hurairah wa Aqlaam al-Haaqideen*. Kuwait: Daar al-Arqam. 1985.

-----*Rijaal al-Shiah fi al-Meezaan*. Kuwait: Daar al-Arqam. 1983.

Feature Article:
Between Islam and *Kufr*

Introduction

One of the grave mistakes made by the Children of Israel was that they developed the belief that they were the chosen of Allah and that Allah would enter them into paradise simply because they were Jews. In *soorah al-Baqarah*, Allah says about them,

وَقَالُوا لَنْ تَمَسَّنَا النَّارُ إِلاَّ أَيَّامًا مَعْدُودَةً

"And they say, 'The fire of punishment will not touch us save for a certain number of days'" (*al-Baqarah* 80). Another verse states,

أَلَمْ تَرَ إِلَى الَّذِينَ أُوتُوا نَصِيبًا مِنْ الْكِتَابِ يُدْعَوْنَ إِلَى كِتَابِ اللَّهِ لِيَحْكُمَ بَيْنَهُمْ ثُمَّ يَتَوَلَّى فَرِيقٌ مِنْهُمْ وَهُمْ مُعْرِضُونَ ذَلِكَ بِأَنَّهُمْ قَالُوا لَنْ تَمَسَّنَا النَّارُ إِلاَّ أَيَّامًا مَعْدُودَاتٍ وَغَرَّهُمْ فِي دِينِهِمْ مَا كَانُوا يَفْتَرُونَ

"Have you not seen how those who have received the Scripture invoke the Scripture of Allah (in their disputes) that it may judge between them: then a faction of them turn away, being opposed to it? That is because they say, 'The Fire will not touch us save for a certain number of days.' That which they

---

[1] This article originally appeared in *al-Basheer*, vol. 1, no. 3 (September 1987).

173

used to invent has deceived them with regard to their religion" (*ali-Imraan* 23-24) Finally, in *soorah al-Jumuah*, Allah clearly challenges them,

قُلْ يَاأَيُّهَا الَّذِينَ هَادُوا إِنْ زَعَمْتُمْ أَنَّكُمْ أَوْلِيَاءُ لِلَّهِ مِنْ دُونِ النَّاسِ فَتَمَنَّوُا الْمَوْتَ إِنْ كُنْتُمْ صَادِقِينَ وَلَا يَتَمَنَّوْنَهُ أَبَدًا بِمَا قَدَّمَتْ أَيْدِيهِمْ وَاللَّهُ عَلِيمٌ بِالظَّالِمِينَ

"Say (O Muhammad), 'O you Jews, if you claim that you are the favored of Allah from all of mankind, then you should long for death if you are truthful.' But they will never long for it because of all that their own hands have sent forth, and Allah is Aware of evildoers" (*al-Jumuah* 6). This concept also developed among the Christians, many of whom now believe that once they are believers in Jesus as the Lord they are saved. The same thing can be said to them, "If you know you are saved and will enter paradise with the Father, then why don't you pray for death today to take you away from this world?"

Allah has shown the Muslims the examples of the Jews and Christians. The Quran clearly implies that it is not the name "Muslim" that matters but it is the belief in and submission to Allah. In one verse in *soorah ali-Imraan* Allah says,

وَمَنْ يَبْتَغِ غَيْرَ الْإِسْلَامِ دِينًا فَلَنْ يُقْبَلَ مِنْهُ وَهُوَ فِي الْآخِرَةِ مِنَ الْخَاسِرِينَ

"Whoever wants a way of life other than that of Islam, it will never be accepted [by Allah] from him and in the Hereafter he will be from among the losers" (*ali-Imraan* 85). The word Islam in this verse implies the submission to the commands of Allah. Furthermore, Allah has also warned the Muslims, and in the same verse has also given them glad tidings, by stating twice in the Quran that He does not forgive *shirk* or ascribing partners to Him but He does forgive what is less than that to whomsoever He will:

إِنَّ اللَّهَ لَا يَغْفِرُ أَنْ يُشْرَكَ بِهِ وَيَغْفِرُ مَا دُونَ ذَلِكَ لِمَنْ يَشَاءُ

"Verily, Allah does not forgive that any partners should be associated with Him but He forgives whatever is less than that for whomever He wills" (*al-Nisaa* 48 and *al-Nisaa* 116). Finally, the Prophet (peace be upon him) has also stated that no one except the believer will enter paradise. (Recorded by al-Bukhari.)

Unfortunately, the idea that the Muslims will enter paradise just because they call themselves Muslims or have Muslim names or live in a Muslim country has also developed among the Muslims. Some poor souls believe that as long as the make the statement, *La ilaaha illa-llah, Muhammadar-rasool-ullah*, they are Muslims and Allah will enter them into paradise regardless of what deeds they perform. What Allah said about the Jews also applies to them, "That which they used to invent has deceived them with regard to their religion." Writing on this point, Saallih al-Fauzaan stated,

> Apostasy from Islam to *kufr* could be by completely leaving the religion of Islam for another religion. Or it could be by performing one of the acts that negates one's Islam although one continues to call himself Muslim and performs some of the obligatory duties of Islam and he considers himself to be one of the Muslims although he is not one of them.... Many people tread into this area because they do not know what denies one's Islam and what is heresy. They think that anyone who performs part of the religion of Islam is a Muslim even if he performs acts of *kufr*.... They use the term Islam for anyone who performs some aspect of the religion even if he also performs one thousand acts of apostasy. They do not

realize that one who calls himself Muslim and performs some acts of worship and also performs acts that negate his Islam is like a person who performs the ablution for prayer (*wudhu*) and then he nullifies his ablution, will there be any affect left from the ablution? Islam is not a claim without any reality to it and it cannot gather together two contradictory actions.... Islam is submission to Allah by declaring His oneness and uniqueness and subservience to Him by obedience and purity from any type of *shirk*.[1]

If one ponders the above, one would realize how important it is to stay within the bounds of Islam in one's beliefs and in one's actions. One must be aware of those deeds or beliefs that will take one from the realm of Islam to the realm of *kufr*. The Muslim scholars have gone through the Quran and the sunnah and they have discussed those things that take a person from Islam to *kufr*. Here, there shall be a discussion of some of these actions that deny one's Islam.

Actions That Take One from Islam to *Kufr*

(1) *Shirk*

Shirk means to associate partners with Allah in one's worship or with respect to any of His characteristics or attributes. Allah clearly emphasizes in a verse in the Quran that for whoever ascribes partners to Allah, paradise will be forbidden to him and he will be in the hell-fire:

---

[1] Saalih al-Fauzaan, *Al-Khutab al-Munbariyyah fi al-Munaasibaat al-Asriyyah* (Beirut: Muasassat al-Risaalah, 1984), p. 22.

إِنَّهُ مَنْ يُشْرِكْ بِاللَّهِ فَقَدْ حَرَّمَ اللَّهُ عَلَيْهِ الْجَنَّةَ وَمَأْوَاهُ النَّارُ وَمَا لِلظَّالِمِينَ مِنْ أَنْصَارٍ

"Whoever joins other gods with Allah, Allah will forbid him the Garden, and the Fire will be his abode. There will be for the wrongdoers no one to help" (*al-Maaidah* 72). Mention has already been made of the verses in which Allah states that He does not forgive the act of associating partners with Him.

Included under this topic is the making of supplications to dead people or seeking aid from dead people or sacrificing animals for anyone other than Allah. If someone believes that a "saint" or "imam" who is dead in the grave can answer his supplication, this is *kufr*. Supplications are only to be made to Allah and aid is only to be sought from Him. The Prophet Muhammad (peace be upon him) said,

الدُّعَاءُ هُوَ الْعِبَادَة

"The act of supplicating is the [real] worship."[1] Unfortunately, this practice of going to the graves and making supplications or sacrifices for dead people is very common in many Muslim countries. There is even a Muslim country that until very recently used to have a week long festival of sacrificing "to the gods of the sea."

This is one of the aspects of *tauheed al-uloohiyyah* or "the oneness of Allah as the Lord." No worship and no supplication may be made to anyone other than Allah. Furthermore, one knowledgeable of the beliefs of Islam will realize that it does not make any sense to pray to anyone other than Allah. Allah has power over all things and no one can do anything without His permission. In a well-known hadith the

---

[1] Recorded by Ahmad, al-Nasaai, al-Tirmidhi, Abu Daawood and others. According to al-Albaani, it is *sahih*. See Muhammad Naasir al-Deen al-Albaani, *Saheeh al-Jaami al-Sagheer* (Beirut: al-Maktab al-Islaami, 1986), vol. 1, p. 641.

Prophet (peace be upon him) told one of his companions that if all of mankind had gathered to help him, they could not do anything if Allah did not will it. Also, if all of mankind had gathered to harm him, they would not be able to do anything to him if Allah did not will it. Therefore, anyone who recognizes this type of *tauheed* will realize that anyone who worships another being or supplicates to another being is in fact negating this type of *tauheed*. If he is negating *tauheed*, how could he still be a Muslim?

(2) Setting Up an Intermediary

Whoever sets up an intermediary between himself and Allah has left the realm of Islam and has entered into the realm of *kufr*. Some of the Christians have done this with the person of Jesus and some of the Muslims have done it with some of the early pious people, "saints," or Imams. This applies to the case where these other beings are being worshipped in, according to the claim, an attempt to get closer to Allah. Muhammad ibn Abdul Wahaab wrote,

> The unbelievers claim that they do not pray to the gods and call on them except to the end that they may intercede on their behalf with Allah, as the verse said, "Those who took gods as patrons besides Allah, claiming that they did so only to come through their intercession nearer to Him, will receive the judgment of Allah in the matter they contend. Allah will not guide the ingrate, the liar" (39:3).[1]

At another place he writes,

> It was to a religious people who worshipped regularly, performed the pilgrimage, gave in charity

---

[1] Muhammad ibn Abdul Wahaab, *Three Essays on Tawhid* (Ismail al-Faruqi, trans., Indianapolis, IN: American Trust Publications, 1979), pp. 22-3.

and remembered Allah constantly that He sent His Prophet Muhammad. Their mistake was one of assigning to some creatures an intermediary role between them and Allah in the hope of realizing closeness to Allah and His pleasure through their intercession. They compared them to the angels who keep Allah constant company, to Jesus and Mary, and many other saints. For this reason, Allah sent Muhammad to revive for them the religion of their ancestor Ibrahim, and to teach them anew that such pietism and devotion as they showed for the saints belonged exclusively to Allah, never to any favorite angel, prophet or any creature. For it must be borne in mind that these associationists did witness that Allah is indeed alone the Creator, without partners in the act of creation...[1]

The point that he is making is that although they believed in Allah as the One Creator, since they set up these intercessors between themselves and Allah, Allah sent the Prophet Muhammad (peace be upon him) to correct this incorrect belief and to bring them back to the straight path. Anyone who reverts to this practice has once again left the true *tauheed* of the prophets Abraham (peace be upon him) and Muhammad (peace be upon him) and is, once again, in need of having his beliefs purified and corrected.

(3) Accepting the False Religions

If someone claims that the religion of the polytheists or of the People of the Book is acceptable and he does not believe those people to be unbelievers, then he has left the

---

[1] Ibid., p. 25.

realm of Islam.[1] This is obviously true because either what Islam says is true or what the others say is true, but both cannot be true. Today, many Muslims are not convinced that the beliefs of the Christians, for example, is *kufr*. This belief itself is *kufr*. Allah says many things about Himself and about Jesus in the Quran and the sunnah that are, for example, contradicted by the beliefs of the Christians. Therefore which is true, what Allah says or what the Christians say? If there is any doubt in anybody's mind about the answer to this question then it means that he has some doubt about the Quran and sunnah and doubt is tantamount to disbelief.

In particular concerning the People of the Book, the Prophet (peace be upon him) himself said,

وَالَّذِي نَفْسُ مُحَمَّدٍ بِيَدِهِ لَا يَسْمَعُ بِي أَحَدٌ مِنْ هَذِهِ الْأُمَّةِ يَهُودِيٌّ وَلَا نَصْرَانِيٌّ ثُمَّ يَمُوتُ وَلَمْ يُؤْمِنْ بِالَّذِي أُرْسِلْتُ بِهِ إِلَّا كَانَ مِنْ أَصْحَابِ النَّارِ

"By the One in whose hand is the soul of Muhammad, no one of this Nation,[2] be he Jew or Christian, hears of me and dies without believing in that which I was sent with except that he will be from the companions of the Hell-fire." (Recorded by Muslim.)

---

[1] This is independent of the question related to those who never heard about Islam and how they will be judged on the Day of Judgment. The point here is that any religion other than the religion of Islam is falsehood and will not be accepted by Allah; its adherents are to be treated as disbelievers in this world.

[2] Here the word "Nation" refers not to the followers of the Prophet (peace be upon him) but to all the people that he was sent to as a messenger, meaning everyone from his time until the Day of Judgment.

(4) Believing that Some Guidance is Superior to the Prophet's Guidance

If anyone believes that there is some guidance that is superior to that which the Prophet Muhammad (peace be upon him) brought or that is superior to what is found in the Quran, he has become an unbeliever. Such a person does not truly believe that this message of Islam was sent by the all-Wise, all-Knowing Creator of this existence. For example, if someone believes that following capitalism is superior to following the laws of Islam, he is no longer a Muslim. Therefore, there is no such thing as a "capitalist Muslim" or a "socialist Muslim" as the choice is between Islam as a whole or no Islam.

Allah says

قُلْ إِنَّ هُدَى اللَّهِ هُوَ الْهُدَى وَلَئِنِ اتَّبَعْتَ أَهْوَاءَهُمْ بَعْدَ الَّذِي جَاءَكَ مِنَ الْعِلْمِ مَا لَكَ مِنَ اللَّهِ مِنْ وَلِيٍّ وَلَا نَصِيرٍ

"Say: 'The Guidance of Allah, that is the (only) Guidance,' were you to follow their desires after the knowledge which has reached thee, then you would not find either a protector or a helper against Allah" (*al-Baqarah* 120). The real guidance is that which comes from Allah; everything that is not consistent with what Allah revealed, no matter how cleverly devised or reasoned, is nothing but the desires of humans. These man made systems are not true guidance and cannot, in any way, be considered superior to Islam.

Actually, this type of *kufr*, on a wide scale, is relatively new. No one thought that Islam was backwards or regressive until the Western countries started to colonize the Muslim lands and the caliphate came to an end. The Muslims who are calling for laws other than that of Islamic laws have been aptly described by Allah in the Quran,

أَفَحُكْمَ الْجَاهِلِيَّةِ يَبْغُونَ وَمَنْ أَحْسَنُ مِنَ اللَّهِ حُكْمًا لِقَوْمٍ يُوقِنُونَ

"Is it a judgment of the time of ignorance that they are seeking? Who is better than Allah for judgment for a people who have certainty (in their belief)?" (al-Maaidah 50). And,

أَلَمْ تَرَ إِلَى الَّذِينَ يَزْعُمُونَ أَنَّهُمْ آمَنُوا بِمَا أُنزِلَ إِلَيْكَ وَمَا أُنزِلَ مِن قَبْلِكَ يُرِيدُونَ أَن يَتَحَاكَمُوا إِلَى الطَّاغُوتِ وَقَدْ أُمِرُوا أَن يَكْفُرُوا بِهِ وَيُرِيدُ الشَّيْطَانُ أَن يُضِلَّهُمْ ضَلَالاً بَعِيدًا وَإِذَا قِيلَ لَهُمْ تَعَالَوْا إِلَى مَا أَنزَلَ اللَّهُ وَإِلَى الرَّسُولِ رَأَيْتَ الْمُنَافِقِينَ يَصُدُّونَ عَنكَ صُدُودًا

"Have you not seen those who pretend that they believe in that which is revealed to you and that which was revealed before you, how they would go for judgment (in their disputes) to false deities when they have been ordered to abjure them? Satan would mislead them far astray. And when it is said unto them, 'Come unto that which Allah has revealed and unto the messenger,' you can see the hypocrites turn from you with aversion" (al-Nisaa 60-61).

This brings up another very important point. What about the rulers who do not apply the guidance of Allah in their lands? Are they all considered unbelievers because of this act? Many people, on both sides of this question, have made mistakes concerning this point. Allah says in the Quran,

وَمَن لَّمْ يَحْكُم بِمَا أَنزَلَ اللَّهُ فَأُولَٰئِكَ هُمُ الْكَافِرُونَ

"Whoever does not rule by what Allah has revealed are unbelievers" (al-Maaidah 44). Ibn Abbaas, in interpreting this verse, was asked about the rulers of his time who did not always apply the Islamic law in everything. He answered that what they are doing does fall under this verse but it is a *kufr* that is less than the great *kufr*; that is, it does not mean that they are no longer to be considered Muslims. Similar statements have also come from Imam Ahmad and ibn al-Qayyim. Others went to an extreme and applied this verse to any ruler who missed any aspect of Islamic law in his reign.

The truth of the matter is that there are different types of rulers—some of them are clearly unbelievers while others cannot be considered such. If a ruler openly performs Islam and sincerely believes that it is obligatory upon him to apply the *Shareeah* yet he does not apply all of it for some worldly reason, then this is what ibn Abbaas was describing when he said, "*Kufr* that is less than *kufr*."[1] This type of ruler is not considered a non-Muslim although he may be considered a *faasiq* or evildoer. Other people openly deny Islam and say that they prefer some other form of government and economy, like socialism or capitalism. This verse also applies to them as these people prefer some guidance to the guidance of Allah and this is clearly the greater *kufr* without any doubt or dispute about it. Allah says in the Quran,

$$\text{فَلَا وَرَبِّكَ لَا يُؤْمِنُونَ حَتَّى يُحَكِّمُوكَ فِيمَا شَجَرَ بَيْنَهُمْ ثُمَّ}$$

$$\text{لَا يَجِدُوا فِي أَنْفُسِهِمْ حَرَجًا مِمَّا قَضَيْتَ وَيُسَلِّمُوا تَسْلِيمًا}$$

"No, by your Lord, they do not believe until they accept you as the decider of their affairs and they do not find any hardship in what you have decided and they submit to you completely" (*al-Nisaa* 65). There are other rulers who do not deny Islam openly yet they do not believe that it is obligatory upon them to enforce the *Shareeah* or they may oppose or refuse to apply the *Shareeah*. This is also a type of *kufr*, the greater kind, and

---

[1] The greater *kufr* takes one out of the fold of Islam. The lesser *kufr* is a great sin, that leads one to the brink of leaving Islam without, in itself, actually taking one out of the fold of Islam.

the person becomes a non-Muslim even if he prays and fasts and performs some of the other rites of Islam. Finally, there are those who claim that they want Islam while in reality they do not want to apply the *Shareeah* and they may even have a hatred in their hearts for Islam. This is clearly a hypocrisy and a type of greater *kufr*.

But this brings up another question: what about those people who live under such *kufr* rulers, have they also left the realm of Islam due to their action of accepting such a ruler? Again, there are different classes of people under such rulers. If the "Muslim" is very happy that the *Shareeah* is not being applied or if he supports the ruler in not applying the *Shareeah*, then this is *kufr* and such a person has left the realm of Islam. If, in his heart, he hates what is going on[1] but he is not able to do anything, then he cannot be considered an unbeliever according to the principles that can be derived from the Quran and the sunnah. The Prophet (peace be upon him) said,

مَنْ رَأَى مِنْكُمْ مُنْكَرًا فَلْيُغَيِّرْهُ بِيَدِهِ فَإِنْ لَمْ يَسْتَطِعْ فَبِلِسَانِهِ فَإِنْ لَمْ يَسْتَطِعْ فَبِقَلْبِهِ وَذَلِكَ أَضْعَفُ الإِيمَانِ

"Whoever of you sees an evil must then change it with his hand. If he is not able to do so, then [he must change it] with his tongue. And if he is not able to do so, then [he must change it] with his heart. And that is the slightest [effect of] faith." (Recorded by Muslim.) If he has some doubt about whether or not he would prefer an Islamic state, then he has also committed *kufr* as doubt is tantamount to disbelief.[2]

---

[1] He hates it not because it goes against his vested interests but because it is a situation hated by Allah.

[2] Cf., Numaan Abdul Razzaaq al-Samuraai, *Al-Takfeer: Judhruhu, Asbaabuhu, Mubarraratuhu* (Riyadh: Al-Manaarah), pp. 139-143.

(5) Disliking What the Prophet (peace be upon him) Taught

If someone dislikes someone that the Prophet (Peace be upon him) brought, even if he acts by it, then he has become a non-Muslim. Allah describes such people in the Quran by saying,

$$ ذَلِكَ بِأَنَّهُمْ كَرِهُوا مَا أَنزَلَ اللَّهُ فَأَحْبَطَ أَعْمَالَهُمْ $$

"And that is because they dislike what Allah reveals and all of their works are therefore rendered vain" (*Muhammad* 9). Anyone familiar with the *tauheed* of Allah's Names and Attributes will understand why this is *kufr*. How could someone realize that Allah is the Compassionate, the Merciful, the Forgiving, the Wise, the Just and the All-Knowing and then dislike something that Allah has revealed? He should realize that everything that Allah revealed comes from His mercy, compassion and wisdom. Therefore, the true believer who realizes this fact will love everything that Allah reveals and will strive his best to fulfill it. He will love it for the sake of Allah.

(6) Ridiculing Any Aspect of the Religion

If someone makes fun of some aspect of Islam or of some reward or punishment, then he becomes a non-Muslim, regardless of whether he was serious in his statement or he was just joking. Today, they are many Muslims who make fun of other Muslims attending the mosque every day and some women make fun of other women who wear the proper Islamic dress, and so on. There is no excuse for making fun of people who are applying the laws of Allah. Allah states in the Quran,

وَلَئِنْ سَأَلْتَهُمْ لَيَقُولُنَّ إِنَّمَا كُنَّا نَخُوضُ وَنَلْعَبُ قُلْ أَبِاللَّهِ
وَآيَاتِهِ وَرَسُولِهِ كُنْتُمْ تَسْتَهْزِئُونَ لا تَعْتَذِرُوا قَدْ كَفَرْتُمْ بَعْدَ
إِيمَانِكُمْ

"If you were to ask them [about their statements], they would declare, 'We were just talking idly and joking.' Say [to them]: Is it Allah or His signs or His Messenger that you are mocking? Make no excuses for yourself. You have made *kufr* after you have had faith" (*al-Taubah* 65-66).

(7) Magic and Sorcery

Magic and similar practices take one from the realm of Islam to the realm of *kufr*. This includes believing in astrologers, fortune tellers and the like. With respect to magic, there is an agreement among the scholars of *ahl al-sunnah wa al-jamaah* that magic is a reality and it has effects. (Actually, there are two types of magic. One is simply illusions while the other is true magic.) If magic were not a reality then the Quran and the Prophet (peace be upon him) would not prohibit it or give stern warnings about it. The Quran gives many references to it, showing that it has been practiced since the time of the Pharaoh. Even the people of Saallih, who lived before the time of Abraham, have been quoted in the Quran as calling their prophet a magician (*al-Shuaraa* 153). Its effects include making people sick, affecting people's mental capabilities, taking a person's eyesight and separating a man from his wife. But it cannot have any effect unless Allah has so willed it. That is to say, it is not a power by itself like another Allah yet in Allah's creation He has allowed the existence and effect of sorcery as a trial for humans. Allah has said,

وَاتَّبَعُوا مَا تَتْلُو الشَّيَاطِينُ عَلَى مُلْكِ سُلَيْمَانَ وَمَا كَفَرَ
سُلَيْمَانُ وَلَكِنَّ الشَّيَاطِينَ كَفَرُوا يُعَلِّمُونَ النَّاسَ السِّحْرَ وَمَا
أُنزِلَ عَلَى الْمَلَكَيْنِ بِبَابِلَ هَارُوتَ وَمَارُوتَ وَمَا يُعَلِّمَانِ مِنْ
أَحَدٍ حَتَّى يَقُولا إِنَّمَا نَحْنُ فِتْنَةٌ فَلا تَكْفُرْ فَيَتَعَلَّمُونَ مِنْهُمَا مَا
يُفَرِّقُونَ بِهِ بَيْنَ الْمَرْءِ وَزَوْجِهِ وَمَا هُمْ بِضَارِّينَ بِهِ مِنْ أَحَدٍ
إِلاَّ بِإِذْنِ اللَّهِ وَيَتَعَلَّمُونَ مَا يَضُرُّهُمْ وَلا يَنفَعُهُمْ وَلَقَدْ عَلِمُوا
لَمَنِ اشْتَرَاهُ مَا لَهُ فِي الآخِرَةِ مِنْ خَلاقٍ وَلَبِئْسَ مَا شَرَوْا بِهِ
أَنفُسَهُمْ لَوْ كَانُوا يَعْلمُونَ

"They followed what the devils gave out (falsely) against the power of Solomon: the blasphemers were not Solomon but the devils, teaching men magic, and such things as came down at Babylon to the angels Harut and Marut. But neither of these taught anyone (such things) without saying: 'We are only for trial; so do not blaspheme.' They learned from them the means to sow discord between man and wife. But they could not thus harm anyone except by Allah's permission. And they learned what harmed them, not what profited them. And they knew that the buyers of (magic) would have no share in the happiness of the Hereafter. And vile was the price for which they did sell their souls, if they but knew" (*al-Baqarah* 102).

This sorcery may cause unnatural things to happen yet it is all within the laws of Allah. Therefore, by itself, magic cannot harm or help anyone—unless Allah wills it so. It is nothing more than another test from Allah to see who will apply magic and who will seek to learn it and who will abstain from it.[1]

(8) Support and Loyalty for the Non-Believers

Supporting the non-believers and helping them against the Muslims takes one out of the fold of Islam. Some people have actually said that they hope that the Muslims do not get control over their country because they do not want to be forced to follow the *Shareeah*. Are these people really Muslims? Allah clearly describes them by saying,

وَمَنْ يَتَوَلَّهُمْ مِنْكُمْ فَإِنَّهُ مِنْهُمْ إِنَّ اللَّهَ لا يَهْدِي الْقَوْمَ الظَّالِمِينَ

"And whoever turns to them [that is, the unbelievers] among you is one of them. Verily, Allah does not guide the evildoers" (*al-Maaidah* 51). Muhammad al-Qahtaani writes,

> *Al-walaa* and *al-baraa*[2] are necessary components of the statement, 'there is no God except Allah.' The proofs for this are many in the Quran and sunnah... [For example,] Allah says, "Let not the believers take disbelievers for their friends in preference to believers. Who does that has no connection with Allah unless it be that you guard yourselves against them, taking as it were security" (*ali-Imraan* 28)[3]...[And from the hadith,] Jareer ibn Abdullah made the oath of allegiance to the Prophet (peace be upon him) to make *naseehah* [sincere deeds and

---

[1] Cf., Haafidh ibn Hakimi, *Maarij al-Qabool* (Beirut: Daar al-Kutub al-Ilmiyyah, 1983), vol. 1, pp. 411-16.

[2] *Al-walaa* means "to take as a friend or patron, support, love, assist," while *al-baraa* means "to take as an enemy, be free of something, hatred, opposition."

[3] Also see *ali-Imraan* 32, *al-Nisaa* 89, *al-Maaidah* 51 and *al-Maaidah* 54.

thoughts] for every Muslim and to be free and
innocent of the unbeliever...[1]

Ibn Taimiyyah wrote,

The fulfillment of the statement, "there is no God
except Allah," is that one does not love except for the
sake of Allah and does not hate except for the sake of
Allah and does not take one as a patron except for the
sake of Allah and does not take one as an enemy
except for the sake of Allah and that one loves
whatever Allah loves and hates whatever Allah
hates.[2]

(9) Believing that Some People are above the *Shareeah*

If someone believes that there are some people in this
world who are not obliged to follow the *Shareeah*, then the
holder of such a belief has left the realm of Islam and has
entered into the fold of disbelief. This message has been sent
to all of mankind and no one, no matter how pious he may be,
is allowed not to follow this religion. Allah clearly states that
if anyone desires a *deen* (religion, way of life) other than that
of Islam it will never be accepted from him. Allah says,

$$\text{وَمَنْ يَبْتَغِ غَيْرَ الْإِسْلَامِ دِينًا فَلَنْ يُقْبَلَ مِنْهُ وَهُوَ فِي الْآخِرَةِ}$$
$$\text{مِنَ الْخَاسِرِينَ}$$

"If anyone desires a religion other than Islam, never will it be
accepted of him; and in the Hereafter he will be in the ranks of
those who have lost" (*ali-Imraan* 85). This type of *kufr* has

---

[1]   Muhammad ibn Saeed al-Qahtaani, *Al-Waraa wa al-Baraa fi al-Islaam*
(Riyadh: Daar al-Taibah, n.d.), pp. 40f.
[2]   Ahmad Ibn Taimiyyah, *Al-Ihtijaaj bi-l-Qadar* (Beirut: al-Maktab al-Islaami,
1973), p. 62.

been most common among some Sufi groups who claim that there are many paths, all equally valid and all leading to God. If there were any truth to this belief, the Messenger of Allah (peace be upon him) himself and his noble Companions should be the first ones allowed not to abide by the laws of the *Shareeah*. However, such was never the case for them and it will never be the case for any human on this earth.

(10) Turning Away from the Religion and Completely Not Practicing It

Turning away from the religion of Allah, not learning it and completely not acting by it make one leave the realm of Islam. Allah says,

$$وَمَنْ أَظْلَمُ مِمَّنْ ذُكِّرَ بِآيَاتِ رَبِّهِ ثُمَّ أَعْرَضَ عَنْهَا إِنَّا مِنَ الْمُجْرِمِينَ مُنتَقِمُونَ$$

"Who does greater wrong than one, when he is reminded of the signs of His lord, turns away from them. Verily, for the sinners there is a grievous punishment awaiting" (*al-Sajdah* 22). Allah also says,

$$وَمَنْ أَظْلَمُ مِمَّنْ ذُكِّرَ بِآيَاتِ رَبِّهِ فَأَعْرَضَ عَنْهَا وَنَسِيَ مَا قَدَّمَتْ يَدَاهُ إِنَّا جَعَلْنَا عَلَى قُلُوبِهِمْ أَكِنَّةً أَنْ يَفْقَهُوهُ وَفِي آذَانِهِمْ وَقْرًا وَإِنْ تَدْعُهُمْ إِلَى الْهُدَى فَلَنْ يَهْتَدُوا إِذًا أَبَدًا$$

"And who does more wrong than one who is reminded of the Signs of his Lord, but turns away from them, forgetting the (deeds) which his hands have sent forth? Verily We have set veils over their hearts lest they should understand this, and over their ears, deafness. If you call them to guidance, even then will they never accept guidance" (*al-Kahf* 57).

How can one call himself a Muslim if he does not even care if he is practicing Islam or not? How many Muslims do not care whether something is permissible or prohibited but only look to their worldly gain to decide if they should perform an act or not? How many Muslims do not even care about the prayer and other essential aspects of the religion and when they are reminded of them they simply turn away?[1]

Commenting on the above ten points, ibn Baaz wrote, "With respect to the above ten, it does not matter if the person performed these acts jokingly or seriously or out of fear—unless he was coerced— [it is still *kufr*]."[2]

(11) Denying Something That is Definitely Part of the Faith

Denying anything that has been established without a doubt by the religion is also *kfur*. For example, if someone says that alcohol or interest is permissible and he denies the clear Quranic commandment concerning it, he is an unbeliever. If someone denies the existence of angels, he is an unbeliever. If someone even rejects just one verse of the Quran, he is considered an unbeliever. This is an agreed upon point among the scholars; they also agree that if someone were new to Islam or living in an area in which all of the teachings of Islam did not reach him, this point especially would not be considered *kufr*.

(12) Not Praying

Leaving the prayers due to thinking that they are not obligatory (which is part of #11 above) or due to laziness or

---

[1] The above mentioned ten points may be found in many books and articles. For example, Abdul Azeez ibn Baaz, *Nawaaqidh al-Islaam* in *Majallat al-Buhooth al-Islaamiyyah*, vol. 7, 1983, pp. 15-18.
[2] Ibid., p. 17.

pride is *kufr* according to the strongest opinion among the scholars.[1] The Prophet (peace be upon him) said,

إِنَّ بَيْنَ الرَّجُلِ وَبَيْنَ الشِّرْكِ وَالْكُفْرِ تَرْكَ الصَّلاةِ

"Between a man and polytheism (*al-shirk*) and disbelief (*al-kufr*) is the abandoning of the prayer." (Recorded by Muslim.) Abdul Azeez ibn Baaz was asked if the funeral prayer should be made for someone who did not pray. His answer was that the prayer should not be made for such a person and the person should not be buried in the Muslim cemetery and the Muslims are not allowed to inherit from such a person.[2] Indeed, according to this opinion, Muslim women married to men who do not pray are automatically divorced due to their husband's apostasy.

These aspects are discussed in greater detail in the works on *aqeedah*, such as *Sharh al-Aqeedah al-Tahaawiyyah* and *Maarij al-Qabool*, and one may refer to them for more information.[3]

---

[1] Allah willing, this question will be discussed in greater detail in a future work published by al-Basheer Company. The reader is referred to Muhammad ibn Uthaimeen's *Hukm Tark al-Salaat* (Riyadh: Daar al-Ifta).

[2] Ibid., p. 12.

[3] Since the publication of this article, a number of more detailed works have been published concerning what negates one's Islam. The first ten points mentioned in this article are discussed in some further detail in: Sulaimaan al-Ulwaan, *Al-Tibyaan Sharh Nawaaqidh al-Islaam* (Riyadh: Daar al-Watan, 1414 A.H.); Muhammad al-Shaibaani, *Sharh Nawaaqidh al-Islaam* (Riyadh: Dar al-Sami'ee, 1991). The question of what takes one out of the fold of Islam in general is discussed in much greater detail in the following dissertations: Muhammad al-Wuhaibi, *Nawaaqidh al-Imaan al-Itiqaadiyyah* (Riyadh: Daar al-Muslim, 1996); Abdul Azeez al-Abdul Lateef, *Nawaaqidh al-Imaan al-Qauliyyah wa al-Amaliyyah* (Riyadh: Daar al-Watan, 1414 A.H.).

Necessary Points

What will be the situation of the person's end in the Hereafter if he avoids the above actions and if he always remains within the realm of Islam? The result will be that Allah will grant him paradise if indeed he had the belief in Islam and he stayed within the realm of Islam. Yes, it is true that many of the Muslims will be punished in Hell and, possibly, for a long time, but in the end Allah will grant them mercy and will enter them into paradise. The Prophet (peace be upon him) said

$$شَفَاعَتِي لِأَهْلِ الْكَبَائِرِ مِنْ أُمَّتِي$$

"My intercession is for the people who committed the major sins of my Nation (*ummati*)."[1] They will be taken out of hell, given a new life, and entered into paradise. In fact, one of the Prophet's companions, Abu Dharr, was shocked when the Prophet (peace be upon him) once said that anyone who dies without associating a partner with Allah will be entered into paradise. Abu Dharr asked the Prophet (peace be upon him) if that was even true for the one who had committed adultery or had been a thief, and so on. And the Prophet (peace be upon him) told him that it even applied to such people. Abu Dharr asked the Prophet (peace be upon him) the same question three times and the Prophet (peace be upon him) told him that it does apply to even them despite the persistence of Abu Dharr. (Recorded by al-Bukhari and Muslim.)

Every Muslim should take the time to think over these facts and to take them seriously before the time of death comes and he is not able to do anything about what he neglected in this life. He should think over the following:

a. Only the believers will be entered into paradise.

---

[1] Recorded by Ahmad, al-Nasaai, Abu Dawood and others. According to al-Albaani, it is *sahih*. See al-Albaani, vol. 1, p. 691.

b. There are many actions or beliefs that will take one from the realm of Islam into the realm of *kufr* and every Muslim should be aware of them and do his best to avoid all such actions or beliefs.

c. If one stays within the realm of Islam then, by the mercy of Allah, he will be entered into paradise; this is a promise that is confirmed by both the Quran and the sunnah, although it may be the case that he may be sent to Hell for some time. [The terrible situation in the hell-fire is well-known and therefore it is not necessary to stress the point that the punishment in the hell-fire is so great that one should be willing to make any sacrifice necessary to avoid being sent to hell even for just one minute.]

d. All of the deeds of the unbeliever or apostate will be worth nothing in the Hereafter. Allah says,

مَثَلُ الَّذِينَ كَفَرُوا بِرَبِّهِمْ أَعْمَالُهُمْ كَرَمَادٍ اشْتَدَّتْ بِهِ الرِّيحُ فِي يَوْمٍ عَاصِفٍ لَا يَقْدِرُونَ مِمَّا كَسَبُوا عَلَى شَيْءٍ ذَلِكَ هُوَ الضَّلَالُ الْبَعِيدُ

"A similitude of those who disbelieve in their Lord: Their works are as ashes which the wind blows hard upon a stormy day. They have no control of aught that they have earned. That is the extreme straying" (*Ibraaheem* 18).

What Is Not *Kufr*

After mentioning the above actions that do take one from the realm of Islam to the realm of *kufr*, it was considered necessary to also point out some actions that are not considered *kufr*. First, Imam al-Tahaawi states in his creed,

"We do not declare anyone of *ahl al-qiblah*[1] an unbeliever because of a sin that he committed."[2] There is a very big difference between committing a sin and committing *kufr*. In the first case, the person remains a Muslim although he may be an evildoer or a disobedient Muslim but he still remains within the fold of Islam as he has not negated the most important thing— Islam or *imaan*. No human being is perfect and everyone will commit some minor or major sin at some time. But as long as the person realizes his mistake, does not declare his illegal deed as legal and does not perform any of the acts of *kufr*, he will remain a Muslim and may yearn for the mercy of Allah on the Day of Judgment. On the other hand, the person who commits *kufr* and willfully exits from the fold of Islam may despair of any mercy from Allah and may look forward to taking his seat in the hell-fire.

There are many hadith that make this point very clear. One is the hadith just recently quoted in which the Prophet (peace be upon him) said,

$$\text{مَا مِنْ عَبْدٍ قَالَ لَا إِلَهَ إِلَّا اللَّهُ ثُمَّ مَاتَ عَلَى ذَلِكَ إِلَّا دَخَلَ الْجَنَّةَ}$$

"There is no slave who says, 'there is no God except Allah,' and then he dies upon that except that he will enter paradise." Abu Dharr asked three times, "Even if he commits adultery or steals?" The Prophet (peace be upon him) answered him three times, "Even if he commits adultery or steals." (Recorded by Muslim.) Furthermore Allah says,

---

[1] That is, those people who pray towards Makkah in the manner that the Prophet (peace be upon him) taught the prayer.

[2] Cf., Ibn Abi al-Izz al-Hanafi, *Sharb al-Aqeedah al-Tahaawiyyah* (Beirut: Maktab al-Islaami, 1983), p. 355.

$$\text{إِنَّ اللَّهَ لا يَغْفِرُ أَنْ يُشْرَكَ بِهِ وَيَغْفِرُ مَا دُونَ ذَلِكَ لِمَنْ يَشَاءُ}$$

$$\text{وَمَنْ يُشْرِكْ بِاللَّهِ فَقَدْ افْتَرَى إِثْمًا عَظِيمًا}$$

"Verily Allah does not forgive that you should ascribe any partner to Him but he forgives whatever is less than that to whomsoever He wills. To set up partners with Allah is to devise a sin most heinous indeed" (*al-Nisaa* 48). This is a point concerning which all of the *ahl al-sunnah wa al-jamaah* are in agreement.

Saying words of *kufr* under duress does not make a person an unbeliever.[1] Allah says in the Quran,

$$\text{مَنْ كَفَرَ بِاللَّهِ مِنْ بَعْدِ إِيمَانِهِ إِلاَّ مَنْ أُكْرِهَ وَقَلْبُهُ مُطْمَئِنٌّ}$$

$$\text{بِالإِيمَانِ وَلَكِنْ مَنْ شَرَحَ بِالْكُفْرِ صَدْرًا فَعَلَيْهِمْ غَضَبٌ مِنْ}$$

$$\text{اللَّهِ وَلَهُمْ عَذَابٌ عَظِيمٌ}$$

"Whoever disbelieves in Allah after his belief— save him who is forced to do so and his heart is still content with faith— but whoso finds ease in disbelief: on them is wrath from Allah. Theirs will be an awful doom" (*al-Nahl* 106). It is recorded in some of the books of Quranic commentary that this verse was revealed with respect to Ammaar ibn Yaasir who was forced to state words of *kufr* after they had tortured his mother. Ammaar came crying to the Prophet (peace be upon him) about that event and the Prophet (peace be upon him) wiped his forehead and said, "If they repeat it, you should also do the same." Then this verse was revealed. Allah knows best.

There is a difference between stating words of *kufr* under duress and concealing one's religion. Concealing one's religion may be done during times of war as a type of strategy.

---

[1] Cf., Abdul Rahmaan Abdul Khaaliq, *Al-Hadd al-Fasl bain al-Imaan wa al-Kufr* (Beirut: Daar al-Qalam, 1983), pp. 77f.

In fact, it was done by the Companions of the Prophet (peace be upon him).[1] There is also a difference between stating words of *kufr* under duress and being forced to harm others. It is not allowed for a Muslim to kill another Muslim—even under duress. Neither Muslim has more of a right to live than the other.

Another action that does not make a person an unbeliever is an incorrect and possible interpretation of the Quran and sunnah. Such a person does not become an unbeliever either by mistaken actions or mistaken conclusions. Commenting on this point, ibn Taimiyyah stated,

> It is well-known among the people concerning mistakes with respect to actions [that it does not make the person an unbeliever] but with respect to creed or beliefs many people call others unbelievers for their mistakes. This is a position that is unheard of among the Companions and their followers and it has not been reported from any of the Imams of the Muslims. In fact, the source for such an opinion is with the people of innovations, such as the Khawaarij, Mutazilah and Jahamiyyah, who innovated something new and then called all of those who differed from them unbelievers.[2]

It is absolutely correct to state, as has been done in this article, that some actions or beliefs are *kufr* but this does not mean that everyone who does or believes in them becomes an unbeliever as the person may act or believe out of ignorance or based on a mistaken interpretation of some verse or hadith. Therefore, they could be believers although they are doing actions or holding beliefs that are outside of the realm of

---

[1] Ibid., p. 78.
[2] Ahmad Ibn Taimiyyah, *Minhaaj al-Sunnah* (Riyadh: Maktabah al-Riyadh al-Hadeethah), vol. 3, p. 27.

Islam.[1] If his mistake was based on an incorrect interpretation of something that is *clear from the Quran and the sunnah*, and his mistake is made clear to him and he is now no longer ignorant yet he insists on following his wrong action or belief, he then becomes an unbeliever.

Finally, a comment is required on a well-known hadith of the Prophet (peace be upon him). The Prophet (peace be upon him) said,

إن بني إسرائيل تفرقت على ثنتين وسبعين ملة وتفترق أمتي على ثلاث وسبعين ملة كلهم في النار إلا ملة واحدة قالوا ومن هي يا رسول الله قال ما أنا عليه وأصحابي

"The tribes of Israel divided into seventy-two sects. My Nation will divide into seventy-three sects, all of them being in the Hell-fire save one." They asked, "What is that [sect], O Messenger of Allah?" He replied, "What I and my Companions are following."[2] So the Prophet (peace be upon him) said that all of these sects would be in the Hell-Fire except one—the one that was following his way and the way of his companions. This one way is known as the way of *ahl al-sunnah wa al-jamaah*. But this hadith does not mean that every member of the other sects will be in the Hell-Fire. As the paragraph above just explained, there may be many believers in the other sects who belong to those sects due to ignorance or due to some mistaken notion. Perhaps, they grew up in a specific area in which a heresy was the dominant belief of that

---

[1] This brings up the very important distinction between *kufr* and *kaafir*. *Kufr* is an act of apostasy while *kaafir* is a disbeliever. It is possible for someone to commit an act of *kufr* yet he is not considered a *kaafir* or disbeliever because, for example, he may have committed that act out of ignorance, unaware that it is an act of *kufr*.

[2] Recorded by al-Tirmidhi. According to al-Albaani, it is *hasan*. See al-Albaani, vol. 2, p. 944.

land and had no idea that what they were believing was incorrect. In such a case, since they have the *imaan* or faith in their heart, they will enter paradise although they were not following the way of the *ahl al-sunnah wa al-jamaah*.

Given this fact, the following statement from Imam al-Tahaawi becomes very clear, "We do not say about anybody that they are from paradise or the hell-fire."[1] This is true because someone who is outwardly and supposedly from *ahl al-sunnah wa al-jamaah* may actually be a hypocrite and not have the true *imaan* and, therefore, he will go to hell. Similarly, one who is not from *ahl al-sunnah wa al-jamaah* may be mistaken or ignorant but he does have *imaan* and, therefore, he will be entered into paradise.

A Final Note

The Prophet (peace be upon him) said,

$$\text{لا يَدْخُلُ الْجَنَّةَ إلاَّ مُؤْمِنٌ}$$

"No one will enter paradise except a believer." (Recorded by al-Bukhari.)

The question of Islam and *kufr* may be the most important question that any individual must face and what has been written here does not cover all that needs to be said on this topic. The reader is encouraged to study this topic in more detail whenever he has the chance to. Furthermore, the purpose of what has been presented here is not that Muslims go around now declaring other Muslims disbelievers. The important goal is for each and every Muslim to realize what these acts of *kufr* are and to do his best to remain as far away from them as he possibly can.

---

[1] Ibn Abi al-Izz al-Hanafi, p. 426.

In the Western countries, sometimes the Muslims spend a lot of time talking about topics like "The Economic System of Islam," "The Social System of Islam," "The Political Role of Muslims in the United States." These are important topics but they are being discussed when many of the Muslims themselves do not even understand the basic concepts of Islam, such as what distinguishes a Muslim from a non-Muslim, what is the real meaning of *tauheed* or of *la ilaaha illa-llah*. These are the topics that need to be driven home first to every Muslim.

The Prophet (peace be upon him) spent thirteen years in Makkah mainly driving home the concept of the oneness of Allah. Today Muslims are giving speeches about Islam to non-Muslims and this essential aspect is never conveyed to the audience. Indeed, most of the literature published in the West barely even mentions the different types of *tauheed* and what exactly they should mean for the Muslims.[1] Even though the ten points mentioned in this article are very well known and have been published in many different books and magazines in Arabic, the author has yet to see them mentioned in any magazine or book in English. If the Muslim is committing *kufr* and does not even realize it, isn't it more important to explain that fact to him than to tell him the beauties of the economic or political system of Islam? Perhaps this is why Muhammad Naasir al-Deen al-Albaani said in a phone conversation with a friend of mine that most of the unbelievers of the West have not received the proper *dawah* or teachings of Islam. That is, the "proof has not been established against them." Of course, it is the Muslim's duty to convey the message of Islam to the non-Muslims but if he himself does not know what the message of Islam is, how will he be able to do it?

---

[1] Note that this article was written in the late 1980s. The situation has improved drastically since then, especially with the numerous publications from al-Hedayah in England and other Muslim publishing companies. May Allah reward them and all who have contributed to this important effort.

References

Abdul Khaaliq, Abdul Rahmaan. *Al-Hadd al-Fasl bain al-Imaan wa al-Kufr*. Beirut: Daar al-Qalam. 1983.

Al-Abdul Lateef, Abdul Azeez. *Nawaaqidh al-Imaan al-Qauliyyah wa al-Amaliyyah*. Riyadh: Daar al-Watan. 1414 A.H.

Al-Albaani, Muhammad Naasir al-Deen. *Saheeh al-Jaami al-Sagheer*. Beirut: Al-Maktab al-Islaami. 1986.

al-Fauzaan, Saalih. *Al-Khutub al-Munbariyyah fi al-Munaasibaat al-Asriyyah*. Muasassat al-Risaalah. Beirut. 1984.

Ibn Abdul Wahaab, Muhammad. *Three Essays on Tawhid*. Ismail al-Faruqi, trans. Indianapolis, IN: American Trust Publications. 1979.

Ibn Abu al-Izz al-Hanafi. *Sharh al-Aqeedah al-Tahaawiyyah*. Beirut: Maktab al-Islaami. 1983.

ibn Baaz, Abdul Azeez. *Nawaaqidh al-Islaam* in *Majallat al-Buhooth al-Islaamiyyah*. vol. 7. 1983.

Ibn Hakimi, Haafidh. *Maarij al-Qabool*. Beirut: Daar al-Kutub al-Ilmiyyah. 1983.

Ibn Taimiyyah, Ahmad. *Al-Ihtijaaj bi-l-Qadar*. Beirut: al-Maktab al-Islaami. 1973.

-----*Minhaaj al-Sunnah*. Riyadh: Maktabah al-Riyadh al-Hadeethah.

Ibn Uthaimeen, Muhammad. *Hukm Tark al-Salaat*. Riyadh: Daar al-Ifta.

al-Qahtaani, Muhammad ibn Saeed. *Al-Walaa wa al-Baraa fi al-Islaam*. Riyadh: Daar al-Taibah.

al-Samuraai, Numaan Abdul Razzaaq. *Al-Takfeer: Judhruhu, Asbaabuhu, Mubarraratuhu*. Riyadh: Al-Manaarah.

al-Shaibaani, Muhammad. *Sharh Nawaaqidh al-Islaam*. Riyadh: Dar al-Sami'ee. 1991.

Al-Ulwaan, Sulaimaan. *Al-Tibyaan Sharh Nawaaqidh al-Islaam*. Riyadh: Daar al-Watan. 1414 A.H.

al-Wuhaibi, Muhammad. *Nawaaqidh al-Imaan al-Itiqaadiyyah*. Riyadh: Daar al-Muslim. 1996.

Feature Article:
Islam and Innovations (I): The Meaning of Bidah[1]

The concept of "innovations," "heresies," or *bidah* is one of the most important topics in Islam. Unfortunately, though, as with many other important topics of Islam, many Muslims do not have a proper understanding of this topic. Many are often confused when one person says, "This act is an innovation," and someone will reply, "Yes, but it is a good innovation." Others are confused about what falls under the category of *bidah* and what does not as the Muslims perform many acts today that the Prophet (peace be upon him) never performed or, perhaps, never conceived of performing. Allah willing, in this article many of the confusing points or misunderstandings about this important concept will be cleared up. An introductory section will cover the textual condemnation of innovation and a short discussion of the different types of sunnah before moving on to the finer questions of the definition of *bidah* and other related topics.

Introductory Points

There are some introductory points that should be noted before the discussion of innovations is begun in earnest.

The first introductory point concerns human intellect. Human intellect is not able to completely determine what is beneficial for itself and what is harmful to itself. This is true for a number of reasons. First, humans are not able to see the

---

[1] This article appeared in *al-Basheer*, vol. 1, no. 4 (November 1987).

entire reality of certain actions. On the outside, an action may seem harmless while it is indeed very harmful for the individual or for society.[1] Second, humans are never completely free from biases, whims and selfish desires that may cloud their conception of an issue. Furthermore, with respect to matters of the Hereafter, that man has no experience with, man is completely in the dark. Therefore, it is necessary for humans to follow divine revelation in order to ensure that they are following what is best for them in both this life and the hereafter. With the help of divine guidance, humans will be able to follow this blessed path. This divine guidance is, of course, the antithesis of innovations.

The second introductory point is concerned with the perfection and completion of Allah's revelation and guidance. Allah says in the Quran,

$$\text{الْيَوْمَ أَكْمَلْتُ لَكُمْ دِينَكُمْ وَأَتْمَمْتُ عَلَيْكُمْ نِعْمَتِي وَرَضِيتُ لَكُمُ الإِسْلامَ دِينًا}$$

"This day have I perfected for you your religion and have completed My blessings upon you and have chosen for you Islam as a religion" (al-Maaidah 3). This means that the guidance is complete. It is all that the Muslims need for happiness in this world and in the Hereafter. It is, therefore, in no need of additions, alterations or deletions. This point has been aptly summarized in two statements of Imam Maalik. Imam Maalik said, "What was not part of the religion during the time of the Prophet (peace be upon him) and his Companions is not part of the religion today." He also said, "If someone innovates something in the religion of Islam that he believes is good, he has, thereby, alleged that the Prophet Muhammad (peace be upon him) has been disloyal to his message. That is true because Allah said, 'This day have I

---

[1] Even atheists or secular philosophers would have to admit that humans can make the completely right decisions *only* if they have all the proper information.

204

perfected for you your religion and have completed My blessings upon you and have chosen for you Islam as a religion [*al-Maaidah* 3]...'"

Finally, the laws of Allah are meant for the complete happiness of mankind. If the person follows the sunnah of the Prophet (peace be upon him) and obeys the commands of Allah in they way that they are to be obeyed, then the person will become purified, his morals refined and his spirit rejuvenated. The situation is quite different with respect to the laws and customs laid down by human beings. Mankind has laid down laws with the intention of purifying the souls or refining their characters or for the best of society as a whole and so on, but they repeatedly fail. In the United States, for example, the people have an adversity for what they call "capital punishment" or "cruel and unusual punishment."[1] They think they are doing what is best for the individual and society by inventing such concepts. The intended results are rarely met, of course. Today, there is such a shortage of prisons in Oregon that they are only keeping the murderers, rapists and kidnappers in jail while merely giving citations to those who commit "lesser crimes." Many other examples can be given but it is enough to look at the history of mankind to know that man cannot attain these noble goals without divine guidance.[2]

These introductory points are meant to instill in the readers the importance of complete obedience to Allah from a logical standpoint. It is only divine guidance that will give the humans what is best for them in this life and the hereafter. There is no room for innovations in the divine scheme of guidance.

---

[1] As they, of course, have defined "cruel and unusual punishment."
[2] This introduction was based on the introduction to Abu Bakr al-Jazaairi's *Hurrimat al-Ibtidaa fi al-Deen* (Idaarah Bina al-Masaajid, 1407), pp. 3-5.

Exhortation to Stick to the Quran and Sunnah and to Avoid Innovations

There are many hadith that clearly demonstrate that the Muslim must avoid any kind of innovation in his religion. The Prophet (peace be upon him) said,

مَنْ أَحْدَثَ فِي أَمْرِنَا هَذَا مَا لَيْسَ مِنْهُ فَهُوَ رَدٌّ

"Whoever introduces anything into this affair of ours that does not belong to it will have it rejected." (Recorded by al-Bukhari and Muslim.) Another version states,

مَنْ عَمِلَ عَمَلاً لَيْسَ عَلَيْهِ أَمْرُنَا فَهُوَ رَدٌّ

"Whoever does a deed that is not consistent with our affairs shall have it rejected." (Recorded by Muslim.) Rejected means that it will not be rewarded by Allah.

When the Prophet (peace be upon him) would deliver a sermon, during the introductory portion he would say,

شَرُّ الأُمُورِ مُحْدَثَاتُهَا وَكُلُّ بِدْعَةٍ ضَلَالَةٌ

"The worst actions are the invented ones. And every innovation is a going astray (Ar., *dhalaalah*)." (Recorded by Muslim.) In other narrations he would say,

وَكُلُّ ضَلَالَةٍ فِي النَّارِ

"And every going astray is in the hell fire." (Recorded by al-Nasaai.) The word *dhaall* means, "Erring, straying, or going astray; deviating from the right way or course, or from that which is right; missing or losing the right way."[1] Perhaps the severity of this description is not appreciated by most Muslims. Al-Shaatibi wrote,

> An innovation is a going astray. And the innovator is straying and leading others astray. *Dhalaalah* is mentioned in many of the reported texts. It is alluded to in the Quranic verses about splitting into sects and breaking up the community and following the errant paths but this is not how other sins are described. The term *dhalaalah* is usually not used except for innovations or things similar to innovations. The intentional mistakes that are made by someone in the *Shareeah*—and these are to be forgiven—are not called *dhalaalah*. The one who makes a mistake or error is not called *dhaall* or misguided. In fact, this term is not even used for those who intentionally commit any of the other sins.[2]

The one who commits sins is different from the innovator as the sinner still accepts the *Shareeah* as the supreme law and decision maker while the innovator takes his own desires or whims as the supreme decision maker. The innovator will always take the somewhat ambiguous (Ar., *mutashaabihaataat*) verses and interpret them according to his desires. Furthermore, the innovator will also interpret the Quranic verses and hadith in such a way that will be compatible with his innovations. After giving many examples of how the term *dhalaalah* is used, al-Shaatibi concludes,

> There are many examples of this nature. All of them point to the fact that *dhalaalah* is usually used for the case where a person follows some doubtful proof or

---

[1] E. W. Lane, *Arabic-English Lexicon* (Cambridge, England: Islamic Texts Society, 1984), vol. 2, p. 1798.

[2] Ibraaheem al-Shaatibi, *Al-Itisaam* (Alexandira: Daar Umar ibn al-Khattaab), vol. 1, p. 133.

he blindly follows a person who is following such. They follow that in place of the *Shareeah* and they take it as their religion although the way of truth is very clear.[1]

The Prophet (peace be upon him) said,

إن الله حجب التوبة عن كل صاحب بدعة حتى يدع بدعته

"Allah keeps repentance away for every companion of innovations until he leaves his innovations." (Recorded by al-Tabaraani.) Al-Shaatibi has offered an explanation for why there is a barrier between the innovator and repentance. He says,

> The reason they are away from repentance is because it is hard for them to obey the *Shareeah* because they are following a way that opposes the *Shareeah* and that is only consistent with their own desires. The truth is very hard on them. Their souls only follow what they like and do not wish to follow any other thing. Every innovation is followed due to the power of desires as its source is their invention and not the *Shareeah*... Furthermore, the innovator claims to be following some proof and claims to be implementing the *Shareeah* [therefore, it is very hard for him to repent and follow the actual truth].[2]

In another hadith, the Prophet (peace be upon him) said,

أَبَى اللَّهُ أَنْ يَقْبَلَ عَمَلَ صَاحِبِ بِدْعَةٍ حَتَّى يَدَعَ بِدْعَتَهُ

---

[1] Ibid., p. 139.
[2] Al-Shatibi, vol. 1, p. 124.

"Allah refuses to accept the deeds of the companion of innovations until he leaves his innovation." (Recorded by ibn Maajah and ibn Abi Asim.[1])

Furthermore, it may be stated that the following of innovations is, first, disobedience to the Quran and sunnah and, secondly, a following of one's desires in preference to the revelation of Allah. Therefore, the following verse readily comes to one's mind:

$$ فَلْيَحْذَرِ الَّذِينَ يُخَالِفُونَ عَنْ أَمْرِهِ أَنْ تُصِيبَهُمْ فِتْنَةٌ أَوْ يُصِيبَهُمْ عَذَابٌ أَلِيمٌ $$

"Let those who conspire to evade orders beware lest a trial (Ar., *fitnah*) or a painful punishment befall them" (*al-Noor* 63). Imam Maalik was once asked about a person who puts on the pilgrim's clothing before he reaches the location designated by the Prophet (peace be upon him). He replied, "That differs from what Allah and His Messenger [have ordered]. I fear that such a person will either get a *fitnah* in this world or a painful punishment in the Hereafter. Have you not heard Allah say, 'Let those who conspire to evade orders beware lest a trial (Ar., *fitnah*) or a painful punishment befall them.'"

From the Quran, one can see that Allah divides people into two groups, those that follow the guidance of Allah and those that follow their own desires. Therefore, all of the following verses also refer to the people of innovations. Allah says,

---

[1] All of the above hadith were taken from Muhammad Naasir al-Deen al-Albaani, *Saheeh al-Targheeb wa al-Tarheeb* (Beirut: al-Maktab al-Islaami, 1982), vol. 1, pp. 22-28, and they are all either *hasan* or *sahih* in his estimation.

فَإِنْ لَمْ يَسْتَجِيبُوا لَكَ فَاعْلَمْ أَنَّمَا يَتَّبِعُونَ أَهْوَاءَهُمْ وَمَنْ
أَضَلُّ مِمَّنْ اتَّبَعَ هَوَاهُ بِغَيْرِ هُدًى مِنْ اللَّهِ إِنَّ اللَّهَ لا يَهْدِي
الْقَوْمَ الظَّالِمِينَ

"And if they answer you not, then know that what they follow is their lusts. And who goes farther astray than he who follows his lust without guidance from Allah? Verily, Allah does not guide the wrongdoing folk" (al-Qasas 50). In another verse Allah clearly states that if one follows his desires, he is not on the path of Allah.

وَلا تَتَّبِعْ الْهَوَى فَيُضِلَّكَ عَنْ سَبِيلِ اللَّه

"And follow not desires that beguile you from the Way of Allah" (Saad 26).

It is true that people who follow innovations are not following the path of Allah and, it should be noted, that the path of Allah is one path and only one path. Abdullah ibn Masood said, "The Prophet (peace be upon him) drew a line and then said, 'This is the path of Allah.' Then he drew some lines on the right and the left of the first one and said, 'These are paths which upon each is a devil calling to it.' Then he recited the verse,

وَأَنَّ هَذَا صِرَاطِي مُسْتَقِيمًا فَاتَّبِعُوهُ وَلَا تَتَّبِعُوا السُّبُلَ فَتَفَرَّقَ
بِكُمْ عَنْ سَبِيلِهِ

'This is My Straight path, so follow it. Follow not other ways, as you will then stray from His way' (al-Anaam 153)."[1] Thus, there is only one path of guidance and that is what is found in the Quran and sunnah and this path is the opposite of the paths of innovations.

---

[1] Recorded by Ahmad, al-Daarimi and ibn Maajah.

In the Hereafter, the innovators will not be allowed to drink from "the cistern of the Prophet," and if anyone drinks from that cistern he will never be thirsty again. The Prophet (peace be upon him) said that he would recognize such people by the marks of ablution on their bodies yet they would be turned away from the cistern. The Prophet (peace be upon him) would say, "My companions, my companions," and he would be told, "You do not know what they innovated after you." He will then say, "Then get away, get away." (Recorded by Muslim.)

By their innovations, the followers of innovations think they are getting closer to Allah while, in reality, their deeds are being rejected. Therefore, they can be considered, to some extent, aptly described in the verse,

$$\text{الَّذِينَ ضَلَّ سَعْيُهُمْ فِي الْحَيَاةِ الدُّنْيَا وَهُمْ يَحْسَبُونَ أَنَّهُمْ يُحْسِنُونَ صُنْعًا}$$

"Those whose efforts are in vain in this world although they think that they are doing good deeds" (*al-Kahf* 104).

Finally, the innovator will not only bear the burden of his own misguidance but he will also bear a share of the burden of all of the people who follow his innovation. The Prophet (peace be upon him) said,

$$\text{مَنْ دَعَا إِلَى هُدًى كَانَ لَهُ مِنَ الأَجْرِ مِثْلُ أُجُورِ مَنْ تَبِعَهُ لَا يَنْقُصُ ذَلِكَ مِنْ أُجُورِهِمْ شَيْئًا وَمَنْ دَعَا إِلَى ضَلَالَةٍ كَانَ عَلَيْهِ مِنَ الإِثْمِ مِثْلُ آثَامِ مَنْ تَبِعَهُ لَا يَنْقُصُ ذَلِكَ مِنْ آثَامِهِمْ شَيْئًا}$$

"Whoever calls to guidance will receive a reward for the one who follows his call with the reward of neither being reduced. And whoever calls to an act of misguidance will share part of the sin of everyone who follows his call with the sin of neither being reduced." (Recorded by Muslim.)

Besides the Quranic verse and hadith of the Prophet (peace be upon him), there are many statements from the Companions and the early scholars exhorting people to stay away from innovations. For the sake of brevity only two will be quoted here. Abdullah ibn Masood said, "Follow our steps and do not innovate and that will be sufficient for you." Hudhaifah said, "Limiting oneself to following the sunnah is better than exerting yourself in following innovations."[1]

From the above the following may be concluded concerning those who follow innovations:

1. They are not following the guidance of Allah.

2. They are following one of the paths of the Satan.

3. Their innovations are rejected by Allah.

4. Their actions are rejected until they give up their innovations.

5. There is no repentance for them until they give up their innovations.

6. What they are doing are astray acts and every astray act will be in the hell fire.

7. They will be turned away from the cistern of the Prophet (peace be upon him) in the Hereafter.

8. They believe they are doing good deeds yet in the Hereafter they will find that their deeds are in vain.

9. Finally, the innovator will also bear some of the burden for everyone who follows his innovation.

Many Muslims do not consider the topic of innovations as an important topic but from the above it should be clear to every sincere Muslim that this topic is a very important topic and every Muslim should be very careful to avoid any innovation in his life lest any or all of the above points be applied to him.

---

[1] For a more complete record of statements from the Quran, the Prophet and early scholars condemning innovations, see al-Shaatibi, vol. 1, pp. 68-91.

Different Types of Sunnah

Before moving on to the definition of innovations and other topics, it will be beneficial to first discuss some aspects of the sunnah of the Prophet (peace be upon him).

The sunnah of the Prophet (peace be upon him) may be divided into the following types:

1. The statements of the Prophet (peace be upon him).
2. The actions of the Prophet (peace be upon him).
3. The actions that the Prophet (peace be upon him) did not perform.
4. The tacit or silent approval of certain acts performed in the presence of the Prophet (peace be upon him).

Concerning the statements of the Prophet (peace be upon him) there is very little difference of opinion or difficulty. If the Prophet (peace be upon him) ordered something, it is considered obligatory or, at least, recommended. If the Prophet (peace be upon him) prohibited something, it is considered impermissible or, at least, reprehensible.

The actions of the Prophet (peace be upon him) concerning which he never made an explicit statement are a different case. If the Prophet (peace be upon him) performed a deed, does that mean that the act is obligatory, recommended or simply permissible? The scholars differ on this point. In order to answer this question, the actions of the Prophet (peace be upon him) must be divided into different categories.[1]

First are those actions of the Prophet (peace be upon him) that the Prophet (peace be upon him) performed due to the fact that he was a human being. They are, therefore, part of his natural disposition and have nothing to do directly with

---

[1] This is not meant to be an exhaustive discussion of this subject and not all of the different categories of the Prophet's actions will be discussed here. The interested reader should consult Muhammad al-Ashqar, *Afaal al-Rasool* (Kuwait: Maktabah al-Manaar al-Islaamiyyah, 1978), vol. 1, pp. 213-321; or Muhammad Abdul Qaadir, *Afaal al-Rasool* (Jeddah: Daar al-Mujtama, 1984), pp. 145-207.

worshipping Allah, such as the way that he stood or sat and so forth. For example, the Prophet (peace be upon him) did not care for eating monitors but this was a personal dislike and had nothing to do with what Allah loves or hates. There is a difference of opinion concerning such actions. Some scholars say that such acts are obligatory upon the Muslims to emulate, but this is a very weak opinion. Most likely, such acts are considered to be either permissible (perhaps this is the strongest opinion) or recommended [1] The important aspect about such deeds of the Prophet (peace be upon him) is that no one may leave them for "religious reasons" as this would be akin to an innovation. For example, the Prophet (peace be upon him) ate meat, thus showing that it is permissible for Muslims to eat meat. That means that it is an innovation to not eat meat claiming that one can come closer to Allah by avoiding such food or by saying that humans should not kill animals and so forth.

Then there are the customary actions that he performed simply because he was alive at a certain time and lived among a certain people. This category would include his exact style of clothing, headdress and so on. All of these actions of the Prophet (peace be upon him) are considered to be permissible by Islamic law but they do not take on any greater significance.

Then there are those actions that cannot be considered just customary but what the Prophet (peace be upon him) performed continually and intentionally, for example, some aspects concerning how he ate or drank or slept and so on. It seems clear that he performed these deeds in such particular manners as a way of pleasing Allah. Such acts are considered recommended by the scholars of hadith while al-Shafi'ee said that they do not have anything to do with the *Shareeah*; that is,

---

[1] This latter opinion was the opinion of ibn Umar and al-Baqillaani; it is based on the fact that the Prophet (peace be upon him) is the best example to follow. Cf., Muhammad ibn Ali al-Shaukaani, *Irshaad al-Fahool* (Beirut: Daar al-Marafah, 1979), p. 35.

they are like the above category. Of course, if the Prophet (peace be upon him) exhorted his followers to perform some act that he used to perform, then the act would not longer be in this category of his actions but would be considered one of his statements, which was discussed above.

Finally, there are those actions that the Prophet (peace be upon him) explicitly performed as part of the *Shareeah* that are meant to be followed. For example, the Prophet (peace be upon him) said,

$$صَلُّوا كَمَا رَأَيْتُمُونِي أُصَلِّي$$

"Pray in the manner that you see me praying" (Recorded by al-Bukhari.) This means that all of his acts related to the prayer are to be followed, that is, they are either recommended or obligatory on the Muslims. He also said,

$$يَا أَيُّهَا النَّاسُ خُذُوا مَنَاسِكَكُمْ فَإِنِّي لا أَدْرِي لَعَلِّي لا أَحُجُّ$$
$$بَعْدَ عَامِي هَذَا$$

"O people, take your rites of pilgrimage for I do not know if I may ever perform the Hajj after this year." (Recorded by Muslim and others.)

The conclusion concerning the acts of the Prophet (peace be upon him), as al-Amidi has stated, is that those acts that were performed out of the intention of getting closer to Allah or pleasing Allah are to be followed by the Muslims as either recommended or obligatory (depending on other related evidence). If the Prophet (peace be upon him) performed an act that was not related to the *Shareeah* or that was not done to get closer to Allah, it simply means that that act is permissible.[1]

---

[1] Ali al-Amidi, *Al-Ihkaam fi Usool al-Ahkaam* (Beirut: Daar al-Kutub al-Ilmiyyah, 1983), vol. 1, p. 249. Note that other categories, such as what was exclusively

The people who best understood the religion of Islam were the Companions of the Prophet (peace be upon him) and they have implemented this distinction between the acts of the Prophet (peace be upon him). For example, when emigrating from Makkah to Madinah, the Prophet (peace be upon him), in order to evade the enemy, was forced to stop in a cave. He worshipped Allah in the cave for that period of time. This was simply the act that was expedient at the time and none of the Companions took it as a virtuous deed that should be followed. Therefore, it is not reported from any of them that they went to that cave or any other cave to worship Allah in order to follow the example of the Prophet (peace be upon him) as they understood that this act was not one that was meant to be followed by the Muslims. Performing such an act as a matter of worship that must or should be performed would be akin to innovation.

A very important topic with respect to innovations and the sunnah are those acts that the Prophet (peace be upon him) did not perform. There are many deeds that the Prophet (peace be upon him) could have easily performed as acts of worship yet he explicitly did not perform them. If these acts were meant to be performed and if they would have brought the Muslims closer to Allah, the Prophet (peace be upon him) would have been commanded to perform them and he would have performed them. If there was a reason to perform some act related to worship yet he explicitly did not perform such act, it means that in the eyes of the *Shareeah* that act is not to be performed and anyone who does perform it, thinking that he is getting closer to Allah by performing it, is doing nothing except performing an innovation. An example could be the stating of the call to prayer before the *Eid* prayers— the Prophet (peace be upon him) never did so although there would have been some purpose in doing it and he could have

---

prohibited or allowed for the Prophet (peace be upon him) only, are not discussed here.

216

easily done so. This means that if anyone does it, he will be performing an innovation.

There are some actions that the Prophet (peace be upon him) did not perform for some constraining reason. For example, the Prophet (peace be upon him) did not gather together the Quran (although his Companions did so after his death). This was because there was a preventive reason that kept him from doing so; that is, the Quran was still being revealed and altered during his lifetime so it was not possible for him to gather it all together before his death. Once that preventive reason has been removed, then there is no harm in performing that act. Another example concerns the performing of the *taraweeh* or Ramadhaan nightly prayers in congregation. The Prophet (peace be upon him) feared that this would become obligatory on the Muslims, that was the preventive reason, and therefore he discontinued this practice. During the time of Umar, the preventive reason no longer existed since Umar is not qualified to make any act obligatory. Therefore, it was possible to revive this sunnah of the Prophet (peace be upon him). It is for this reason that al-Shaatibi wrote,

> What the Prophet (peace be upon him) avoided is of two types. One, what the *Shareeah* was silent about because there was no need to mention it at that time—such as rules concerning things that happened after the death of the Prophet (peace be upon him). The scholars must look at these matters based on the general principles of the *Shareeah* to decide [if they are lawful or not]. This category includes all of the acts of the early generations such as collecting together the Quran, recording the *Shareeah* and other acts that were not called for during the time of the Prophet (peace be upon him)... Second, those particular actions that the lawgiver was silent about or actions that were not performed although there may have been some "need" or reason to perform

them during the time of revelation... These actions are considered innovations by the *Shareeah*. Examples include "the prostration of thanks' according to Imam Maalik. Maalik reasoned that this is an innovation since there was a reason for its performance during the time of the Prophet but it was not performed...[1]

Ibn al-Qayyim, in his excellent work *Ilaam al-Muwaqieen*, also has an illuminating discussion of this point. He says that what the Prophet (peace be upon him) avoided is of two types and both of them lead to a sunnah. First are those actions that have been *reported not to have been performed by the Prophet* (peace be upon him). For example, the Prophet (peace be upon him) did not wash the bodies of the martyrs at Uhud nor did he pray over them; the Prophet (peace be upon him) also did not use to have the *adhaan* or *iqaamah* given for the *Eid* prayers, and so on. Second, those actions that *have not been reported by anyone from the Prophet (peace be upon him) or from the Companions*. For example, it is not reported that any of them pronounced the intention before beginning the prayer, or that the Imam would make supplications aloud while facing the followers after the prayers and them saying *ameen* to his supplications, and so on. He then says, "If anyone says that any act like them is recommended, he is contradicting the sunnah. What the Prophet (peace be upon him) avoided is sunnah in the same way as what he did is sunnah. [Therefore, it is actually recommended to leave these actions and not to perform them.]"[2]

This is an important concept as many of the innovations of Islam have appeared due to ignorance concerning this point. Any action, especially any action related

---

[1] Al-Shatibi, vol. 1, p. 168. Other scholars do not consider the "prostration of thanks" to be an innovation due to the hadith that lend support for that practice.
[2] Muhammad Ibn al-Qayyim, *Ilaam al-Muwaqieen* (Beirut: Daar al-Jeel), vol. 2, p. 166.

to worship, that the Prophet (peace be upon him) could have performed and that may have been called for but was explicitly not performed by the Prophet (peace be upon him) should also not be performed by the Muslims. If such acts are performed, they are innovations. Examples of this nature will be given later.[1]

Finally, there are the "tacit or silent approvals" of the Prophet (peace be upon him). That refers to any action that was done in his presence that he did not object to. Such actions are considered permissible at the very least. It was the duty of the Prophet (peace be upon him), in fulfilling his mission, that if any action was done in his presence that was incorrect or illegal, he must correct that action. Therefore, his silence or approval of any act means that the act is, at the very least, permissible.[2]

The Meaning of *Bidah*

One of the reasons for confusion concerning innovations is that there is more than one definition given by the scholars for the term *bidah*. From a lexical point of view, the meaning of *bidah* is,

> An innovation; a novelty; anything originated, invented or innovated; anything made, done, produced, caused to be or exist, or brought into existence, namely, for the first time, it not having been or existed before, and not after the similitude of anything pre-existing.[3]

In the Quran, Allah uses the term in this sense when He says,

---

[1] Cf., Muhammad Ahmad al-Adawi, *Usool fi al-Bidah wa al-Sunan* (Beirut: al-Maktab al-Islaami, 1986), pp. 71-86.
[2] This paragraph is sufficient for the purposes of this article. For more details see al-Shaukaani, p. 41.
[3] Lane, vol. 1, p. 167.

$$\text{قُلْ مَا كُنْتُ بِدْعًا مِنَ الرُّسُلِ}$$

"Say: I am not a new thing [Ar., *bidaan*] among the Messengers" (*al-Ahqaaf* 9). But, of course, the *Shareeah* or legal definition of *bidah* may not be the same as the lexical definition; that is a very important distinction that must be made and that has confused some people concerning innovations.

It could be stated that there are three popular legal definitions for *bidah* among the scholars, some are much more "extensive" or "encompassing" than others.

The First Definition

The first group gives a broad definition for *bidah* that encompasses every new thing that has appeared after the time of the Prophet (peace be upon him). For example, Al-Shafi'ee has divided innovations into good and evil ones, praiseworthy and blameworthy ones. He said, "Innovations are of two types: a praiseworthy innovation and a blameworthy innovation. Whatever is in agreement with the sunnah is praiseworthy and whatever is in disagreement with the sunnah is blameworthy."[1] Ibn Hazm has given a similar definition stating, "Innovations in the religion are everything that is not found in the Quran or in the sunnah of the Prophet (peace be upon him) but for some of them the person who performs them will receive a reward due to his goal of performing what is good... These are those acts that are in essence permissible... Then there are some that are blameworthy."[2] Al-Ghazaali, ibn al-Atheer, Abdul Haqq al-Dahlaawi, al-Izz ibn Abdul Salaam, al-Nawawi and Abu Shaamah have all given similar definitions.[3] As shall be shown

---

[1] Quoted in Abdul Rahmaan Abu Shaamah, *Al-Baath ala Inkaar al-Bidah wa al-Hawaadith* (Cairo: Daar al-Huda, 1978), p.22.
[2] Quoted in Izzat Atiyya, *Al-Bidah* (Cairo: Daar al-Kutub al-Hadeethiyyah), p. 196.
[3] Ibid., pp. 196-198.

later, this definition implies that there are some innovations that are obligatory, recommended or permissible.

The Second Definition

The second group can be divided into two subgroups with the common point between them being that they do not ascribe to the view that there is such a thing as a "permissible innovation." In other words, all innovations are blameworthy according to the *Shareeah*. The first of these subgroups, according to Atiyya, define *bidah* as anything that is in contradiction to the sunnah. For example, ibn Rajab defined *bidah* as, "Any innovation that has no source whatsoever in the *Shareeah* that points to it. If something has some source in the *Shareeah* that points to it, it is not a *bidah* according to the legal definition [of *bidah*] although it is a *bidah* according to the word's lexical definition."[1] Ibn Hajr al-Asqilaani, ibn Hajr al-Haithami, al-Zarkashi and Muhammad Bukhait have all given similar definitions.[2] Therefore, according to this group a *bidah* is any blameworthy innovation but this does not imply everything that occurred after the time of the Prophet (peace be upon him), but only those acts that are in contradiction to the basic sources of Islam, the Quran and the sunnah.

The Third Definition

The second subgroup is led by al-Shaatibi and his thoughts as expressed in the excellent exposition *al-Itisaam*. According to this group, a *bidah* is any innovated act that differs from the sunnah and that is taken as part of the religion and as being along the straight path. This can include actions

---

[1] Abdul Rahmaan Ibn Rajab, *Jaami al-Uloom wa al-Hikm* (Riyadh: Daar al-Ifta) p. 52.
[2] They were all quoted in Atiyya, pp. 198-200.

of worship as well as other actions. Al-Shaatibi has given two clear definitions for *bidah* in *al-Itisaam*. He wrote,

> A *bidah* is any invented act or path that is meant to resemble part of the *Shareeah* and it is followed as an act of worship of Allah. This definition is according to those who are of the opinion that customary acts[1] do not fall under the category of innovations. It is only concerned with acts of worship. But the definition according to those that would include customary acts under the topic of *bidah* is any invented act or way in the religion that is made to resemble the *Shareeah* and that is followed for the same reason that the *Shareeah* is supposed to be followed.[2]

According to the first definition, any action that is not related to the religion in any way, that is, what is purely related to worldly needs, is not considered a *bidah*. Similarly, if there is some direct source for an action in the Quran or sunnah, it will also not be considered an innovation.

Any action that has no precedence in the *Shareeah* is an innovation. In other words, any action that lies outside of what has been spanned by the *Shareeah* is an innovation. With this constraint, many of the actions that some people claim to be innovations are not so in reality. Al-Shaatibi refers to the study of grammar, vocabulary, *usool al-fiqh* and the sciences of hadith as studies that, although not completely present during the time of the Prophet (peace be upon him), were alluded to by the *Shareeah*. For example, the Muslim is instructed to ponder over the meanings of the verses of the Quran and this can only be done through a knowledge of Arabic grammar, vocabulary and rhetoric. Hence, the study of

---

[1] Or, non-religious acts.
[2] Al-Shaatibi, vol. 1, p. 37.

these topics is not an innovation as the *Shareeah* has alluded to its study.[1]

The act must be in resemblance to the way of the *Shareeah* although, in fact, it is the antithesis of the *Shareeah*. Therefore, any act that has nothing to do with getting closer to Allah or non-religious acts that are done for some worldly benefit and that does not contradict the laws of the *Shareeah* would not be considered an innovation. Al-Shaatibi states that,

> the *Shareeah* was revealed for the temporal and eternal benefit of mankind, that is, for mankind's happiness in both this world and the Hereafter. And this is also the goal of the innovator when he invents something. An innovation is either related to non-religious acts or it is related to acts of worship. If the innovation is related to worship, it is meant to get the person the greatest reward in the Hereafter according to what [the innovator] alleges. Similarly, if it is related to non-religious actions, it is meant for the person's maximum benefit in this life [but, in fact, this can only be attained by following the pure *Shareeah*].[2]

A Discussion of the Three Definitions

The first definition is strictly based on the lexical meaning of the term *bidah*. It was not this group's intention just to give the legal definition of *bidah*. They took this approach because of reports like Umar ibn al-Khattaabi's saying, "What a good *bidah* this is."[3] Therefore, it can be argued that there is nothing essentially wrong with their definition as they clearly state that any innovation that

---

[1] Cf., al-Shaatibi, vol. 1, pp. 37-39.
[2] Al-Shatibi, vol. 1, p. 41.
[3] This statement shall be discussed in detail later.

contradicts the sunnah is blameworthy and this is exactly what the second definition states. According to al-Ali,

> In sum, though, it is clear to us that the two groups[1] are in agreement that the *bidah* that is blameworthy is that act that has no source in the *Shareeah*, as made up of the Quran, sunnah, consensus and analogy [based on those], that could make the act or belief something that can be considered as taking one closer to Allah. Concerning other ["praiseworthy"] innovations that appeared after the time of the Prophet (peace be upon him), the first group will still call them *bidah*... The second group would not call them *bidah* but would include them under one of the general principles of the *Shareeah*, such as *masaalih al-mursalah* or *istihsaan*[2] or "that which is a must for something that is obligatory, also becomes obligatory" or "blocking the means to some evil" and so on. The important thing is that they agree that what has been invented in the religion that has no source in the *Shareeah* is forbidden.[3]

But it is true that the *Shareeah* itself has stated that every *bidah* is a going astray, as mentioned in the hadith recorded earlier. Therefore, since this condition is from the *Shareeah* itself, it should be applied in the definition in order to avoid any confusion. Saallih al-Ali writes, "To say that every *bidah* is blameworthy according to the *Shareeah* is better and more correct as the acts of innovation are all blameworthy.... The texts that are related concerning *bidah* say that they are all blameworthy."[4]

---

[1] That is, the people who ascribe to the first definition and the people who ascribe to either of the second or third definitions.
[2] These terms will be discussed and defined later.
[3] Saalih al-Ali, "Al-Bidah Taan fi al-Deen," *Majallat al-Buhooth al-Islaamiyyah* (vol. 14, Dhu al-Qaadah, 1405), p. 166.
[4] Al-Ali, p. 161.

Al-Shaatibi is a bit more adamant on this point saying, "You should know— may Allah have mercy on you— that what we have presented as evidence is proof through many means that all innovations are blameworthy." His points are: (1) All of the texts state the word *bidah* in an unrestricted sense without any qualifier or in general terms without any particularization. (2) It is a fundamental principle that any absolute predicate or absolute legal evidence that is repeated in many places and that has lots of supporting evidence for it with nothing that confines it or makes it specific is evidence that it applies in general without any restriction.[1] (3) There is a consensus among the Companions and their Followers that *every* innovation is a going astray and misguidance. (4) The innovator has invented his act himself[2] in opposition to what the *Shareeah* has decreed. Therefore, it is not logically possible to say that some such innovations are good while others are bad. This is an insult to the *Shareeah*. Therefore, all innovations are bad.[3]

Therefore, it may be said that "the first definition", although correct lexically speaking and according to what they had in mind, is not the proper definition from the *Shareeah* point of view. Furthermore, the author has witnessed that such a definition has led to confusion among today's Muslims and has been used by some as an excuse to follow some innovations, claiming that they are "good *bidah*s." This point was also noticed by al-Ali who wrote,

> Concerning what the first group says, that innovations may be forbidden or may be legal, that is

---

[1] What al-Shaatibi is saying here is that if a principle is repeated often in the Quran and hadith and nowhere is this principle particularized and there is no evidence that suggests that it does not apply to every case, then it does apply to every case. An example is the principle that "no person shall bear the burden of another" which is mentioned a few times in the Quran and which is not particularized in any verse or hadith. Hence, it is true for all situations.

[2] Or he is following someone who has invented an act.

[3] Al-Shatibi, vol. 1, pp. 141-5. Also see his discussion on pp. 191-211.

a terminology that grants the forbidden innovations
something of insignificance and makes the warnings
about them seem exaggerated and makes some of the
people accept them as something customary or
excusable. This is true because the innovation may be
forbidden or it may be legal, therefore they reduce
the emphasis on rejecting the act.[1]

Atiyya, in his doctoral dissertation on innovations,
concludes that the second definition stated above is the correct
definition for *bidah*. Concerning the third definition (from
al-Shaatibi), Atiyya writes, "[This definition] is not acceptable
because he particularizes *bidah* as being only those acts that
resemble the religion from other acts that do not do so. But all
of the evidence presented does not support this condition."[2]
The evidence he presents to support his refutation of
al-Shaatibi is not very strong. His strongest point, for example,
is probably his fourth point that states that many of the actions
that the early scholars called innovations were not actions that
resembled the *Shareeah*, such as the rulers delaying the
prayers beyond their proper time limits.[3] If the rulers delayed
the prayers due to laziness or being busy, this would be a sin
and not an innovation. If the rulers did so believing that it was
permissible for them to delay the prayers, then they did make a
ruling "resembling the *Shareeah*" which contradicts the
sunnah and which is, therefore, a *bidah*.

---

[1] Al-Ali, p. 162.
[2] Atiyya, p. 215.
[3] Atiyya, pp. 218-219. The delaying of the prayers is the only example that he
presents for this point. He quotes a hadith in a footnote about the rulers that
states that, "[they will] act according to innovations and they will delay the
prayers." He seems to imply that the hadith calls the delaying of the prayers "an
innovation" but this is not exactly true. The hadith simply states that they will
follow innovations and they will *also* delay the prayers. The other hadith he
quotes concerning their delaying of the prayers does not mention *bidah* at all.
Furthermore, it should be noted that many of the early scholars would use many
specific terms in a much wider sense than can be derived from the Quran or
sunnah.

As alluded to in the previous two sentences, a problem with the second definition of *bidah* is that it does not differentiate between a sin and an innovation as it simply states that any act that contradicts the sunnah, regardless of the intention behind it, is a *bidah*. Before making a conclusion about the definition of *bidah*, it is important to understand the difference between a sin and a *bidah*.

Difference between a Sin and an Innovation

"Sin" and "innovation" are not synonymous terms although the usage of some of the early scholars and the second definition might lead one to believe they are. It could be stated, though, that an innovation is a particular type of sin.

Suppose someone does not perform an act that is obligatory, recommended or permissible, is this a type of innovation? The answer depends on the case and there are two cases possible. (A) If the person did not perform the act due to some personal weakness like laziness or heedlessness, that is, not due to any "religious" reason, and the action was an obligatory duty, he has committed a sin. If the action was simply a recommended or permissible act, he did not commit a sin. In either case, it would not be an innovation. (B) If the person left such acts intentionally believing or claiming that by doing so he was pleasing Allah and getting closer to Allah, then he has innovated something in the religion and this would be both a sin and an innovation. This has been brought out by a hadith in which one person decided to pray all night, another decided to fast every day and a third decided not to marry, thinking that by doing so they would be pleasing Allah. These people decided to leave permissible acts (sleeping, eating and marriage) for "religious purposes." The Prophet (peace be upon him) pointed out that there deeds were mistaken and said,

$$ فَمَنْ رَغِبَ عَنْ سُنَّتِي فَلَيْسَ مِنِّي $$

"Whoever turns away my sunnah is not from me." (Recorded by al-Bukhari and Muslim.) Hence, what they were planning on doing is considered *bidah*.

That simple question and response should demonstrate the difference between an innovation and a sin. The scholars have also pointed out some other differences between the two. They are:

1. The one who commits a sin to satisfy a fleeting desire is still hoping for Allah's forgiveness concerning that deed. He still believes that the deed is unlawful and he has some fear of Allah and hope for His forgiveness. Fear and hope are two of the essential components of *imaan* or faith. This fear and hope is not present when an innovator performs an innovation because he claims that there is nothing wrong with the act he performed.

2. The sinner does not believe that the deed he performs is lawful and, therefore, in no way does he "challenge" the truthfulness or validity of the *Shareeah*. The innovator, on the other hand, claims that his innovation (that he or another invented) is supposed to be part of the *Shareeah*, thus claiming that there is some shortcoming in the *Shareeah* as preached by the Messenger of Allah (peace be upon him). If someone intentionally claims that there is some shortcoming or imperfection in the *Shareeah*, he becomes an unbeliever. If this is done due to some weak or erroneous interpretation of the Quran or hadith, the person is either mistaken or a sinner (because he made *ijtihaad* without being qualified to do so). In any case, the act he is following is still an innovation.

3. The person who commits a sin still loves Allah and His Messenger although he commits sins. This is not true for the innovator. The proof for this contention is in the following two hadith. Al-Bukhari recorded the hadith about the Companion who drank alcohol on a number of occasions and afterwards he would be punished by the Prophet (peace be upon him). Another Companion cursed the one who drank alcohol and the Prophet (peace be upon him) told him,

$$\text{لا تَلْعُنُوهُ فَوَاللَّهِ مَا عَلِمْتُ إِنَّهُ يُحِبُّ اللَّهَ وَرَسُولَهُ}$$

"Do not curse him for I know he loves Allah and His Messenger." (Recorded by al-Bukhari.) The Prophet (peace be upon him) showed that although the person sinned, he will still be in the graces of Allah due to his belief and faith.

As opposed to this hadith, the Prophet (peace be upon him) described the Khawaarij, one of the people of *bidah*,[1] as people with whom the Muslims could not compare their prayers, fasting and reciting of the Quran with. Yet the Prophet (peace be upon him) also said,

$$\text{قَوْمٌ يَقْرَعُونَ الْقُرْآنَ لا يُجَاوِزُ حَنَاجِرَهُمْ يَمْرُقُونَ مِنَ الدِّينِ}$$
$$\text{مُرُوقَ السَّهْمِ مِنَ الرَّمِيَّةِ يَقْتُلُونَ أَهْلَ الإِسْلامِ وَيَدَعُونَ أَهْلَ}$$
$$\text{الأَوْثَانِ لَئِنْ أَنَا أَدْرَكْتُهُمْ لأَقْتُلَنَّهُمْ قَتْلَ عَادٍ}$$

"[They] are a people who will recite the Quran but it will not pass their throats. They will swerve from Islam as an arrow goes through the animal shot at. They will kill the followers of Islam and leave the worshippers of idols alone but if I live to their time I shall certainly kill them like the killing of Ad." (Recorded by al-Bukhari and Muslim.) The difference here is notable. Although they prayed, fasted and recited the Quran often, the Prophet (peace be upon him) did not say that they loved Allah and His Messenger but, instead, ordered them to be killed because of their innovations in the religion.

Indeed, the position of the believing sinner is far superior to that of the innovator. Ahmad ibn Hanbal once said,

---

[1] The phrase, "people of innovations and desires," refers to those people who innovate the beliefs and actions, who try to support their innovations from Quranic verses and hadith, who blame others for not following their innovations and who may also claim that those who do not follow their innovations are not along the true path. Cf., al-Shaatibi, vol. 1, pp. 162-3.

"The evildoers of 'the people of the sunnah and congregation' (Ar., *ahl al-sunnah wa al-jamaah*) are among the patrons of Allah. And the most devout of the people of *bidah* are among the enemies of Allah."

Therefore, it is true that, as ibn Muflih wrote, "innovations are worse and more harmful than sins because the person who performs or follows innovations believes them to be true and obedience to Allah but this is a lie against Allah and it is a position concerning His religion that is not based on any fact and it is very rare that such an innovator should repent."[1] This is why ibn Taimiyyah has stated that innovations are "more evil than adultery, theft and drinking alcohol."[2]

Sufyaan al-Thauri once said, "Innovations are more beloved to the Satan than sins because one may repent from sins but one does not repent from innovations." This is yet another difference between sins and innovations about which there is some difference of opinion: Is there repentance for innovators?

Conclusions on the Definition of *Bidah*

(1) *Bidah* or innovations, from a *Shareeah* point of view, are only blameworthy as the Prophet (peace be upon him) said,

$$\text{كُلُّ بِدْعَةٍ ضَلَالَةٌ}$$

"Every innovation is a going astray." Therefore the *bidah* that are referred to in the hadith quoted earlier are not that as defined by Imam al-Shafi'ee and others, although their definition may be lexically acceptable.

---

[1] Ibn Muflih is quoted in al-Ali, p. 175.
[2] Ahmad ibn Taimiyyah, *Majmooat Fataawa ibn Taimiyyah*, (Riyadh: Daar al-Ifta, Riyadh) vol. 11, p. 474. Also see al-Ali, pp. 173-175.

(2) Since the *Shareeah* has constrained the definition of *bidah* to be only blameworthy acts, it is best and less confusing, if not a must, to apply this constraint in the definition of *bidah*.

(3) There is definitely a difference between sins, in general, and innovations. Again, the definition of *bidah* must encompass this fact.

Given these points, it is concluded that al-Shaatibi's definitions of *bidah* are the soundest. His definitions, once again, are

> a *bidah* is any invented act or path that is made to resemble part of the *Shareeah* and it is followed as an act of worship of Allah. This definition is according to those who are of the opinion that customary acts[1] do not fall under the category of innovations. It is only concerned with acts of worship. But the definition according to those who would include customary acts under the topic of *bidah* is any invented act or way in the religion that is made to resemble the *Shareeah* and that is followed for the same reason that the *Shareeah* is supposed to be followed.[2]

It should be noted again that his definition is not completely incompatible with the first definition described above. As stated in the quote from Saallih al-Ali, both of these definitions are in agreement that any act that has no supporting source in the *Shareeah* is a *bidah* and is blameworthy.

Finally, the second and third definitions agree that if the *Shareeah* alludes to something, it is not an innovation. And if the *Shareeah* in no way alludes to something, it is an innovation. In the author's opinion, the second definition (quoted from ibn Rajab, ibn Hajr al-Asqilaani, ibn Hajr

---

[1] Or, "non-religious acts."
[2] Al-Shatibi, vol. 1, p. 37.

al-Haithami and others) is not to be taken at face value as these scholars themselves, in many of their writings, distinguished between sins and innovations. It could be argued that they simply left something out of their definitions.

Therefore, if this suggestion is correct, the three definitions are compatible although al-Shaatibi's statement of the definition is the best and most complete.

References

Abdul Qaadir, Muhammad. *Afaal al-Rasool*. Jeddah: Daar al-Mujtama. 1984.

Abu Shaama, Abdul Rahmaan. *Al-Baath ala Inkaar al-Bidah wa al-Hawaadith*. Cairo: Daar al-Huda. 1978.

al-Adawi, Muhammad Ahmad. *Usool fi al-Bidah wa al-Sunan*. Beirut: al-Maktab al-Islaami. 1986.

al-Albaani, Muhammad Naasir al-Deen. *Saheeh al-Targheeb wa al-Tarheeb*. Beirut: al-Maktab al-Islaami. 1982.

al-Ali, Saallih. "Al-Bidah Taan fi al-Deen" in *Majallat al-Buhooth al-Islaamiyyah*. Vol. 14, Dhu al-Qaadah, 1405.

al-Amidi, Ali. *Al-Ihkaam fi Usool al-Ahkaam*. Beirut: Daar al-Kutub al-Ilmiyyah. 1983.

al-Ashqar, Muhammad. *Afaal al-Rasool*. Kuwait: Maktabah al-Manaar al-Islaamiyyah. 1978.

Atiyya, Izzat. *Al-Bidah*. Cairo: Daar al-Kutub al-Hadeethiyyah.

Ibn al-Qayyim, Muhammad. *Ilaam al-Muwaqieen*. Beirut: Daar al-Jeel.

Ibn Rajab, Abdul Rahmaan. *Jaami al-Uloom wa al-Hikm* Riyadh: Daar al-Ifta.

Ibn Taimiyyah, Ahmad. *Majmooat Fataawa ibn Taimiyyah*. Riyadh: Daar al-Ifta.

al-Jazaairi, Abu Bakr. *Hurimat al-Ibtidaa fi al-Deen*. Idaarat Bina al-Masaajid. 1407.

Lane, E. W. *Arabic-English Lexicon*. Cambridge, England: Islamic Texts Society. 1984.

al-Shaatibi, Ibraaheem. *Al-Itisaam*. Alexandria: Daar Umar ibn al-Khattaab.

al-Shaukaani, Muhammad ibn Ali. *Irshaad al-Fahool.* Beirut: Daar al-Marafah. 1979.

Feature Article:
The Importance of the Sunnah and Hadith in Islam[1]

Introduction

The proofs concerning the importance of the sunnah may be divided into four categories: proofs from the Quran, proofs from the sunnah itself, corroborating evidence in the statements of the Companions of the Prophet, and conclusions of the leading scholars of Islam.[2]

The Importance of the Sunnah from the Quran

Obviously, if somebody denies the importance of the sunnah *in toto* hadith cannot be used as arguments to prove the importance of the sunnah. Instead, one must derive some proof from the Quran itself concerning the position of the sunnah in Islam. There exist many verses in the Quran that point to the

---

[1] This article appeared in *al-Basheer*, vol. 1, no. 6 (Apr.-March 1988). By the grace and mercy of Allah, this author has just completed another work entitled, *The Authority and Importance of the Sunnah* (Boulder, CO: Basheer Publications, 1999). That book touches upon a number of issues not discussed in this article. Although the bulk of this article is captured in that book, due to the importance of the topic, it was decided to leave this article in this work also.

[2] Of course, the consensus of the Companions and of later scholars is definitely a proof, while individual statements of scholars are not actually proofs. (Actually, there is a difference of opinion among the scholars concerning the authority of the statements of individual Companions.) However, they are presented as supporting arguments.

importance of the sunnah. In fact, many verses give a clear indication that it is obligatory for a person who believes in Allah to follow the sunnah.[1] Many of these verses are so emphatic that no conscientious person can deny their implications concerning the sunnah.[2]

The following is a discussion of just some of these verses:

Allah says in the Quran,

يَاأَيُّهَا الَّذِينَ آمَنُوا أَطِيعُوا اللَّهَ وَأَطِيعُوا الرَّسُولَ وَأُولِي الْأَمْرِ مِنْكُمْ فَإِنْ تَنَازَعْتُمْ فِي شَيْءٍ فَرُدُّوهُ إِلَى اللَّهِ وَالرَّسُولِ إِنْ كُنْتُمْ تُؤْمِنُونَ بِاللَّهِ وَالْيَوْمِ الْآخِرِ ذَلِكَ خَيْرٌ وَأَحْسَنُ تَأْوِيلاً

"O you who believe, obey Allah and obey the Messenger and those in authority among you. And if you are in dispute over any matter, refer it to Allah and His Messenger if you are actually believers in Allah and the Last Day. That is better for you and more seemly in the end" (al-Nisaa 59). Many important points may be deduced from this one verse of the

---

[1] Ibn Taimiyyah stated that the position of the sunnah has been confirmed in over forty places in the Quran. Cf., Ahmad Ibn Taimiyyah, *Majmooat al-Fataawa ibn Taimiyyah* (collected by Abdul Rahmaan ibn Qaasim and his son Muhammad, Riyadh: Daar al-Ifta 1978), vol. 19, pp. 93f.

[2] Unfortunately there has arisen among Muslims recently a group who attempt to divorce the sunnah from Islam. They claim that the sunnah was only applicable during the time of the Prophet (peace be upon him) and it need not be followed today. Such people are going against many verses of the Quran as well as many hadith and the consensus of believers. It is for this reason that many scholars have stated that anyone who denies that the sunnah is the pattern of behavior for Muslims and the second source of legislation in Islam has left the fold of Islam. Some people also try to live only by the Quran and call themselves "Quranists" but, as will be shown, it is not possible to understand the Quran without reference to the sunnah. Furthermore, it is also not possible to follow the Quran without following the sunnah, as it is the Quran itself that obliges the Muslim to follow the sunnah. Their claim is nothing, in essence, but a sort of oxymoron.

Quran. First, it must be noted that Allah explicitly uses the command "to obey" (Ar., *ateeu*) not only for Himself but also for the Messenger (peace be upon him), that is, "*obey* Allah and *obey* the Messenger." (The same verb or command does not directly precede "those in authority among you."[1]) This establishes the Messenger of Allah (peace be upon him) as an independent object of obedience while obedience to anyone else is conditional upon consistency with the Quran or sunnah. Second, Muslims are commanded to take any dispute that they may have to only two arbiters: Allah and His Messenger (peace be upon him). According to the understanding of the Companions of the Prophet (peace be upon him) and later scholars, "refer it to Allah" means "to refer it to the Book of Allah." And referring the matter to the Messenger of Allah (peace be upon him) means to refer it directly to him during his lifetime and to his sunnah after his death.

Note that the two, the Book of Allah and the sunnah of the Messenger (peace be upon him), are placed together here and the verse does not say, "refer the matter to Allah and if you do not find the answer there, refer the matter to the Messenger." Third, Allah clearly states that the true believers are the ones who refer their disputes not to Allah only but to Allah and His Messenger (peace be upon him). Fourth, the believer knows that the important life is that of the Hereafter. Allah states in this verse that it is better in the end (that is, in the Hereafter), when the person must face Allah, for the believer to refer any dispute to both Allah and His Messenger and not to Allah only by denying the position of the sunnah of the Prophet (peace be upon him). Finally, one should realize that this verse refers to all types of disputes, whether concerning matters of worship, business or other worldly affairs. Some scholars mention that this verse was revealed

---

[1] Of course, this is not proper according to English syntax which requires that the items in the position following *obey* be the objects of *obey*. But in Arabic, such a construction can be done to emphasize the obedience to those stated directly after the command.

with respect to some of the deputies of the Messenger of Allah (peace be upon him). Before the time of the Prophet, the Arabs had no real idea of governmental authority and, hence, this led to disputes concerning which, Allah states, the solution was to refer the matter to Allah and His Messenger (peace be upon him).

Allah also states in the Quran,

فَلَا وَرَبِّكَ لَا يُؤْمِنُونَ حَتَّى يُحَكِّمُوكَ فِيمَا شَجَرَ بَيْنَهُمْ ثُمَّ لَا يَجِدُوا فِي أَنفُسِهِمْ حَرَجًا مِمَّا قَضَيْتَ وَيُسَلِّمُوا تَسْلِيمًا

"But nay, by thy Lord, they will not actually believe until they make you the judge of what is in dispute between them and find within themselves no dislike of that which you decide and they submit with full submission" (al-Nisaa 65). The occasion for the revelation of this verse—or, at least, a case that it explicitly applies to—is recorded in *Sahih al-Bukhari* as:

> Al-Zubair quarreled with a man from the Ansaar because of a natural mountain stream at al-Harra. The Prophet (peace be upon him) said, "O Zubair, irrigate your land and then let the water flow to your neighbor." The Ansaar said, "O Allah's Apostle, (is this because) he is your cousin?" At that the Prophet's face became red (with anger) and he said, "Zubair, irrigate your land and then withhold the water until it fills the land up to the walls and then let if flow to your neighbor." So the Prophet (peace be upon him) enabled al-Zubair to take his full right after the Ansaari had provoked his anger. The Prophet (peace be upon him) had previously given an order that was in favor of both of them. Al-Zubair said, "I do not think that this verse, 'Nay, by thy Lord...', was revealed except on this occasion."

Al-Shaukaani points out that one's belief is not perfected until one completely accepts the Messenger of Allah (peace be upon him) as the decider of affairs. By the word *haraj* (translated above as "dislike") is meant, according to some authorities, doubt concerning any decision made by the Prophet (peace be upon him); others say that it means "sin"— by finding in their hearts the desire to reject the decision of the Prophet (peace be upon him). The last part of the verse means that the true Muslim will have no doubt concerning what the Messenger of Allah (peace be upon him) said or ordered and will submit and accept his authority without any hesitation, rationalization or false excuses. In conclusion, a Muslim cannot truthfully call himself a believer until, in his heart, he completely accepts the Messenger of Allah's (peace be upon him) his way of life, his sunnah and his decisions.[1]

Another point that deserves attention is that Allah begins this verse by swearing. This is fairly common in the Quran, but in this particular instance Allah swears by the Lord of the Prophet (peace be upon him). This swearing is much more tremendous than any other found in the Quran, and it is after this great swearing that Allah tells the believers that it is necessary for them to completely accept the authority of the Prophet (peace be upon him). In commenting on this verse, Ibn Katheer quotes the hadith of the Prophet (peace be upon him), "None of you truly believes until his desires are subservient to what I have come with."[2]

Another verse in the Quran states,

---

[1] Muhammad ibn Ali al-Shaukaani, *Fath al-Qadeer* (Mustafa al-Babi al-Halabi, 1964), vol. 1, p. 483.

[2] Imaad al-Deen ibn Katheer, *Tafseer al-Quran al-Adheem* (Daar Ihya al-Kutub al-Arabi, no date or city), vol. 1, p. 560. Unfortunately, there is a difference of opinion concerning this hadith. Some of the scholars, for example, al-Albaani, consider it weak while others, such as al-Nawawi, consider it *hasan*.

قُلْ إِنْ كُنْتُمْ تُحِبُّونَ اللَّهَ فَاتَّبِعُونِي يُحْبِبْكُمُ اللَّهُ وَيَغْفِرْ لَكُمْ
ذُنُوبَكُمْ وَاللَّهُ غَفُورٌ رَحِيمٌ

"Say (O Muhammad): If you truly love Allah then follow me
and Allah will love you and forgive your sins. Allah is the
Forgiving, the Merciful" (*ali-Imraan* 31). The one who truly
loves Allah will seek to find the actions that will lead Allah to
love him. According to this verse, in order to gain Allah's love
one need only follow and obey the Messenger (peace be upon
him) and then Allah will love him and forgive his sins.
Al-Shaukaani wrote that "to love Allah" implies to desire to
obey Allah completely and to do anything that Allah orders.
He quoted al-Azhaari, who said, "The love of Allah and His
Messenger by a slave means (that the slave) obeys the two
completely and follows them in his actions."[1] Ibn Katheer adds
that this verse makes it a fact that anyone who claims to love
Allah yet refuses to obey or follow the Messenger is a liar.[2]

Allah also revealed to His Prophet,

مَنْ يُطِعِ الرَّسُولَ فَقَدْ أَطَاعَ اللَّهَ وَمَنْ تَوَلَّى فَمَا أَرْسَلْنَاكَ
عَلَيْهِمْ حَفِيظًا

"Whoever obeys the Messenger verily obeys Allah; but if any
turn away, We have not sent you to watch over their (evil
deeds)." (*al-Nisaa* 80). In this verse, Allah clearly states that
obedience to the Messenger (peace be upon him) is nothing
less than obedience to Allah. The verse is so clear it cannot be
construed in any other manner.

In the *Sahih*s of al-Bukhari and Muslim it is recorded
that the Messenger of Allah (peace be upon him) said,

---

[1] Al-Shaukaani, *Fath al-Qadeer*, vol. 1, p. 338.
[2] Ibn Katheer, *Tafseer*, vol. 1, p. 358.

مَنْ أَطَاعَنِي فَقَدْ أَطَاعَ اللَّهَ وَمَنْ عَصَانِي فَقَدْ عَصَى اللَّهَ

"Whoever obeys me, obeys Allah. Whoever disobeys me, disobeys Allah." Not following the sunnah or the commands of the Prophet (peace be upon him) is exactly the same as not following the commands of Allah. Ibn Katheer noted that it is the Prophet's job only to convey the message and it is up to each person to accept or to reject his message. The one who follows his message will be saved. Hence, whoever obeys Allah and His Messenger is guided; whoever disobeys Allah and His Messenger harms no one except himself.[1] Al-Shaukaani points out that this verse proves that anything that comes from the Messenger (peace be upon him) actually originated with Allah.[2]

Allah says,

وَأَطِيعُوا اللَّهَ وَالرَّسُولَ لَعَلَّكُمْ تُرْحَمُونَ

"O you who believe, obey Allah and His Messenger that you may attain mercy" (*ali-Imraan* 132). In this verse, Allah states that the Mercy in the next life will be showered upon those who obeyed Allah and His Messenger (peace be upon him).

Allah also revealed,

وَمَا كَانَ لِمُؤْمِنٍ وَلَا مُؤْمِنَةٍ إِذَا قَضَى اللَّهُ وَرَسُولُهُ أَمْرًا أَنْ يَكُونَ لَهُمُ الْخِيَرَةُ مِنْ أَمْرِهِمْ وَمَنْ يَعْصِ اللَّهَ وَرَسُولَهُ فَقَدْ ضَلَّ ضَلَالًا مُبِينًا

"It does not become a believing man or believing woman, when Allah and His Messenger have decided any matter that they should (after that) claim any say in their affair; and whoever is disobedient to Allah and His Messenger has

---

[1] Ibid., vol. 1, p. 568.
[2] Al-Shaukawni, *Fath*, vol. 1, p. 489.

certainly gone astray in manifest error" (*al-Ahzaab* 36). If Allah or His Messenger has made a decision on any matter, then the believer has no choice but to submit himself to the decrees of Allah and His Messenger (peace be upon him).

Al-Suyooti has recorded the occasion for the revelation of this verse: Qataadah narrated that the Messenger of Allah (peace be upon him) asked Zainab to marry Zaid, but instead she wished to marry the Prophet (peace be upon him) himself, and, therefore, she refused to accept the Prophet's choice. This verse was then revealed, and she became pleased and submitted to the Prophet's decision. Such was also narrated through a couple of chains on the authority of ibn Abbaas.[1] Ibn Katheer stated a number of authorities who mentioned this incident as the occasion behind the revelation of this verse. If these narrations are correct, a couple of points should be noted with respect to this verse. First, it was revealed in connection with a decision made by the Prophet (peace be upon him). No Quranic commandment had been revealed about this request of the Prophet (peace be upon him); yet Allah describes the Prophet's decision as coming from both Allah and His Messenger, "when Allah and His Messenger have decided a matter." This clearly proves that the Prophet's commands were not from himself but were inspired by Allah. Second, and even more profound, is that this verse was revealed with respect to marriage and the personal desires of the heart. Allah states that even in these delicate matters one must completely submit to the commands of Allah and His Messenger (peace be upon him). Thus the obedience to the

---

[1] Al-Suyooti, *Lubaab*, p. 174. The incident was recorded by al-Tabaraani with a *sahih* chain back to Qataadah. Qataadah, however, was not a Companion of the Prophet (peace be upon him) and, hence, that chain traced back to the Prophet (peace be upon him) is broken. The narrations from ibn Abbaas all have some weakness to them. Other narrations state that it was revealed with respect to a different woman; however, the gist of that story is the same as the one presented above.

Messenger (peace be upon him) must permeate even the most private aspects of our lives.

One can also find the following verse in the Quran,

$$\text{يَاأَيُّهَا الَّذِينَ آمَنُوا اسْتَجِيبُوا لِلَّهِ وَلِلرَّسُولِ إِذَا دَعَاكُمْ لِمَا يُحْيِيكُمْ}$$

"O you who believe, respond to Allah and His Messenger when they call you to that which gives you life" (*al-Anfaal* 24). Al-Shaukaani commented that "to respond to" means "to obey" Allah and His Messenger (peace be upon him) when they make a command. The *Shareeah*, which is embodied in the Quran and sunnah, are the proclamations of Allah and His Messenger (peace be upon him). It is this *Shareeah* that gives true meaning and true life to this worldly existence. Ignoring or not responding to this call and guidance is, in fact, a type of death. Al-Shaukaani pointed out that this verse proves that it is obligatory for every Muslim to obey any command (that is, call) that he hears from Allah or His Messenger (peace be upon him), even if the command should go against his own desires, opinion or against popular opinion. The manner in which one should respond to the commands of Allah or His Prophet (peace be upon him) has been exemplified in the story of Abu Saeed ibn Mualla. While Abu Saeed was praying, the Prophet (peace be upon him) summoned him, but he did not respond until he had finished the prayer. Upon finally coming to the Prophet (peace be upon him), the Messenger of Allah recited the above verse to him showing his behavior towards the call of the Prophet (peace be upon him) was incorrect.[1]

Verse seven of *soorah al-Hashr* states,

---

[1] Al-Shaukaani, *Fath*, vol. 2, p. 299-300.

$$\text{وَمَا آتَاكُمُ الرَّسُولُ فَخُذُوهُ وَمَا نَهَاكُمْ عَنْهُ فَانْتَهُوا وَاتَّقُوا}$$
$$\text{اللَّهَ}$$

"Whatsoever the Messenger gives you, take it; and whatsoever he forbids for you, abstain from it. And be aware of Allah." This verse was revealed specifically with respect to the spoils of war: "what the Messenger gives you of the spoils, take it; and what he does not give you of the spoils, abstain from it." No scholar has argued that this verse pertains only to the spoils of war. Ibn Juraij said that its meaning is general, that whatever the Messenger (peace be upon him) orders you to do, you must do; and whatever he shuns for you, you must also shun. Al-Shaukaani said that the wording of the verse is general and the occasion behind the revelation does not confine the ruling of the verse. He said that the verse has a general application and applies to all of the regulations, commands or prohibitions that come from the Prophet (peace be upon him).[1] Allah ends this verse with a warning, "And be aware of Allah." This is a clear warning to those who do not respect the limits laid down by the Prophet (peace be upon him).

Allah also stated,

$$\text{فَلْيَحْذَرِ الَّذِينَ يُخَالِفُونَ عَنْ أَمْرِهِ أَنْ تُصِيبَهُمْ فِتْنَةٌ أَوْ}$$
$$\text{يُصِيبَهُمْ عَذَابٌ أَلِيمٌ}$$

"Let those who conspire to evade orders beware lest a calamity or painful punishment should befall them" (al-Noor 63). Al-Qurtubi said that jurists point to this verse as a proof that it is obligatory to follow the commands and orders that come from Allah and His Messenger (peace be upon him). In this same verse, al-Qurtubi added, Allah warns of a punishment to

---

[1] Ibid., vol. 5, p. 198.

befall anyone who decides not to follow Allah's or His Prophet's commands.[1]

In another relevant verse, Allah states,

لَقَدْ مَنَّ اللَّهُ عَلَى الْمُؤْمِنِينَ إِذْ بَعَثَ فِيهِمْ رَسُولاً مِنْ أَنْفُسِهِمْ يَتْلُوا عَلَيْهِمْ آيَاتِهِ وَيُزَكِّيهِمْ وَيُعَلِّمُهُمُ الْكِتَابَ وَالْحِكْمَةَ وَإِنْ كَانُوا مِنْ قَبْلُ لَفِي ضَلالٍ مُبِينٍ

"Allah has clearly shown grace to the believers by sending unto them a Messenger of their own who recites unto them His revelations, and causes them to grow and teaches them the Book and the *Hikmah*,[2] although before they were in flagrant error" (*ali-Imraan* 164). This is a beautiful verse from which may be derived many important points,[3] but, unfortunately, the discussion here will have to be quite brief. One important phrase of this verse is, "he teaches them the Book and the *Hikmah*." This refers to something that the Messenger of Allah (peace be upon him) was sent with in addition to the Quran. The obvious question is then: What was it that the Prophet Muhammad (peace be upon him) was sent in addition to the Quran? As in *al-Nisaa* 113 (mentioned below) what else was *revealed* to the Prophet (peace be upon him)? The answer can only be the sunnah. It is part of the blessing upon the believers

---

[1] Abu Abdillah al-Qurtubi, *al-Jaami li-Ahkaam al-Quran* (Beirut: Daar Ihya al-Turaath al-Arabi, no date), Vol. 12, p. 322.

[2] The word *hikmah* literally means wisdom. However, in these verses it refers to what was revealed along with the Book. It is understood to refer to the Sunnah of the Prophet (peace be upon him) and, therefore, it has been left untranslated as *hikmah*.

[3] This verse is an answer to Abraham's prayer that is recorded in *soorah al-Baqarah* verse 129. The words "of their own" refer to the fact that the Prophet (peace be upon him) was a human being and could, therefore, be a perfect example for the rest of mankind. Cf., ibn Katheer, *Tafseer*, vol. 1., p. 130. For example, given the Christian doctrine of trinity, it would be ridiculous for Christians to consider Jesus (peace be upon him) as a perfect example for the humans to follow.

that the Prophet taught them both the book (the Quran) and the *Hikmah* (the sunnah).

Commenting on this verse, Imam al-Shafi'ee recorded the following verses:

رَبَّنَا وَابْعَثْ فِيهِمْ رَسُولاً مِنْهُمْ يَتْلُو عَلَيْهِمْ آيَاتِكَ وَيُعَلِّمُهُمُ الْكِتَابَ وَالْحِكْمَةَ وَيُزَكِّيهِمْ

"O our Lord! Raise up in their midst a Messenger from among them who shall recite unto them Your revelations and shall instruct them in the scripture and in the *Hikmah* and shall make them grow" (*al-Baqarah* 129).

كَمَا أَرْسَلْنَا فِيكُمْ رَسُولاً مِنْكُمْ يَتْلُو عَلَيْكُمْ آيَاتِنَا وَيُزَكِّيكُمْ وَيُعَلِّمُكُمُ الْكِتَابَ وَالْحِكْمَةَ وَيُعَلِّمُكُمْ مَا لَمْ تَكُونُوا تَعْلَمُونَ

"Even as We have sent unto you a messenger from among you, who recites to you Our revelations and causes you to grow, and teaches you the scripture and the *Hikmah* and teaches you what which you knew not" (*al-Baqarah* 151).

هُوَ الَّذِي بَعَثَ فِي الْأُمِّيِّينَ رَسُولاً مِنْهُمْ يَتْلُو عَلَيْهِمْ آيَاتِهِ وَيُزَكِّيهِمْ وَيُعَلِّمُهُمُ الْكِتَابَ وَالْحِكْمَةَ وَإِنْ كَانُوا مِنْ قَبْلُ لَفِي ضَلَالٍ مُبِينٍ

"He it is who has sent among the unlettered ones a messenger of their own to recite to them His revelations and to make them grow. And to teach them the Book and the *Hikmah*, though heretofore they were indeed in error manifest" (*al-Jumuah* 2).

وَاذْكُرُوا نِعْمَةَ اللَّهِ عَلَيْكُمْ وَمَا أَنزَلَ عَلَيْكُم مِّنْ الْكِتَابِ
وَالْحِكْمَةِ يَعِظُكُم بِهِ

"Remember Allah's grace upon you and that which He has revealed unto you of the Book and the *Hikmah*, whereby he does exhort you" (al-Baqarah 231).

وَاذْكُرْنَ مَا يُتْلَى فِي بُيُوتِكُنَّ مِنْ آيَاتِ اللَّهِ وَالْحِكْمَةِ

"And recite that which is rehearsed in your houses of the revelations of Allah and the *Hikmah*" (al-Ahzaab 34).

After quoting these verses, al-Shafi'ee wrote,

> So God mentioned His Book—which is the Quran—and *Hikmah*, and I have heard that those who are learned in the Quran—whom I approve—hold that *Hikmah* is the sunnah of the Apostle of God. This is like what [God Himself] said; but God knows best! For the Quran is mentioned [first], followed by *Hikmah*; [then] God mentioned His favor to mankind by teaching them the Quran and *Hikmah*. So it is not permissible for *Hikmah* to be called here [anything] save the sunnah of the Apostle of God. For [*Hikmah*] is closely linked to the Book of God, and God has imposed the duty of obedience to His Apostle, and imposed on men the obligation to obey his orders. So it is not permissible to regard anything as a duty save that set forth in the Quran and the sunnah of His Apostle. For [God], as we have [just] stated, prescribed that the belief in His Apostle shall be associated with belief in Him.

> The sunnah of the Apostle makes evident what God means [in the text of His Book], indicating His general and particular [commands]. He associated the *Hikmah* [embodied] in the sunnah with his Book, but

made it subordinate [to the book]. Never has God done this for any of His creatures save His Apostle.[1]

In another verse, Allah describes the swearing of allegiance to the Prophet (peace be upon him) as swearing allegiance to Himself in the following verse,

$$\text{إِنَّ الَّذِينَ يُبَايِعُونَكَ إِنَّمَا يُبَايِعُونَ اللَّهَ يَدُ اللَّهِ فَوْقَ أَيْدِيهِمْ}$$

$$\text{فَمَنْ نَكَثَ فَإِنَّمَا يَنْكُثُ عَلَى نَفْسِهِ وَمَنْ أَوْفَى بِمَا عَاهَدَ}$$

$$\text{عَلَيْهُ اللَّهَ فَسَيُؤْتِيهِ أَجْرًا عَظِيمًا}$$

"Lo those who swear allegiance to you (Muhammad), swear allegiance only unto Allah. The Hand of Allah is above their hands. So whosoever breaks his oath, breaks it only to his soul's hurt; while whosoever keeps his covenant with Allah, on him will He bestow immense reward" (al-Fath 10). Here Allah describes the making of an oath of allegiance to the Messenger of Allah (peace be upon him) as being the same as swearing allegiance to Allah. This implies that obeying the Messenger (peace be upon him) is the same as obeying Allah.

The last relevant verses that shall be discussed in this section are from al-Hujuraat,

$$\text{يَاأَيُّهَا الَّذِينَ آمَنُوا لا تُقَدِّمُوا بَيْنَ يَدَيْ اللَّهِ وَرَسُولِهِ وَاتَّقُوا}$$

$$\text{اللَّهَ إِنَّ اللَّهَ سَمِيعٌ عَلِيمٌ يَاأَيُّهَا الَّذِينَ آمَنُوا لا تَرْفَعُوا}$$

$$\text{أَصْوَاتَكُمْ فَوْقَ صَوْتِ النَّبِيِّ وَلا تَجْهَرُوا لَهُ بِالْقَوْلِ كَجَهْرِ}$$

$$\text{بَعْضِكُمْ لِبَعْضٍ أَنْ تَحْبَطَ أَعْمَالُكُمْ وَأَنْتُمْ لا تَشْعُرُونَ}$$

---

[1] Majid Khadduri, *Islamic Jurisprudence: Shafi'i's Risala* (Baltimore: Johns Hopkins Press, 1961), pp. 111-112. Heretofore referred to al-Shafi'ee. Note that Khadduri had translated the word *hikmah* into wisdom in the above passage but it has been changed here for the sake of consistency.

"O you who believe, be not forward in the presence of Allah and His Messenger. O you who believe, lift not up your voices above the voice of the Prophet, nor speak aloud to him in talk as you speak loudly one to another, lest your works be rendered vain while you perceive not" (*al-Hujuraat* 1-2). Al-Qurtubi stated in his commentary to this verse, "Do not be forward with any statement or action in the presence of Allah or the statements of His Messenger and his actions in those things that you should take from them regarding your religion or worldly life. Whoever prefers his speech or actions over that of the Messenger (peace be upon him) also puts his speech over that of Allah as the Messenger (peace be upon him) is only ordering what Allah has ordered."[1] The latter part of these two verses states that just raising one's voice above the Prophet's voice may lead to the destruction of one's deeds. If that is the case with just raising one's voice above the Prophet's voice, what might be the case of the person who turns away from the Prophet's words, refuses to listen to the commands of the Prophet (peace be upon him) or puts his opinion above the statement of the Messenger of Allah (peace be upon him)?

Before continuing on to discuss some of the hadith of the Prophet (peace be upon him), what one msut conclude from the above verses should be stated.[2]

---

[1] Al-Qurtubi, vol. 16, p. 300.

[2] The reader should note that missing from the above discussion is a set of verses usually used as a proof that the sunnah is divinely inspired. These verses are, "Your companion errs not nor is he deceived. Nor does he speak out of his own desires. It is only an inspiration that is being revealed to him" (*al-Najm* 2-4). The author has not included these verses because there is a difference of opinion over whether they refer to everything the Prophet (peace be upon him) said or specifically to only the Quran. In this discussion, only the verses about which the scholars agree are concerning the sunnah are mentioned. Concerning these verses from *al-Najm*, Al-Saadi said, "This [verse] points out that the sunnah is a revelation of Allah to His Messenger...And he is protected [from making a mistake] in what he relates about Allah and His law as his speech is not derived from his own desires but it is derived from what is being revealed to him." Al-Saadi never mentions that other scholars do not agree with this interpretation.

Based solely on the text of the Quran, one may conclude:

a. It is Allah Himself who has ordered the Muslims to follow and to obey the Prophet Muhammad (peace be upon him). This notion was not a innovation of later jurists, nor is it something open to debate or discussion.

b. If anyone claims to follow the Quran, then he must also follow the sunnah of the Prophet (peace be upon him), as it is the Quran itself that orders the Muslims to follow the Prophet (peace be upon him). Therefore, it is inconsistent to claim to follow the Quran while denying one's obligation to follow the sunnah.

c. Allah has stated severe warnings for anyone who refuses to follow the Messenger (peace be upon him); on the other hand, Allah has promised mercy and forgiveness for those who do follow the way of the Prophet (peace be upon him).

The Prophet's Own Statements Concerning the Importance of the Sunnah

Besides the above verses that point to the necessity of obeying the Messenger of Allah (peace be upon him) and the importance of his sunnah, the Prophet (peace be upon him)

Al-Qaasimi mentions both opinions (that it refers to only to the Quran or to everything the Prophet said) and states that the stronger opinion is that the pronoun (*huwa*, "it") refers only to the Quran, "The object is the Quran, as can be understood from the context as the people who were rejecting [the mission] were referring to the Quran." Al-Raazi has the longest discussion on this point, and he also concludes that the verses refer to the Quran. Cf., Abdul Rahmaan al-Saadi, *Taiseer al-Kareem al-Rahmaan fi Tafseer Kalaam al-Mannaan* (Riyadh: Al-Muasassah al-Saeediyyah), vol. 7, p. 204; Jamaal al-Deen al-Qaasimi, *Mahaasan al-Ta'weel* (Beirut: Daar al-Fikr, 1978), vol. 15, pp. 222-23; Fakhr al-Deen al-Raazi, *Tafseer al-Kabeer* (Beirut: Daar Ihya al-Turaath al-Arabi), vol. 28, pp. 282-83. The verses quoted earlier concerning the revelation of the *Hikmah* are sufficient to prove that the Sunnah is also divinely inspired.

himself clearly stated the importance of his own sunnah and warned about abandoning his sunnah. Now that it has been established that the Quran itself tells Muslims to follow the sunnah, it will be acceptable to use the statements of the Prophet himself as further proof of the importance of the sunnah in Islam and of the obligation to follow the sunnah. What follows are some examples from the hadith of the Prophet (peace be upon him).

The Messenger of Allah (peace be upon him) said,

لا أُلْفِيَنَّ أَحَدَكُمْ مُتَّكِئًا عَلَى أَرِيكَتِهِ يَأْتِيهِ أَمْرٌ مِمَّا أَمَرْتُ بِهِ أَوْ نَهَيْتُ عَنْهُ فَيَقُولُ لا أَدْرِي مَا وَجَدْنَا فِي كِتَابِ اللَّهِ اتَّبَعْنَاهُ

"I do not wish to find anyone of you reclining on a couch and there comes to him one of my commandments or one of my prohibitions and he says about it, 'I do not know, what we find in the book of Allah (only) do we follow.'"[1]

In a similar hadith the Messenger of Allah (peace be upon him) is reported to have prohibited the flesh of domestic donkeys and said,

يُوشِكُ الرَّجُلُ مُتَّكِئًا عَلَى أَرِيكَتِهِ يُحَدَّثُ بِحَدِيثٍ مِنْ حَدِيثِي فَيَقُولُ بَيْنَنَا وَبَيْنَكُمْ كِتَابُ اللَّهِ عَزَّ وَجَلَّ مَا وَجَدْنَا فِيهِ مِنْ حَلَالٍ اسْتَحْلَلْنَاهُ وَمَا وَجَدْنَا فِيهِ مِنْ حَرَامٍ حَرَّمْنَاهُ أَلَّا وَإِنَّ مَا حَرَّمَ رَسُولُ اللَّهِ صَلَّى اللَّهُمَّ عَلَيْهِ وَسَلَّمَ مِثْلُ مَا حَرَّمَ اللَّهُ

"Soon it will be that a man will recline on his couch and will be told a hadith of my hadith and will say, 'Between us and

---

[1] Recorded by al-Baihaqi, al-Shafi'ee, al-Humaidi, Ahmad, Abu Daawood, al-Tirmidhi, Ibn Maajah, Ibn Hibbaan and al-Haakim with a *sahib* chain. According to al-Albaani, it is *sahib*. See Muhammad Naasir al-Deen al-Albaani, *Saheeh al-Jaami al-Sagheer* (Beirut: al-Maktab al-Islaami, 1986), vol. 2, p. 1204.

you is the Book of Allah. What we find allowed therein, we allow. What we find prohibited therein, we prohibit.' But truly, what the Messenger of Allah has forbidden is similar to what Allah has forbidden."[1]

In these two hadith, the Messenger of Allah (peace be upon him) has warned Muslims about people who will neglect the sunnah of the Prophet (peace be upon him) and claim that they need only live by the injunctions of the Quran. In the second hadith, he has stated that what he pronounces as illegal should be treated in the same way as that which Allah has declared illegal. In the latter hadith, the Messenger of Allah (peace be upon him) prohibited the eating of donkey flesh. Nowhere in the Quran is such a prohibition found. But, from the Quran itself, it is known that it is sufficient for the Prophet (peace be upon him) to declare it illegal; no one may consider it legal because it is not mentioned as illegal in the Quran.

The Messenger of Allah (peace be upon him) said,

أَلا إِنِّي أُوتِيتُ الْكِتَابَ وَمِثْلَهُ مَعَهُ

"Verily I have been given the Book and something similar to it with it..."[2] Badr al-Badr said,

> There can be two meanings for this [hadith]: (a) The meaning is that the Messenger of Allah has been given a *batin* (hidden) revelation that is not recited, in the same way that he has been given an apparent [revelation] that is recited. (b) Another meaning it carries is that he has been given the Book which is a revelation that is recited and he has been given its explanation. That is, he has been given the permission to explain what is in the Book, what has

---

[1] Recorded by al-Baihaqi, Ahmad, al-Tirmidhi and ibn Maajah. According to al-Albaani, it is authentic. See al-Albaani, *Saheeh al-Jaami*, vol. 2, p. 1360.
[2] Recorded by Abu Daawood with a *sahih* chain. The rest of the hadith is similar to the first hadith mentioned above.

> general and specific application, and he can increase
> upon its legislation in matters not mentioned by the
> Quran. In that manner lies his duty to order and for
> others to obey his orders in exactly the same manner
> in which [it is obligatory] to follow the clear
> recitation of the Quran.[1]

This hadith can be read together with the verses recorded above concerning the *Hikmah*. This hadith supports the view of al-Shafi'ee that the Prophet (peace be upon him) was not only given the Book but he was also given along with it another type of revelation: the *Hikmah* or sunnah.

The Messenger of Allah (peace be upon him) said, during the farewell pilgrimage,

$$ تَرَكْتُ فِيكُمْ أَمْرَيْنِ لَنْ تَضِلُّوا مَا تَمَسَّكْتُمْ بِهِمَا كِتَابَ اللَّهِ وَسُنَّةَ نَبِيِّهِ $$

"I have left among you two matters that if you adhere to them you will never be misguided: the Book of Allah and the sunnah of His prophet."[2] In another version he stated, "O mankind, listen to what I say and live by it."[3] These hadith and other similar hadith have been narrated by a large number of Companions, and there is, therefore, no doubt about their authenticity. In this hadith the Messenger of Allah (peace be upon him) gave Muslims clear advice: if they wish never to be misguided they need only follow the Book of Allah and the sunnah of the Prophet (peace be upon him). Note that he gave this advice during his final pilgrimage when he knew that his

---

[1] Commentary by Badr al-Badr in Jalaal al-Deen al-Suyooti, *Miftaah al-Jannah fi al-Ihtijaaj bi al-Sunnah* (Kuwait: Daar al-Huda al-Nubuwwa, no date), p. 22, fn. 47. Most of the hadith and other statements found in this chapter may be found in this excellent work by al-Suyooti. Note, however, that many of the reports he uses have weak chains; those have not been used in this work.

[2] Recorded by Maalik, al-Haakim and al-Baihaqi. It is *sahih*.

[3] Recorded by al-Baihaqi with a *hasan* chain.

death was near and it was a farewell advice to the thousands that thronged around him. (Note also that if his sunnah was only to be followed during his lifetime it would have been his duty to tell that to his followers. Otherwise, he would not be fulfilling his mission of conveying the message. Instead, at a time when he knew his death was near he reiterated that Muslims must cling to both the Book of Allah and the sunnah of His Prophet.)

The Messenger of Allah (peace be upon him) said,

لكل عمل شرة ولكل شرة فترة فمن كانت فترته إلى سنتي
فقد اهتدى ومن كانت فترته إلى غير ذلك فقد هلك

"Every action has its period of extreme activity and every action has its period of inactivity. Whosoever keeps his period of inactivity within the limits of my sunnah has been guided aright; whoever goes beyond this limit will, in fact, be destroyed."[1] In this hadith, the Messenger of Allah (peace be upon him) has pointed to the fact that the ones who are truly guided and who will be saved in the Hereafter are those whose periods of inactivity—in doing good deeds, voluntary work and so on—are within the limits of the sunnah of the Prophet (peace be upon him). It is often the case that some people are very active for a period of time and then experience a lack of enthusiasm, and their deeds begin to diminish. If the low points are beyond the limits established by the sunnah (for example, the person completely stops praying in congregation) then these low points will lead to destruction. According to this hadith, for a person to be rightly guided he must always stay within the limits established by the sunnah of the Prophet Muhammad (peace be upon him). Actually, even in periods of

---

[1]   Recorded by Ahmad, ibn Hibbaan and others with a *sahih* chain. According to al-Albaani, it is *sahih*. See Muhammad Naasir al-Deen al-Albaani, *Sahih al-Targheb wa al-Tarheeb* (Riyadh: Maktabah al-Maarif, 1988), vol. 1, p. 98.

enthusiasm the person must be careful to stay within the limits set by the Prophet (peace be upon him), since his sunnah is the standard by which acts are judged. Thus, at either extreme, of activity or inactivity, the Muslim must stay within the sunnah. This is a clear warning for those who abandon the sunnah altogether and for those who introduce new concepts into the religion and try to add to the sunnah of the Prophet (peace be upon him).

In the following hadith the Messenger of Allah (peace be upon him) referred to his own judgment as "judging by the Book of Allah." Abu Hurairah and Zaid ibn Khaalid Juhani reported that two people quarreled and came to the Messenger of Allah (peace be upon him). One said, "O Messenger of Allah, decide between us in accordance with the Book of Allah." The other, who was more sensible, said, "Yes, Messenger of Allah, decide in accordance with the Book of Allah and permit me to speak." The Messenger of Allah (peace be upon him) allowed him to speak. He said, "My son was employed by this man and he [my son] committed adultery with his wife. The people said that my son deserves to be stoned. I gave the man one hundred sheep and a slave girl as a ransom on my son's behalf. I then asked the learned men and they said that my son should be whipped a hundred times and exiled for a year and that his wife is liable to be stoned to death as a punishment for her action." The Messenger of Allah (peace be upon him) said, "I will make a decision for you both in accordance with the Book of Allah. Your sheep and the slave girl are your property, take them back. The son shall be whipped a hundred times and exiled for a year." He then asked Unais Aslami to go to the other man's wife and see if she admitted to the crime, in which case he should have her stoned. She confessed and was stoned to death. (Recorded by Maalik.) This judgment, whipping a hundred times *with* an exile for a year, is not to be found in the Quran; yet the Prophet (peace be upon him) called it "deciding in accordance with the Book of Allah." This is because the commands of the

Prophet (peace be upon him) are, in fact, on the same level in
Islamic law, with respect to implementation, as the Quran,
both being inspired by Allah. This is a result of the legislative
authority of the Messenger (peace be upon him) that comes
from Allah Himself in the Quran.

Al-Bukhari records the following moving hadith:

جَاءَتْ مَلائِكَةٌ إِلَى النَّبِيِّ صَلَّى اللَّهم عَلَيْهِ وَسَلَّمَ وَهُوَ نَائِمٌ
فَقَالَ بَعْضُهُمْ إِنَّهُ نَائِمٌ وَقَالَ بَعْضُهُمْ إِنَّ الْعَيْنَ نَائِمَةٌ وَالْقَلْبَ
يَقْظَانُ فَقَالُوا إِنَّ لِصَاحِبِكُمْ هَذَا مَثَلاً فَاضْرِبُوا لَهُ مَثَلاً فَقَالَ
بَعْضُهُمْ إِنَّهُ نَائِمٌ وَقَالَ بَعْضُهُمْ إِنَّ الْعَيْنَ نَائِمَةٌ وَالْقَلْبَ يَقْظَانُ
فَقَالُوا مَثَلُهُ كَمَثَلِ رَجُلٍ بَنَى دَارًا وَجَعَلَ فِيهَا مَأْدُبَةً وَبَعَثَ
دَاعِيًا فَمَنْ أَجَابَ الدَّاعِيَ دَخَلَ الدَّارَ وَأَكَلَ مِنَ الْمَأْدُبَةِ وَمَنْ
لَمْ يُجِب الدَّاعِيَ لَمْ يَدْخُلِ الدَّارَ وَلَمْ يَأْكُلْ مِنَ الْمَأْدُبَةِ فَقَالُوا
أَوِّلُوهَا لَهُ يَفْقَهْهَا فَقَالَ بَعْضُهُمْ إِنَّهُ نَائِمٌ وَقَالَ بَعْضُهُمْ إِنَّ
الْعَيْنَ نَائِمَةٌ وَالْقَلْبَ يَقْظَانُ فَقَالُوا فَالدَّارُ الْجَنَّةُ وَالدَّاعِي
مُحَمَّدٌ صَلَّى اللَّهم عَلَيْهِ وَسَلَّمَ فَمَنْ أَطَاعَ مُحَمَّدًا صَلَّى اللَّهم
عَلَيْهِ وَسَلَّمَ فَقَدْ أَطَاعَ اللَّهَ وَمَنْ عَصَى مُحَمَّدًا صَلَّى اللَّهم
عَلَيْهِ وَسَلَّمَ فَقَدْ عَصَى اللَّهَ وَمُحَمَّدٌ صَلَّى اللَّهم عَلَيْهِ وَسَلَّمَ
فَرْقٌ بَيْنَ النَّاسِ

Some angels came to the Messenger of Allah (peace be upon
him) while he was sleeping. Some of the angels said, "He is
sleeping [therefore leave him]." The others answered, "His

eyes sleep but his heart is alert." They said, "Your companion is like this" and they propounded a similitude. They said, "His similitude is like a person who builds a house and provides a tablespread filled with provisions and calls the other people to it. Those who respond to his call enter the house and eat from the tablespread. Those who do not respond to his call do not enter the house nor do they eat from the tablespread." Some of the angels said, "Give him its interpretation." Others replied, "He is sleeping." They were answered by others who said, "His eyes sleep but his heart is alert." So they explained the parable to him, saying, "The house is the paradise and the one inviting is Muhammad (peace be upon him). Whoever obeys Muhammad (peace be upon him) has verily obeyed Allah. Whoever disobeys Muhammad (peace be upon him) has verily disobeyed Allah. And Muhammad (peace be upon him) is a separator of humanity." In this hadith one can see the mistake committed by those who deny the sunnah or who give it little importance. The Prophet Muhammad (peace be upon him) with his perfect example, his orders and prohibitions, has made the way clear for Muslims and has called them to the path to paradise in the same way that a person invites another to dinner. By ignoring this call a person would be ignoring, in fact, the path to Allah. The end result for those who do not bother to pattern their lives after the sunnah of the Prophet (peace be upon him) is that they will not be allowed to enjoy the fruits of paradise. Lastly, the angels said that the Messenger of Allah (peace be upon him) separates mankind. That is to say that his message distinguishes the believers from the unbelievers—those who accept his invitation by following him and those who reject his invitation by rejecting his sunnah and way of life. This hadith, therefore, establishes the following of the sunnah as one of the vital signs of faith.

The Messenger of Allah (peace be upon him) said,

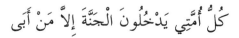

كُلُّ أُمَّتِي يَدْخُلُونَ الْجَنَّةَ إِلاَّ مَنْ أَبَى

"All of my nation will enter paradise except those who refuse."
His companions asked, "Who would refuse?" He answered,

مَنْ أَطَاعَنِي دَخَلَ الْجَنَّةَ وَمَنْ عَصَانِي فَقَدْ أَبَى

"Those who obey me will enter paradise; those who disobey
me have refused (to enter paradise)." (Recorded by al-Bukhari
and others.) Here again one can see the true and simple beauty
of the Prophet's role. The Messenger of Allah (peace be upon
him), by his sunnah or way of life, showed the path for
Muslims that leads them directly to paradise. If the Muslim
accepts to follow him, he will not be refusing the invitation to
paradise. If the Muslim refuses to follow him, he is, in effect,
refusing to enter paradise. Note that the Prophet (peace be
upon him) was referring to the people who believe in him ("his
nation"), thus showing, as in other hadith, that Allah had
informed the Prophet (peace be upon him) that there would
exist people who would refuse to follow his sunnah.

Many more hadith can be added to the ones mentioned
above but for the sake of brevity it will be best to stop here.
The following are the conclusions that can be made from the
hadith of the Prophet (peace be upon him):

(a) The Prophet (peace be upon him), in conveying the
message as he was commissioned to by Allah, made it
explicitly clear on many occasions that the Muslim must
follow his sunnah in order to be rightly guided.

(b) Allah vouchsafed to the Prophet (peace be upon
him) the knowledge that in later times there would come
people who would reject his sunnah and refuse to follow his
way of life. Therefore, the Prophet (peace be upon him)
warned his followers about such people and about such
concepts.

(c) From the hadith of the Prophet (peace be upon
him), a Muslim can be certain that if he is following the
Prophet's sunnah he is, in fact, on the straight path, the path
leading directly to Allah's pleasure, forgiveness and Paradise.

The Prophet's Companions' View of the Sunnah

Next to the Messenger of Allah, it was his Companions who best understood the true meaning of the Quran and who best understood in what manner a believer should behave. The Messenger of Allah (peace be upon him) himself described his generation as the best of all generations. Indeed, it was through the Companions that Allah safeguarded the Quran, and it was through them that the following generations learned vital and detailed aspects of Islam. Below are mentioned some of the most prominent and knowledgeable Companions and their positions toward the sunnah of the Prophet (peace be upon him).

Al-Bukhari and Muslim record in their *Sahih*s that the companion Abdullah ibn Masood said, "Allah curses the one who tattoos, the one who asks to be tattooed, the one who plucks the eyebrows and the one who files her teeth in order to change the creation of Allah." This statement reached Umm Yaqoob, who came to him and said, "It has come to me that you said such and such." He answered her, "What is wrong with me if I curse what the Messenger of Allah has cursed and is to be found in the Book of Allah." She told him, "I have read [the Quran] from cover to cover yet I did not find [in there what you have stated]." Abdullah told her, "If you have read it you would have found it there. Did you not read, 'Verily, what the Messenger gives you take and what he forbids for you, abstain from' [*al-Hashr* 7]?" She said, "Yes." He replied, "He [the Messenger of Allah (peace be upon him)] forbade these things." In this incident there is a Companion mentioning a ruling of the Prophet (peace be upon him) as a ruling of Allah. The lady, Umm Yaqoob, misunderstood Abdullah and thought that he was referring to a specific verse wherein the actions he stated were specifically mentioned. In Abdullah's explanation he shows that what the Messenger of Allah (peace be upon him) prohibited has, in fact, the same status as something that Allah explicitly prohibited in the Quran. His proof was the seventh verse of *al-Hashr* that was discussed earlier.

Abu Daawood recorded from Saeed ibn al-Musayyab that Umar said, "The divorced wife is not entitled to any inheritance out of the blood money [paid due to] her husband [having been killed]." Al-Dhuhaak ibn Sufyaan told Umar that the Messenger of Allah (peace be upon him) had once written to him that the wife of Ashyam al-Dhahabi was to be given an inheritance from the blood money of her husband. Umar then reversed his decision and gave a portion of the blood money to the widow. This incident reveals the view of the sunnah held by Umar ibn al-Khattaab, the second caliph of Islam, who was known for his knowledge and insight into the religion. Unknowingly, he had taken a position that was contrary to the decision of the Messenger of Allah (peace be upon him). Upon finding out that his decision contradicted the sunnah, he immediately abandoned his opinion and completely submitted to the decision of the Prophet (peace be upon him).

In another situation involving Umar[1] a certain decision was made because one Companion reported a hadith of the Prophet (peace be upon him) concerning a similar incident. After this, Umar stated, "If we did not hear this [hadith] we would have given a different judgment. We would have judged according to our opinions." Here again, as al-Shafi'ee commented, Umar's decision would not have been the same as the decision of the Prophet's but since he knew the decision of the Prophet (peace be upon him), Umar knew that there was no say for him in the matter and, furthermore, he knew that the believer must accept the decision of the Prophet (peace be upon him) even if it goes against his own opinion.

In an incident recorded in the *Sahih*s of al-Bukhari and Muslim, it is reported that Umar had the intention to travel to al-Shaam ("Greater Syria"), where a plague had broken out.

---

[1] Quoted in al-Suyooti, *Miftaah al-Jannah*, pp. 49-50.

When he came upon the Companion Abdul Rahmaan ibn Auf, Abdul Rahmaan told him that the Prophet (peace be upon him) said, "If you hear that there is a plague in a certain land, do not set out for that land; and if you happen to be in that land, do not depart from that land." Upon hearing this Umar knew that it would not be right for him to proceed to al-Shaam; so he returned to Madinah. In another incident, also recorded by al-Bukhari, it is said that Umar abstained from taking the *jizyah* (the poll tax) from the Magians until Abdul Rahmaan ibn Auf bore testimony that the Prophet (peace be upon him) took it from them. This incident demonstrates that even the most important affairs of government are subservient to the commands and sunnah of the Prophet (peace be upon him). By hesitating in accepting the *jizyah* from the Magians (until he could confirm that the Prophet had actually done so), Umar was adversely affecting the budget of the expanding Islamic state.

Al-Baihaqi and al-Haakim record, with *sahih* chains, that Taawoos used to pray two units (Ar., *rakah*) after the obligatory afternoon prayer. Ibn Abbaas told him to refrain from doing so. He replied that he would not abandon them. Ibn Abbaas then said, "The Messenger of Allah (peace be upon him) forbade praying after the afternoon prayer. Therefore I do not know if you will be punished or rewarded [for this prayer that you perform]. Verily Allah said, 'It is not becoming of a believing man or believing woman, after Allah and His Messenger have decided an affair, that they should have any choice in the matter' [*al-Ahzaab* 36]." From this incident one can see the importance of the commands of the Prophet (peace be upon him). Even in the virtuous acts of worship one must be aware of the regulations laid down by the Prophet (peace be upon him). Ibn Abbaas told Taawoos, "I do not know if you will be rewarded or punished" for the prayer Taawoos performed. How could it be that he might be punished for praying? It is because he was, in fact, violating the commands of the Prophet (peace be upon him). This shows that all deeds, no matter how virtuous they may seem, must be approved by the Quran or sunnah to be acceptable.

Ibn Umar narrated that the Messenger of Allah (peace be upon him) said, "Permit your women to go to the mosques at night." One of Abdullah's sons stated that he would not do so. Upon hearing this Abdullah struck his chest and said, "I relate a hadith of the Messenger of Allah (peace be upon him) to you and you say, 'No.'"[1] In this incident Abdullah ibn Umar, son of Umar ibn al-Khattaab, one of the most knowledgeable of the Companions, struck his son's chest because his son showed some inclination not to abide by a command from the Prophet (peace be upon him). In Abdullah's statement it is clear that he was implying, "I am telling you a statement of the Messenger (peace be upon him) and you think you have some say in the matter. Indeed, you do not."

The following incident was recorded by al-Bukhari and Muslim (the wording of the report is Muslim's): Qataadah narrated, "We were sitting in a group with Imraan ibn Husain and Bushair ibn Kaab. Imraan narrated to us that on a certain occasion the Messenger of Allah (peace be upon him) said, 'Modesty is a virtue through and through,' or said, 'Modesty is completely good.' Upon hearing this Bushair ibn Kaab said, 'We find in certain books or books [of wisdom] that it is God-inspired peace of mind or sobriety for the sake of Allah and there is also some weakness in it.' Imraan was so much enraged that his eyes became red and he said, 'I am narrating to you a hadith of the Messenger of Allah (peace be upon him) and you are contradicting it.'" Abdul Hamid Siddique commented on this hadith, saying,

> This hadith explains the status of a Prophet. The source of prophetic knowledge is divine; it is, therefore, perfect and free from all kinds of error. Human wisdom is based on observation, experience

---

[1] This was recorded by Ahmad, Muslim and Abu Daawood. It is also recorded that ibn Umar refused to talk to his son after this incident.

and inference and can, therefore, be never infallible. This is the reason why humanity has always been exhorted to follow the commands of the Prophets and not those of the philosophers. This hadith also clearly brings into light the position of the Hadith. It is a part of divine knowledge and, therefore, it should be accepted with religious devotion.[1]

In this hadith Bushair is referring to some of the old books of the Arabs which contained their "wisdom." But how can it be wisdom when it contradicts what the All-Wise has revealed? How could it be considered wisdom when the Messenger (peace be upon him) has stated the opposite to be true? How can one respect any contradictory statement after the Prophet (peace be upon him) has spoken?[2]

Al-Bukhari recorded that Ali and Uthmaan were on the road between Makkah and Madinah. At the time Uthmaan was preventing, for specific reasons, people from performing *muta* (that is, combining the *hajj* and *umrah* under one visit but with a break between them and with only one intention). Ali had made the intention: "We are coming for *hajj* and *umrah* together with a break in between them." Uthmaan said to him, "You see that I am preventing the people from doing so yet you do it?" Ali answered him, "I cannot leave the sunnah of the Messenger of Allah (peace be upon him) for the statement of anyone of mankind." In this incident one again sees that the Companions of the Prophet (peace be upon him) would accept no authority save that of Allah or His Messenger (peace be upon him). In this case Ali found Uthmaan's juristic reasoning

---

[1] Abdul Hamid Siddiqui, trans. and commentator, *Sahih Muslim* (Lahore: Sh. Muhammad Ashraf, 1972), vol. 1, p. 28, fn. 87.

[2] Unfortunately, one can find Muslims who follow ideas that contradict what the Prophet (peace be upon him) has stated. For some, especially from lesser developed countries, anything that comes from the "scientific West" is considered superior to what they have of "traditional wisdom." In some cases, this may be due to some kind of inferiority complex. All Muslims must realize that what they possess is the truth and there is no knowledge superior to what they have.

to be wrong, as he noted that Uthmaan did not correctly understand the sunnah concerning *muta*. One point that should be noted is that this incident occurred while Uthmaan was the caliph of the Islamic state. This incident demonstrates that the Companions knew that even the highest authority in the land, as pious as he might be, cannot impose a law that goes against the sunnah of the Prophet (peace be upon him).

It is recorded concerning many Companions, through a number of authentic chains, that if any problem arose they would seek its solution, first, in the Book of Allah. If they did not find the solution there, they would search the sunnah of the Prophet (peace be upon him) for the answer.[1] Failing to find a solution, then, and only then, would they resort to personal reasoning. This was the way of Abu Bakr, the first caliph, and of Umar, Abu Bakr's successor, and, in fact, of all of the Companions of the Prophet (peace be upon him).[2]

From the above one may conclude the following:

(a) There was a consensus of opinion among the Companions (the best and most knowledgeable of all generations) that it was obligatory for them to follow the sunnah of the Prophet (peace be upon him), and none of them ever claimed to be free of this obligation.

(b) After the death of the Prophet (peace be upon him), Muslims still agreed that they must follow the sunnah of the Prophet (peace be upon him).

(c) The sunnah of the Prophet (peace be upon him) is to be applied to all aspects of life, from worship to government, and even the leader of the state does not have the

---

[1] Whether the Quran should be looked to first and then the sunnah or if both of them should be taken together is a matter of dispute. A complete and detailed discussion of this question is beyond the scope of this work. However, it is clear that the above reports do not mean that the sunnah does not explain and further clarify the meaning of the Quran.

[2] One can find no report whatsoever of any of the Companions not behaving in this manner.

right to rule in contradiction to the sunnah of the Prophet (peace be upon him).

Scholarly Opinion Regarding the Sunnah

In this section, commentary will be kept to minimum. After the above three sections, lengthy comments should not be necessary. Here will be recorded statements from some of the leading scholars throughout the ages to show that all of the great scholars of Islam have agreed that it is obligatory for all Muslims to follow the sunnah, or way, of the Prophet Muhammad (peace be upon him).[1]

Ibn Khuzaimah said, "No one can say anything if the Messenger of Allah (peace be upon him) has already spoken [on a topic] and it comes to us through a sound chain."

The famous scholar Mujaahid said, "We accept some sayings and reject others of everybody save the Messenger of Allah (peace be upon him)." In other words, all of his statements are to be accepted.

Ibn al-Mubaarak reported that he heard Imam Abu Haneefah say, "If a report comes from the Messenger of Allah, then it is the head and eye [of the matter: there is no room for dispute in such a case]. If reports come from the Companions of the Prophet, we choose from among their statements. If reports come from the Followers [the generation after that of the Companions], they are men and we are men."

Urwah said, "Following the sunnah is the establishing of the religion."

Uthmaan ibn Umar reported that a man came to Imam Maalik and asked him a question. Imam Maalik replied, "The Messenger of Allah (peace be upon him) said such and such." The man asked, "What is your opinion?" Maalik simply

---

[1] The following statements can be found in al-Suyooti, *Miftah al-Jannah*, pp. 74f.

answered him with the following verse of the Quran which contains a stern warning,

فَلْيَحْذَرِ الَّذِينَ يُخَالِفُونَ عَنْ أَمْرِهِ أَنْ تُصِيبَهُمْ فِتْنَةٌ أَوْ يُصِيبَهُمْ عَذَابٌ أَلِيمٌ

"Let those who conspire to evade orders beware lest a trial (Ar., *fitnah*) or a painful punishment befall them" (*al-Noor* 63).

Al-Rabeeah reported that Imam al-Shafi'ee said, "If you find anything in my book that differs from the sunnah of the Messenger of Allah (peace be upon him), then speak according to the sunnah of the Messenger and leave what I have said."

Sufyaan al-Auzaaee said, "The Companions of the Messenger of Allah and those who followed them in good deeds based their lives on five [principles]: sticking to the community, following the sunnah, building [and attending] the mosques, reciting the Quran and jihad in the way of Allah."

Ibn al-Mubaarak mentioned the hadith, "A group of my nation will not cease being victorious in the truth and will not be harmed by others until the Hour arrives," and stated, "In my opinion this group could only be the people of hadith."

Abu Sulaimaan al-Daarimi said, "Perhaps there pricks my heart the problems and discussions of my day and I never accept anything except with the testimony of the two just witnesses: the Book and the sunnah."

Ahmad ibn Abu al-Huwari said, "Whoever does a deed that is not in accordance with the sunnah has, in fact, done a vain deed."

Hasan ibn Attiyah said, "The Angel Gabriel used to reveal to the Messenger of Allah (peace be upon him) the sunnah in the same way that he revealed to him the Quran. He taught it to him like he taught him the Quran."

Note that although all of the above scholars (and thousands of other scholars) lived after the death of the Messenger of Allah (peace be upon him), none of them ever even remotely hinted at the possibility that the sunnah was only to be obeyed during the Prophet's lifetime and not for all time until the Day of Judgment. Indeed, such a thought is an innovation of recent times that has no foundation whatsoever, as can be seen from the preceding three sections.

The Roles of the Messenger (peace be upon him)

Those who want to attack Islam try to separate the Quran and Islam from the sunnah of the Prophet (peace be upon him). Such people are clearly wrong. The sunnah is, in fact, the living Quran and its embodied spirit. As Aishah said, "The character of the Messenger of Allah was the Quran." (Recorded by al-Bukhari and others.) The enemies of Islam know the value and the importance of the sunnah to the whole structure of Islam. This is why they have spared no efforts in attacking it during the past few centuries. Unfortunately, among Muslims themselves are people who have taken up this call of the enemies of Islam. The Quran, the hadith and the consensus of all of the Companions and scholars of Islam clearly demonstrate that the sunnah of the Messenger of Allah (peace be upon him) must be obeyed by Muslims. It is that way of life that is the life *par excellence* of the believer in Allah, the Last Day, the Resurrection and the Final Judgment.

Upon further study of the above Quranic verses, as well as others, one can see that the importance of the Messenger of Allah lies in certain roles that he fulfills for the nation of Islam. These roles further establish the indispensability of following the sunnah and hadith. Many scholars have enumerated these roles. Although many roles of the Prophet (peace be upon him) could be discussed, the discussion here will be limited to the following four roles:

267

explainer of the Quran, independent legislator, perfect example, and object of obedience.

The Prophet Muhammad (peace be upon him) as the Explainer of the Quran

This topic was discussed in greater detail in an earlier issue of *al-Basheer*.[1] Due to space limitations, this material will not all be repeated here. The following are just some summary statements.

Allah says in the Quran,

$$وَأَنزَلْنَا إِلَيْكَ الذِّكْرَ لِتُبَيِّنَ لِلنَّاسِ مَا نُزِّلَ إِلَيْهِمْ وَلَعَلَّهُمْ يَتَفَكَّرُونَ$$

"And We have revealed unto you (Muhammad) the reminder so you may expound unto all of mankind that which has been revealed for them. So perchance they may ponder" (*al-Nahl* 44). Al-Albaani writes that this verse has two meanings. First, the Messenger of Allah (peace be upon him) is not to conceal anything of the revelation that he has received but he must convey all of it to mankind. Second, it means that the Messenger of Allah (peace be upon him) has the duty of explaining the finer details of the Quran and of demonstrating how the Quran is to be applied.[2]

Obviously, Allah would not burden the Messenger (peace be upon him) with that duty unless He also gave the Prophet (peace be upon him) the necessary knowledge to explain the Quran. Otherwise, "expounding unto mankind

---

[1] See Jamaal al-Deen Zarabozo, "The Basics of *Tafseer*" (*al-Basheer*, Vol. 1, No. 2, July 1987), pp. 16-19. Such a discussion may also be found in Jamaal al-Deen Zarabozo, *How to Approach and Undersand the Quran* (Boulder, CO: Al-Basheer Company for Publications and Translations, 1999), pp. 212-224.

[2] See Muhammad Naasir al-Deen al-Albaani, *Manzalat al-Sunnah fi al-Islaam* (Kuwait: al-Daar al-Salafiyyah, 1980), p. 6.

what has been revealed" would be an impossible task and Allah does not burden any soul beyond what it can bear. Thus the Prophet (peace be upon him), when he spoke or acted, was implementing and explaining the Quran according to the knowledge that Allah had bestowed upon him for this purpose. This was in order for him to fulfill the role of "the explainer of the revelation." Hence, whenever the Messenger of Allah (peace be upon him) explained or applied any verse, this explanation or application was based on Allah's intention or purpose behind the verse, the knowledge of which Allah had vouchsafed unto the Prophet (peace be upon him).

The verse also states that if anyone truly seeks Allah's explanation and application of the Quran, then, as Allah states, he must look to the sunnah of the Messenger of Allah (peace be upon him). In the above verse it is clearly stated that this is one of the roles of the Prophet (peace be upon him); he is to explain the Quran to mankind. If such a role was not necessary, the Quran could have been revealed unto a mountain with no need for a Messenger to accompany it. But Allah, in His infinite wisdom, did not do so and left it to mankind to ponder over the reason for this action.

The functions of the Prophet (peace be upon him) with respect to the Quran may be summarized as follows:

(1) explaining the general and specific ordinances of the Quran,

(2) explaining the details and applications of the Quranic commandments or prohibitions,

(3) giving the exact meaning of some phrases whose meanings were ambiguous or had many possible meanings,

(4) giving additional ordinances and regulations that are not to be found in the Quran but which make up part of the religion of Islam,

(5) clarifying which verses are abrogated and which are not, and

(6) emphasizing and stressing, by his own speech, the meanings of numerous Quranic verses.

The correct understanding of the Quran cannot be achieved without reference to the Prophet (peace be upon him) and the manner in which he applied the Quran. This is why all scholars of Quranic exegesis are in agreement that the first source of finding the meaning of the verses of the Quran is other relevant verses of the Quran itself. The second source is, undoubtedly, the sayings and actions of the Messenger of Allah (peace be upon him), as, indeed, it was one of his roles that he should explain the Quran and put it into practice in the exact manner in which it was meant to be put into practice. After Saeed ibn Jubair related some hadith of the Prophet (peace be upon him), a man came to him and said, "In the Book of Allah is something that differs from what you have said," to which Saeed replied, "The Messenger of Allah knows the Book of Allah much better than you do." He was absolutely correct. Indeed, the Messenger of Allah (peace be upon him) knows the Book of Allah better than anyone of this creation and anyone who claims to know it or understand it better than the Prophet (peace be upon him) is an apostate.

The Messenger of Allah (peace be upon him) as an "Independent Source of Law"

One of the roles of the Messenger of Allah (peace be upon him) was to be a source of law and what he decreed must be accepted as part of the Islamic law or *Shareeah*. In previous pages, there are examples in which the Prophet (peace be upon him) stated legislation that was not found in the Quran. Allah, the Most High, did not include all of the laws of Islam in the Quran. Some of the Islamic laws Allah instituted only through the sayings and deeds of His Messenger (peace be upon him).

Allah says in the Quran,

يَأْمُرُهُمْ بِالْمَعْرُوفِ وَيَنْهَاهُمْ عَنِ الْمُنكَرِ وَيُحِلُّ لَهُمُ
الطَّيِّبَاتِ وَيُحَرِّمُ عَلَيْهِمُ الْخَبَائِثَ وَيَضَعُ عَنْهُمْ إِصْرَهُمْ
وَالأَغْلالَ الَّتِي كَانَتْ عَلَيْهِمْ

"For he [the Prophet (peace be upon him)] commands them what is just and forbids them what is evil; He allows them as lawful what is good and pure and prohibits them from what is bad and impure. He releases them from their heavy burdens and from the yokes that are upon them" (*al-Araaf* 157). This verse is a description of the Messenger of Allah (peace be upon him). In this verse Allah describes the Messenger of Allah as being the one who "allows them as lawful..." This is because the Messenger of Allah (peace be upon him) himself has been commissioned by Allah to give commandments and issue regulations. In this manner, what the Messenger of Allah (peace be upon him) ordered is similar to what Allah has ordered.

Al-Baihaqi recorded that Imraan ibn Husain mentioned the intercession of the Prophet (peace be upon him). A person said to him, "O Abu Najeed, you relate hadith [concerning topics] not found in the Quran." Imraan became angered and told that person, "Have you read the Quran?" The man answered, "Yes!" Imraan told him, "Did you find therein that the night prayer is four units, and the sunset prayer is three and the morning prayer is two and the noon prayer is four and the afternoon prayer is four?" Imraan told him further, "From whom do you take these ordinances? Do you not take them from the Messenger of Allah?"[1] No Muslim claims that the morning prayer's being only two units is not part of the Islamic law because it is not explicitly mentioned in the Quran. Hence, one is forced to admit that this ordinance came not

---

[1] For the rest of the incident see al-Suyooti, *Miftaah al-Jannah*, p. 21.

from the Quran but from the Messenger of Allah (peace be upon him) who is, therefore, an independent source of law.

It is because the Messenger of Allah (peace be upon him) is an independent source of Islamic law that one can find certain sunnah actions that seem to have no source or related text in the Quran. On this point Imam al-Shafi'ee has written,

> For the Apostle has laid down a sunnah [on matters] for which there is a text in the Book of God as well as for others concerning which there is no [specific] text. But whatever he laid down in the sunnah God has ordered us to obey, and He regards [our] obedience to him as obedience to Him, and [our] refusal to obey him as disobedience to Him for which no man will be forgiven.[1]

The Prophet Muhammad (peace be upon him) as a Model of Behavior

Allah says in the Quran,

لَقَدْ كَانَ لَكُمْ فِي رَسُولِ اللَّهِ أُسْوَةٌ حَسَنَةٌ لِمَنْ كَانَ يَرْجُو
اللَّهَ وَالْيَوْمَ الْآخِرَ وَذَكَرَ اللَّهَ كَثِيرًا

"An excellent model you have in Allah's Messenger, for all whose hope is in Allah, and in the Final Day and who often remember Allah" (*al-Ahzaab* 21). This verse brings to light another role of the Messenger of Allah (peace be upon him). Instead of sending an angel or something similar to an angel with the message of Islam, Allah always sent only human beings as messengers and prophets. Allah states in the Quran that these humans married and had children and lived among the people. Allah alone knows the complete wisdom behind

---

[1] Al-Shafi'ee, *Risala*, p. 119.

this course of action. Some scholars point to the fact that Allah sent such humans in order to give the believers a perfect example of how the message is to be applied in everyday human affairs. Believers have an actual human example before them. The example has shown believers their capabilities as human beings (as well as their limitations) and proves to them that they are, in fact, capable of fulfilling the requirements and commands of the religion in a manner comparable to the manner in which the Prophet (peace be upon him) himself had performed them.

Imagine the problem the believers would have faced if they had not been given such a perfect example. One can look to the example of the ascetics of Christianity (who no longer possessed the perfect example of their messenger because of the loss of historic material) to see to what extremes many may go to "please their Lord." Allah praises fasting, but how often should one fast? Possibly every day? What about continuous fasting? In Islam, the answers to all of these types of questions are found in the example of the Prophet (peace be upon him). His exact mode of behavior is known and captured in the hadith literature. Therefore, a Muslim knows "how far" he needs to go to please His Lord.

One is reminded by *al-Ahzaab*, verse 21, of the story of the three who, upon asking about the Messenger of Allah's sunnah, said that they could do more than what the Prophet (peace be upon him) was doing. One said that he would fast every day, another would spend the whole night in prayer, while the other would never marry. Upon hearing this the Messenger of Allah (peace be upon him) became angry and stated that sometimes he would fast and sometimes he would not, he would sleep part of the night and pray part of the night, and he would wed. After stating this the Prophet (peace be upon him) clearly warned,

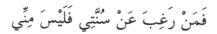

"One who turns away from my sunnah is not of me."[1] In other words, one who rejects the Prophet's sunnah is, in fact, rejecting his role as Messenger and Example for the believers and is in effect rejecting him as the Prophet of Allah (peace be upon him). On another occasion a Companion asked about kissing while fasting. A wife of the Prophet (peace be upon him) informed him that she and the Prophet (peace be upon him) would kiss while he was fasting. The Companion replied that he was not of the same nature as the Messenger of Allah (peace be upon him) and therefore he would refrain from kissing while fasting although he knew that the Prophet (peace be upon him) considered it lawful. The Prophet (peace be upon him) replied to this man's misconception by stating that he was the most aware of Allah and the most knowledgeable regarding Allah and He likes and dislikes. He clearly stated,

$$ مَا بَالُ أَقْوَامٍ يَتَنَزَّهُونَ عَنِ الشَّيْءِ أَصْنَعُهُ فَوَاللَّهِ إِنِّي أَعْلَمُهُمْ بِاللَّهِ وَأَشَدُّهُمْ لَهُ خَشْيَةً $$

"What is wrong with a people that they refrain from doing something that I do. By Allah, I am certainly the most knowledgeable of Allah and the most fearful of Him." (Recorded by al-Bukhari.) Hence, he is the example that the believer must follow.

A Muslim, by the grace of Allah, can read the hadith of the Messenger of Allah (peace be upon him) and practically visualize the actions of this perfect model. This is a special blessing that has been vouchsafed to the nation of Muhammad (peace be upon him) only. The previous communities never established the system of reports from their prophets that allowed them to preserve the details of their prophets' lives. That valuable information has been lost for them but it has been saved in the case of the final prophet (peace be upon

---

[1] Recorded by al-Bukhari and Muslim.

274

him), so that all of mankind may learn this information and follow that excellent example.

Al-Shaukaani wrote that "the one who hopes for Allah," in this verse from *al-Ahzaab*, is the one who believes in Allah and is seeking His pleasure and reward. Hence the verse implies that if one truly believes in Allah and the Last Day and remembers Allah often, he should pattern his life after the one whom Allah Himself called "the excellent example."[1]

Allah also says about the Prophet (peace be upon him),

وَكَذَلِكَ أَوْحَيْنَا إِلَيْكَ رُوحًا مِنْ أَمْرِنَا مَا كُنْتَ تَدْرِي مَا الْكِتَابُ وَلَا الْإِيمَانُ وَلَكِنْ جَعَلْنَاهُ نُورًا نَهْدِي بِهِ مَنْ نَشَاءُ مِنْ عِبَادِنَا وَإِنَّكَ لَتَهْدِي إِلَى صِرَاطٍ مُسْتَقِيمٍ

"And thus have We inspired in you [Muhammad] a spirit of Our command, you knew not what the scripture was, nor what the faith was. But We have made it a light whereby We guide whom We will of Our bondmen. *And lo! You verily do guide unto a right path*" (al-Shooraa 52). In the Quran, Allah describes two very general types of guidance: the type of guidance that only Allah gives which is actually an opening of the heart to the truth, as in the verse, "Allah guides whomsoever He wills;" and a second type of guidance in the form of showing what is the correct path to follow, as in the verses,

ذَلِكَ الْكِتَابُ لَا رَيْبَ فِيهِ هُدًى لِلْمُتَّقِينَ

"This is the book in which there is no doubt. Guidance for those who are aware of Allah..." (al-Baqarah 2). From the verse of *soorah al-Shuaraa*, quoted above, one can conclude that the Prophet (peace be upon him), by his behavior, speech and example, is establishing for believers a "guide to the

---

[1] Al-Shaukaani, *Fath*, vol. 4. p. 270.

straight path," as in the second type of guidance mentioned above. All Muslims supplicate to Allah in their prayers, "Guide us to the straight path..." Allah has clearly answered this prayer with the Quran[1] and with the sunnah of the Messenger (as is clear from *al-Shooraa* 52). Hence, the Muslim has the Book and the sunnah; these are the two guides that Allah has revealed to guide mankind to the straight path.

The Prophet Muhammad (peace be upon him) as a Recipient of Obedience

The last role of the Messenger of Allah (peace be upon him) to be discussed here is related to the Prophet's (peace be upon him) having been sent by Allah to be obeyed. Allah says in the Quran,

$$ وَمَا أَرْسَلْنَا مِنْ رَسُولٍ إِلاَّ لِيُطَاعَ بِإِذْنِ اللَّهِ $$

"We never sent any messenger except for him to be obeyed, by Allah's leave" (*al-Nisaa* 64). Allah has sent the message of Islam in a clear and beautiful manner in order for all of mankind to respond to the call of Allah and His guidance. Allah has left man free to choose between truth and falsehood. Allah says in the Quran,

$$ تَبَارَكَ الَّذِي بِيَدِهِ الْمُلْكُ وَهُوَ عَلَى كُلِّ شَيْءٍ قَدِيرٌ الَّذِي خَلَقَ الْمَوْتَ وَالْحَيَاةَ لِيَبْلُوَكُمْ أَيُّكُمْ أَحْسَنُ عَمَلاً وَهُوَ الْعَزِيزُ الْغَفُورُ $$

"Blessed is He in whose hand is the Sovereignty, and He is able to do all things— Who has created life and death that He may try you [and see] which of you is best in conduct; and He

---

[1] As is clear from *al-Baqarah* 2, "This is the book in which there is no doubt, a guidance for the pious..."

is the Mighty, the Forgiving" (*al-Mulk* 1-2). In the same way that Allah created all of mankind and is testing them to see if they follow His Book, He is also testing them to see if they will follow and obey the sunnah of the Prophet (peace be upon him). It is not enough for them to claim by their tongues that they are believers, but they must also demonstrate their truthfulness by willingly submitting to the complete truth of the Quran and the sunnah. Allah says,

أَحَسِبَ النَّاسُ أَنْ يُتْرَكُوا أَنْ يَقُولُوا آمَنَّا وَهُمْ لا يُفْتَنُونَ
وَلَقَدْ فَتَنَّا الَّذِينَ مِنْ قَبْلِهِمْ فَلَيَعْلَمَنَّ اللَّهُ الَّذِينَ صَدَقُوا
وَلَيَعْلَمَنَّ الْكَاذِبِينَ

"Do the people think that they will be left alone on saying, 'We believe,' and that they will not be tested? We did test those before them, and Allah will certainly know those who are true from those who are false" (*al-Ankaboot* 2-3).

Until recent times, very few Muslims who passed the first test of following the Quran failed to pass the second test of following the sunnah. Only recently have many people claimed that they are following the Quran and they need not follow the sunnah. It is a prerequisite of belief for a person to follow both the Quran and the sunnah. This fact can be proven by many verses of the Quran, some of which have already been discussed.

In the Quran one may find the following:

قُلْ أَطِيعُوا اللَّهَ وَالرَّسُولَ فَإِنْ تَوَلَّوْا فَإِنَّ اللَّهَ لا يُحِبُّ
الْكَافِرِينَ

"Say: Obey Allah and the Messenger. And if you turn away [know that] verily Allah does not love the unbelievers" (*ali-Imraan* 32). In this verse those who turn away from Allah and the Messenger are implicitly referred to as unbelievers. Ibn Katheer points out that this verse proves that whoever differs from the Messenger (peace be upon him) and refuses to follow his sunnah becomes an unbeliever.[1] There is, in fact, no way to get close to Allah and to receive His love save by following the Messenger (peace be upon him), as is stated in the verse,

قُلْ إِنْ كُنْتُمْ تُحِبُّونَ اللَّهَ فَاتَّبِعُونِي يُحْبِبْكُمُ اللَّهُ وَيَغْفِرْ لَكُمْ ذُنُوبَكُمْ

"Say [O Muhammad]: If you truly love Allah, then follow me and Allah will love you and forgive your sins" (*ali-Imraan* 31).
Allah says in the Quran,

مَنْ يُطِعِ الرَّسُولَ فَقَدْ أَطَاعَ اللَّهَ

"Whoever obeys the Messenger verily obeys Allah" (*al-Nisaa* 80). The Messenger of Allah (peace be upon him) added that whoever disobeys the Messenger has disobeyed Allah. This verse needs no further amplification.

Imam al-Shafi'ee perceptibly noted,

> In whatever form it may take, God made it clear that He imposed the duty of obedience to His Apostle, and has given none of mankind an excuse to reject any order he knows to be the order of the Apostle of God. God has rather made men have a need for him in [all matters of] religion and He has given the proof for it by providing that the sunnah of the Apostle make clear the meanings of the duties laid down in His Book, so that it might be known that the sunnah—whether in the form specifying the meaning of God's commands as provided in the text of the Book which they can read or in the form of legislation in the absence of such a text—in either

---

[1] Ibn Katheer, *Tafseer*, vol. 1, p. 358.

form represents God's command and is in [full] agreement with that of His Apostle; both are [equally] binding in all circumstances.[1]

Allah's Preservation of the Sunnah

Proofs that Allah preserved the sunnah are both textual (Ar., *naqli*) and logical (Ar., *aqli*). The textual argument is based on the verse,

$$إِنَّا نَحْنُ نَزَّلْنَا الذِّكْرَ وَإِنَّا لَهُ لَحَافِظُونَ$$

"We reveal the Reminder (Ar., *al-dhikr*) and We, verily, are its Guardian" (*al-Hijr* 9). The word *al-dhikr* and its derivatives have many meanings in the Quran.[2] It is sometimes used for the Quran, as in,

$$وَهَذَا ذِكْرٌ مُبَارَكٌ أَنزَلْنَاهُ$$

"This is a blessed Reminder that We have revealed" (*al-Anbiyaa* 50); and it is sometimes used for the sunnah, as in,

$$وَأَنزَلْنَا إِلَيْكَ الذِّكْرَ لِتُبَيِّنَ لِلنَّاسِ مَا نُزِّلَ إِلَيْهِمْ وَلَعَلَّهُمْ يَتَفَكَّرُونَ$$

"We have revealed to you the Reminder that you may explain to mankind that which has been revealed for them" (*al-Nahl* 44). Therefore, *a priori*, it cannot be stated that *al-dhikr* in,

$$إِنَّا نَحْنُ نَزَّلْنَا الذِّكْرَ وَإِنَّا لَهُ لَحَافِظُونَ$$

"We reveal the Reminder and We, verily are its Guardian," is referring only to the Quran. In fact, in this verse *al-dhikr* is either referring to both the Quran and the sunnah or only the

---

[1] Al-Shafi'ee, pp. 121-2.
[2] See Majud al-Deen al-Fairoozabaadi, *Basaair Dhuwi al-Tamyeez* (Beirut: al-Maktabah al-Ilmiyyah, n.d.), vol. 3, pp. 9-17.

sunnah; it is not possible that it is referring to the Quran only. This is true because it is inconceivable that only the wording of the Quran would be preserved. Preserving the Quran must imply preserving both its wording and meaning. But, as was shown earlier, the meaning of the Quran is captured in the sunnah of the Prophet (peace be upon him); that is, its meaning cannot be had without the sunnah. Therefore, when Allah promises to preserve the *dhikr*, He is talking about both the Quran and the sunnah or just the sunnah by itself.[1]

The logical argument runs as follows. According to Islamic belief, the Quran is Allah's final revelation and the Prophet Muhammad (peace be upon him) is Allah's final messenger. Allah orders Muslims to follow the sunnah of the Prophet (peace be upon him), as has been shown in this chapter. If Allah did not preserve the sunnah, the true sunnah would have been lost and Allah would be ordering Muslims to follow something that they could not possibly follow. This would not be consistent with what is known of the mercy, wisdom and justice of Allah. Therefore, logically speaking, Allah must have preserved the sunnah.

These arguments do not mean that Allah did not use some earthly means to preserve the Quran and the sunnah. The manner in which Allah, through the Companions, preserved the Quran is well-known and fairly clear.[2] The manner in which Allah preserved the sunnah is a bit more involved is beyond the scope of this work.

---

[1] There are many other verses that state that the Quran cannot be tampered with. Therefore, there is no compelling argument for this verse (*al-Hijr* 15) to be applied to the Quran.

[2] Cf. Ahmad von Denffer, *Ulum al-Quran: An Introduction to the Sciences of the Quran* (Leicester, England: The Islamic Foundation, 1983), pp. 31-56.

The Ruling Concerning One Who Rejects the Sunnah of the Prophet (peace be upon him)

The scholars of Islam who have discussed what distinguishes a Muslim from a non-Muslim are in agreement that whoever refuses to accept the Prophet's sunnah as a binding perfect example becomes an apostate. Ibn Hazm wrote, "If a person says, 'We only follow what we find in the Quran,' then he has become an unbeliever according to the consensus of this nation [of Islam]."[1] Al-Shaukaani said, "The stand of the sunnah and its being an independent source of law is part of the knowledge that is known to every Muslim and no one differs from this point except for those people who have nothing to do with Islam."[2]

Shaikh al-Dausiri was asked about the ruling concerning a person who rejects the sunnah and lives only according to the Quran. He said that "this is the claim of the *zandiqa*[3] and heretics who deny half of the faith and fool the people by claiming that they are honoring the Quran. They are liars as the Quran itself orders the obedience to the Messenger and this can only be done by following his sunnah...and there is no difference of opinion on this point except from those people who have no relationship to the religion of Islam whatsoever."[4]

Abdul Azeez ibn Baaz has written, "The denial of the sunnah...and rendering it inapplicable is an act of *kufr* and apostasy due to the fact that whoever denies the sunnah

---

[1] Quoted in Abdul Rahmaan Itr, *Maalim al-Sunnah al-Nabawiyya* (Jordan: Maktabah al-Manaar, 1986), p. 32.
[2] Muhammad Ali al-Shaukaani, *Irshaad al-Fahool* (Beirut: Daar al-Marifa, 1979), p. 33.
[3] The *zandiqa* are those people who entered into Islam without a sincere belief; in fact, their only intention was to destroy Islam from within.
[4] Abdul Rahmaan al-Dausiri, *Al-Ajuba al-Mufeedah limuhimmat al-Aqeedah* (Beirut: Maktabah Daar al-Arqam, 1982), pp. 62-63.

actually denies the Quran and whoever denies either or both of them is a disbeliever according to all of the schools of thought in Islam."[1]

Al-Suyooti stated, "You should know, may Allah have mercy on all of you, that whosoever rejects the fact that the hadith of the Prophet (peace be upon him), being a report of his statement or action that meets the well-known conditions, is an authority has become an unbeliever and he shall be gathered with the Jews and Christians or with whomsoever Allah wishes to gather him with of the non-believing groups [on the Day of Judgment]."[2]

Conclusion: The Importance of the Sunnah and Hadith

Now that the role and the importance of the sunnah in Islam have been made clear, the importance of the hadith should be, by now, very obvious. How does one know what the sunnah of the Prophet (peace be upon him) is? Where does one look to find the statements of the Prophet (peace be upon him)? By the grace of Allah, unlike the messengers who preceded the Prophet Muhammad (peace be upon him), Allah has preserved for Muslims the actual statements and actions of His last Prophet (peace be upon him). The Prophet's statements, actions and even his physical appearance are all captured in the body of literature known as the hadith literature. Virtually nothing has been lost from his noble life. A Muslim can know exactly how he prayed, fasted, engaged in sport and participated in daily matters with his fellow

---

[1] *In Defence of the Quran and Sunnah* (Majlis of al-Haq Publication Society, S. Burnaby, Canada), p. 5. Cf., Abdul Azeez ibn Baaz, *Wujoob al-Amal bisunnat al-Rasool wa kufr man inkaaraha* (Riyadh: Shaarikah al-Taba al-Arabiya al-Saudiya, 1400 A. H.), pp. 13-14.

[2] Ibn Baaz, ibid., p. 30, quoting from *Miftah al-Jannah*.

companions. He can visualize how he ate, drank and sat. Such a miraculous and complete record cannot be found for any other historical figure since man's creation. (This is actually another sign of the truth of the prophethood of Muhammad, peace be upon him.)

Anyone who refuses to follow the sunnah of the Prophet (peace be upon him) as embodied in the authentic hadith has left the fold of Islam.

References

al-Albaani, Muhammad Naasir al-Deen. *Manzalat al-Sunnah fi al-Islaam.* Kuwait: al-Daar al-Salafiyyah. 1980.

-----*Saheeh al-Jaami al-Sagheer.* Beirut: al-Maktab al-Islaami. 1986.

-----*Sahih al-Targheb wa al-Tarheeb.* Riyadh: Maktabah al-Maarif. 1988.

-----*Silsilat al-Ahaadeeth al-Dhaeefah.* Beirut: al-Maktab al-Islaami. 1978.

Itr, Abdul Rahmaan. *Maalim al-Sunnah al-Nabawiyya.* Jordan: Maktabah al-Manaar. 1986.

al-Dausiri, Abdul Rahmaan. *Al-Ajuba al-Mufeedah limuhimmat al-Aqeedah.* Beirut: Maktabah Daar al-Arqam. 1982.

al-Fairoozabaadi, Majud al-Deen. *Basaair Dhuwi al-Tamyeez.* Beirut: al-Maktabah al-Ilmiyyah.

ibn Baaz, Abdul Azeez. *Wujoob al-Amal bisunnat al-Rasool wa kufr man Ankaaraha.* Riyadh: Shaarikah al-Taba al-Arabiya al-Saudiya. 1400 A. H.

Ibn Katheer, Imaad al-Deen. *Tafseer al-Quran al-Adheem.* Daar Ihya al-Kutub al-Arabi.

Ibn Taimiyyah, Ahmad. *Majmooat al-Fataawa ibn Taimiyyah.* Collected by Abdul Rahmaan ibn Qasim and his son Muhammad. Riyadh: Daar al-Ifta. 1978.

Khadduri, Majid. *Islamic Jurisprudence: Shafi'i's Risala.* Baltimore: Johns Hopkins Press. 1961.

Majlis of al-Haq Publication Society. *In Defence of the Quran and Sunnah.* S. Burnaby, Canada.

al-Qaasimi, Jamaal al-Deen. *Mahaasan al-Ta'weel.* Beirut: Daar al-Fikr. 1978.

al-Qurtubi, Abu Abdullah. *al-Jaami li-Ahkaam al-Quran.* Beirut: Daar Ihya al-Turaath al-Arabi.

al-Raazi, Fakhr al-Deen. *Tafseer al-Kabeer.* Beirut: Daar Ihya al-Turaath al-Arabi.

al-Saadi, Abdul-Rahmaan. *Taiseer al-Kareem al-Rahmaan fi Tafseer Kalaam al-Mannaan.* Riyadh: Al-Muasassah al-Saeediyyah.

al-Shafi'ee- See Khadduri.

al-Shaukaani, Muhammad ibn Ali. *Fath al-Qadeer.* Mustafa al-Babi al-Halabi. 1964.

-----*Irshad al-Fahool.* Beirut: Daar al-Marifa. 1979.

Siddiqui, Abdul Hamid, trans. and commentator. *Sahih Muslim.* Lahore, Pakistan: Sh. Muhammad Ashraf. 1972.

al-Suyooti, Jalaal al-Deen. *Lubaab al-Naqool fi Asbaab al-Nuzool.* Beirut: Daar Ihya al-Uloom. 1980.

-----*Miftaah al-Jannah fi al-Ihtijaaj bi al-Sunnah.* Badr al-Badr, ed. Kuwait: Daar al-Huda al-Nubuwwa.

von Denffer, Ahmad. *Ulum al-Quran: An Introduction to the Sciences of the Quran.* Leicester, England: The Islamic Foundation. 1983.

Zarabozo, Jamaal al-Din. "The Basics of Tafsir." *Al-Basheer.* Vol. 1, No. 2. July 1987.

Feature Article:
The Importance of Jihad in the Life of a Muslim[1]

Introduction

It is somewhat surprising that although jihad plays an essential role in Islam there are few works in English that deal with it in detail.[2] Most of these works are very short and do not discuss many important topics concerning jihad. Therefore, there is still a large void in the English literature concerning this very important topic. In a number of future issues of *Al-Basheer* we hope to fill some of this void.

---

[1] This article appeared in *al-Basheer*, vol. 2, no. 2 (July-Aug. 1988).

[2] The few decent works in English that do cover this topic include: Linda Kay Jitmoud, "An Intellectual Historical Study of Islamic Jihad During the Life of Muhammad and in the Twentieth Century" (Ph. D. dissertation, Ball State University, 1985) (although this is a fine work it is amazing that someone can be given a Ph.D. for a thesis on jihad that never refers to a reference in Arabic, the language in which the greatest works on Islam may be found. In fact, it is probably due to her want of authentic references in Arabic that she made some questionable conclusions in her dissertation); Abul Ala Maudoodi, *Jihad in Islam* (Lahore: Islamic Publications, Ltd. 1976); Abdul Hameed Siddiqi, *Jihad in Islam* (Lahore: Kazi Publications, 1979); Hassan al-Banna, "On Jihad," in Hassan al-Banna, *Five Tracts of Hassan al-Banna*, Charles Wendell, tr. (Berkeley: University of California Press, n.d.), pp. 133-162; Abdullah ibn Muhammad ibn Humaid, "The Call to Jihad in the Holy Quran" in M. M. Khan, trans., *Sahih al-Bukhari* (Chicago: Kazi Publications, 1976), vol. 1, pp. xxiii-xlii. Note that it is respect to jihad that many people go to extremes. It is therefore imperative that there be a serious study on the fiqh of jihad so that people can recognize the difference between, for example, jihad and terrorism.

Importance of *Imaan* and Jihad

Allah says in the Quran,

يَاأَيُّهَا الَّذِينَ آمَنُوا هَلْ أَدُلُّكُمْ عَلَى تِجَارَةٍ تُنجِيكُمْ مِنْ
عَذَابٍ أَلِيمٍ تُؤْمِنُونَ بِاللَّهِ وَرَسُولِهِ وَتُجَاهِدُونَ فِي سَبِيلِ اللَّهِ
بِأَمْوَالِكُمْ وَأَنفُسِكُمْ ذَلِكُمْ خَيْرٌ لَكُمْ إِنْ كُنتُمْ تَعْلَمُونَ

"O you who believe! Shall I show you a commerce that will save you from a painful doom? You should believe in Allah and His Messenger, and should strive (Ar., *jaahidoo*) for the cause of Allah with your wealth and your lives. That is better for you, if you did but know" (*al-Saff* 10-11).

This verse points to the importance of two concepts: *imaan* or *aqeedah* ("faith") and jihad. It states that in addition to *imaan* or belief, jihad is an essential component of this trade that will save the Muslim from a grievous punishment.

The essential question in any person's life is whether he is a believer or an unbeliever. The Prophet (peace be upon him) said,

لا يدخل الجنة إلا مؤمن

"No one shall enter paradise except the believer." (Recorded by Muslim.) But this verse also points out that an essential aspect of this "trade" is the jihad which goes hand in hand with the true and complete belief in Allah. In another verse, Allah states,

إن الله اشترى من المؤمنين أنفسهم وأموالهم بأن لهم
الجنة يقاتلون في سبيل الله فيقتلون ويقتلون وعدا عليه

حَقًّا فِي التَّوْرَاةِ وَالإِنْجِيلِ وَالْقُرْآنِ وَمَنْ أَوْفَى بِعَهْدِهِ مِنَ اللَّهِ فَاسْتَبْشِرُوا بِبَيْعِكُمُ الَّذِي بَايَعْتُمْ بِهِ وَذَلِكَ هُوَ الْفَوْزُ الْعَظِيمُ

"Lo, Allah has bought from the believers their lives and their wealth because the Garden will be theirs: they shall fight in the way of Allah and shall slay and be slain. It is a promise which is binding on Him in the Torah and the Gospel and the Quran. Who fulfills His covenant better than Allah? Rejoice then in your bargain that you have made, for that is the supreme triumph" (*al-Tauba* 111).

These verses clearly show the importance of jihad in the life of a Muslim. Allah mentions jihad in conjunction with *imaan* or belief, paradise and His pleasure. These two verses quoted above should be enough to encourage anybody with the slightest amount of faith in his heart to strive and sacrifice for the sake of Allah.

Allah seals the relationship between being a believer and performing jihad when He describes the believers in the following verse:

إِنَّمَا الْمُؤْمِنُونَ الَّذِينَ آمَنُوا بِاللَّهِ وَرَسُولِهِ ثُمَّ لَمْ يَرْتَابُوا وَجَاهَدُوا بِأَمْوَالِهِمْ وَأَنْفُسِهِمْ فِي سَبِيلِ اللَّهِ أُولَئِكَ هُمُ الصَّادِقُونَ

"The [true and complete] believers are only those who believe in Allah and His Messenger and afterward doubt not, but strive (Ar., *jaahadoo*) with their wealth and their lives for the cause of Allah. Such are the sincere" (*al-Hujuraat* 15). Nimat Siddeeqi wrote,

> Allah stresses in this noble verse that the jihad in His path is sign of a sincere faith. The believer in Allah, who possesses the true faith, does not have any doubt about His existence and is certain about His promise

and His warnings. It is, therefore, impossible for such a person to be stingy with his wealth and his life and not to call others to the way of Allah and to support the truth... These are the people who are true in their claims to faith.[1]

In fact, this verse was revealed after some bedouins stated that they believed in Allah and then Allah answered them with the following words,

قَالَتِ الْأَعْرَابُ آمَنَّا قُلْ لَمْ تُؤْمِنُوا وَلَكِنْ قُولُوا أَسْلَمْنَا وَلَمَّا يَدْخُلِ الْإِيمَانُ فِي قُلُوبِكُمْ

"The bedouins say: 'We believe.' Say to them: 'You believe not, but rather say, 'We submit,' for faith has not yet entered into your hearts'..." (*al-Hujuraat* 14). According to al-Shaukaani, "After Allah stated that those who claimed to be believers were not [complete] believers and that faith had not entered their hearts, Allah makes it clear who those people are who are true believers"[2] and revealed the next verse (al-Hujuraat 15 quoted above). In a similar vein, Sawwaaf wrote,

These verses expound the true nature of *imaan* and the attributes of the sincere believers, their statements and actions, as if Allah was saying to those who made a claim to belief, 'Belief is not what you people think it is,' i.e., a statement without any sincerity in the heart or a claim that is not followed by deeds and obedience.[3]

---

[1] Nimat Siddeeqi, *Al-Jihaad fi Sabeel Allah* (Cairo: Daar al-Itisaam, 1979), pp. 9-10.

[2] Muhammad ibn Ali al-Shaukaani, *Fath al-Qadeer* (Cairo: Mustafa al-Baba, 1964), vol. 5, p. 68.

[3] Muhammad Mahmood al-Sawwaaf, *Nadharaat fi Soorah al-Hujuraat* (Beirut: Muasassah al-Risaalah, 1980), pp. 170-171.

Therefore, any person who claims to be a sincere believer in Allah should understand the obligation of jihad. What exactly is jihad? What are the types of jihad? What types of jihad are obligatory on every Muslim? As well as many other questions. If the person does not concern himself with these questions, then he is similar to those bedouins who claim to have faith yet the true and complete faith had not actually entered into their hearts. They say that they believe but they do not meet Allah's description of the believers. Again, these verses state,

قَالَتِ الْأَعْرَابُ آمَنَّا قُلْ لَمْ تُؤْمِنُوا وَلَكِنْ قُولُوا أَسْلَمْنَا وَلَمَّا يَدْخُلِ الْإِيمَانُ فِي قُلُوبِكُمْ وَإِنْ تُطِيعُوا اللَّهَ وَرَسُولَهُ لَا يَلِتْكُمْ مِنْ أَعْمَالِكُمْ شَيْئًا إِنَّ اللَّهَ غَفُورٌ رَحِيمٌ إِنَّمَا الْمُؤْمِنُونَ الَّذِينَ آمَنُوا بِاللَّهِ وَرَسُولِهِ ثُمَّ لَمْ يَرْتَابُوا وَجَاهَدُوا بِأَمْوَالِهِمْ وَأَنْفُسِهِمْ فِي سَبِيلِ اللَّهِ أُولَئِكَ هُمُ الصَّادِقُونَ

"The bedouins say: 'We believe.' Say to them: 'You believe not, but rather say, 'We submit,' for faith has not yet entered into your hearts. Yet if you obey Allah and His Messenger, He will not withhold from you anything of the rewards of your deeds.[1] Lo, Allah is Forgiving, Merciful. The true believers are only those who believe in Allah and His Messenger and afterward doubt not, but strive (Ar., *jaahadoo*) with their wealth and their lives for the cause of Allah. Such are the sincere" (*al-Hujuraat* 14-15).

---

[1] This portion of the verse proves that those bedouins were not disbelievers or hypocrites. Their faith was simply not at a level of completeness for them to be called true believers.

Jihad, *Imaan* and Hypocrisy

How could anyone claim to be a believer and claim to be deserving of paradise yet he is not even willing to sacrifice the time and effort needed to learn about his religion and the obligations upon him? How can anyone claim to be a believer and deserving of paradise and he is not even willing to perform the most basic deed of the religion, the prayers? How can anyone claim to be deserving of paradise while he is not even willing to sacrifice the smallest thing for the sake of Allah? When thinking about questions like these the astute person should realize that, yes, jihad—striving for the sake of Allah—and *imaan* definitely go hand and hand. Perhaps this is why the Prophet (peace be upon him) said,

$$\text{مَنْ مَاتَ وَلَمْ يَغْزُ وَلَمْ يُحَدِّثْ بِهِ نَفْسَهُ مَاتَ عَلَى شُعْبَةٍ مِنْ نِفَاقٍ}$$

"Whoever dies and had not fought [for the sake of Allah] or did not even consider fighting [for the sake of Allah], dies upon a branch of hypocrisy."[1] Imam al-Nawawi commented, "Whoever does that [does not participate in a battle or intends to do so] is similar to the hypocrites who do not participate in jihad. Therefore, not participating in jihad is a branch of hypocrisy."[2]

---

[1] Recorded by Muslim, Ahmad, Abu Daawood and al-Nasaai. Note that the word used in this hadith is a form of the word *ghazu* which implies actual fighting, a specific type of jihad. Abdullah ibn al-Mubaarak stated that this hadith only applies to the time of the Prophet (peace be upon him) but there is no evidence for his opinion and, therefore, the generality of the hadith's application must be considered correct.

[2] Yahya al-Nawawi, *Sharh Saheeh Muslim* (Beirut: Daar al-Fikr, 1978), vol. 13, p. 56.

In fact, it is characteristic of the hypocrites that they become very happy whenever they are able to avoid any kind of jihad. Allah says about them,

فَرِحَ الْمُخَلَّفُونَ بِمَقْعَدِهِمْ خِلافَ رَسُولِ اللَّهِ وَكَرِهُوا أَنْ يُجَاهِدُوا بِأَمْوَالِهِمْ وَأَنْفُسِهِمْ فِي سَبِيلِ اللَّهِ وَقَالُوا لا تَنفِرُوا فِي الْحَرِّ قُلْ نَارُ جَهَنَّمَ أَشَدُّ حَرًّا لَوْ كَانُوا يَفْقَهُونَ فَلْيَضْحَكُوا قَلِيلاً وَلْيَبْكُوا كَثِيرًا جَزَاءً بِمَا كَانُوا يَكْسِبُونَ فَإِنْ رَجَعَكَ اللَّهُ إِلَى طَائِفَةٍ مِنْهُمْ فَاسْتَأْذَنُوكَ لِلْخُرُوجِ فَقُلْ لَنْ تَخْرُجُوا مَعِيَ أَبَدًا وَلَنْ تُقَاتِلُوا مَعِيَ عَدُوًّا إِنَّكُمْ رَضِيتُمْ بِالْقُعُودِ أَوَّلَ مَرَّةٍ فَاقْعُدُوا مَعَ الْخَالِفِينَ وَلا تُصَلِّ عَلَى أَحَدٍ مِنْهُمْ مَاتَ أَبَدًا وَلا تَقُمْ عَلَى قَبْرِه إِنَّهُمْ كَفَرُوا بِاللَّهِ وَرَسُولِهِ وَمَاتُوا وَهُمْ فَاسِقُونَ

"Those who were left behind [from the jihad] rejoiced at sitting still behind the messenger of Allah, and were averse to striving with their wealth and their lives in Allah's way. And they said: Go not forth in the heat! Say: The heat of hell is more intense, if they but understood. Then let them laugh a little; they will weep much, as the reward of what they used to earn. If Allah brings you back (from the campaign) unto a party of them and they ask of you permission to go out (to fight) then say unto them: 'You shall never more go out with me nor fight with me against a foe. You were content with sitting still the first time. So sit still, with those who stay behind.' And never pray for one of them who dies, nor stand by his grave. Lo, they disbelieved in Allah and His Messenger, and they died while they were evildoers" (*al-Taubah* 81-84).

With respect to jihad, the hypocrites have some particular characteristics.[1] First, they claim to believe in jihad and in Islam but, in reality, this is a false claim. This was also true for the hypocrites during the time of the Prophet (peace be upon him). They almost died from fear when verses concerning fighting were finally revealed. Allah states,

وَيَقُولُ الَّذِينَ آمَنُوا لَوْلَا نُزِّلَتْ سُورَةٌ فَإِذَا أُنزِلَتْ سُورَةٌ مُحْكَمَةٌ وَذُكِرَ فِيهَا الْقِتَالُ رَأَيْتَ الَّذِينَ فِي قُلُوبِهِم مَّرَضٌ يَنظُرُونَ إِلَيْكَ نَظَرَ الْمَغْشِيِّ عَلَيْهِ مِنَ الْمَوْتِ فَأَوْلَى لَهُمْ

"And when those who believe say: If only a *soorah* were revealed. But when a decisive *soorah* is revealed and war is mentioned therein, you see those in whose hearts is a disease [the hypocrites] looking at you with the look of men fainting unto death. Woe unto them" (*Muhammad* 20).

Second, they try their best to avoid the jihad and make excuses for their lack of participation in the jihad. Again, this was true during the Prophet's time also. Allah says,

لَا يَسْتَأْذِنُكَ الَّذِينَ يُؤْمِنُونَ بِاللَّهِ وَالْيَوْمِ الْآخِرِ أَنْ يُجَاهِدُوا بِأَمْوَالِهِمْ وَأَنفُسِهِمْ وَاللَّهُ عَلِيمٌ بِالْمُتَّقِينَ إِنَّمَا يَسْتَأْذِنُكَ الَّذِينَ لَا يُؤْمِنُونَ بِاللَّهِ وَالْيَوْمِ الْآخِرِ وَارْتَابَتْ قُلُوبُهُمْ فَهُمْ فِي رَيْبِهِمْ يَتَرَدَّدُونَ

"Those who believe in Allah and the Last Day ask no leave of you lest they should strive with their wealth and their lives. Allah is aware of those who keep their duty (to Him). They alone ask leave of you who believe not in Allah and the Last

---

[1] Cf., Ibraaheem Ali Saalim, *Al-Nifaaq wa al-Munaafiqoon* (Cairo: Daar al-Shaab, 1970), pp. 389-393.

Day, and whose hearts feel doubt, so in their doubt they waver" (*al-Tauba* 44-45). Commenting on this verse, Sayyid Qutb wrote,

> This is a principle that is never contradicted. Those who believe in Allah and are certain about the Day of Judgment do not try to be excused from performing the obligation of jihad and they do not hesitate in responding to the call to go out in the way of Allah with their wealth and souls. In fact, they rush to the call, whether strong or weak, in the way that Allah had ordered them to obey His orders and with certainty in their meeting with Him and certain of His reward and desiring His pleasure. In fact, they go out willingly and there is no need to encourage them to go; therefore, there is no question of them asking for permission not to take part in the jihad. The only ones who ask to be excused are those whose hearts are not filled with certainty. These people hesitate and offer excuses in order to avoid their obligation.[1]

Finally, if they are actually forced to take part in the jihad, they will do their best to cause as much mischief as possible among the Muslims and, if possible, make them retreat from fighting. On this point, a verse states,

لَوْ خَرَجُوا فِيكُمْ مَا زَادُوكُمْ إِلاَّ خَبَالاً وَلأَوْضَعُوا خِلَالَكُمْ يَبْغُونَكُمُ الْفِتْنَةَ وَفِيكُمْ سَمَّاعُونَ لَهُمْ وَاللَّهُ عَلِيمٌ بِالظَّالِمِينَ

"Had they [the hypocrites] gone forth among you they would have added to you nothing but trouble and had hurried to and fro among you, seeking to cause sedition among you, and among you there are some who would have listened to them. Allah is aware of evildoers" (*al-Taubah* 47).

---

[1] Sayyid Qutb, *Fi Dhilaal al-Quran* (Beirut: Daar al-Shurooq, 1977), vol. 3, p. 1662.

Therefore, jihad is not just a way to get closer to Allah and to earn His pleasure but it is a dividing line between faith and disbelief, between sincerity and hypocrisy. In fact, it seems that it is only the unbeliever or hypocrite who is completely unwilling to sacrifice for the sake of Allah.

Jihad, *Imaan* and Hypocrisy Today

The Prophet (peace be upon him) said,

لَا يُؤْمِنُ أَحَدُكُمْ حَتَّى يُحِبَّ لأَخِيهِ مَا يُحِبُّ لِنَفْسِه

"None of you [truly] believes until he loves for his brother what he loves for himself." (Recorded by al-Bukhari and Muslim.) Any Muslim who has any faith in his heart cannot rest if he sees his brother starving or oppressed. His belief in Allah, his love for the believers in Allah and his understanding of his duty to Allah will drive him to struggle against what is happening and do his best to change it. This is an essential aspect of one's faith. The Prophet (peace be upon him) said,

مَنْ رَأَى مِنْكُمْ مُنْكَرًا فَلْيُغَيِّرْهُ بِيَدِهِ فَإِنْ لَمْ يَسْتَطِعْ فَبِلِسَانِهِ فَإِنْ لَمْ يَسْتَطِعْ فَبِقَلْبِهِ وَذَلِكَ أَضْعَفُ الإِيمَانِ

"Whoever of you sees an evil must then change it with his hand. If he is not able to do so, then [he must change it] with his tongue. And if he is not able to do so, then [he must change it] with his heart. And that is the slightest [effect of] faith." (Recorded by Muslim.)

Allah asks the believers,

وَمَا لَكُمْ لا تُقَاتِلُونَ فِي سَبِيلِ اللَّهِ وَالْمُسْتَضْعَفِينَ

294

عٌ مِنْ الرِّجَالِ وَالنِّسَاءِ وَالْوِلْدَانِ الَّذِينَ يَقُولُونَ رَبَّنَا
أَخْرِجْنَا مِنْ هَذِهِ الْقَرْيَةِ الظَّالِمِ أَهْلُهَا وَاجْعَلْ لَنَا مِنْ لَدُنْكَ
وَلِيًّا وَاجْعَلْ لَنَا مِنْ لَدُنْكَ نَصِيرًا

"How can you not fight for the cause of Allah and of the feeble among men and of the women and the children who are crying: Our Lord, bring us forth from this town of which the people are oppressors and raise for us from You one who will protect; and raise for us from You one who will help..." (*al-Nisaa* 75). How can the people who claim to be believers today read this verse and other similar verses and not be moved to sacrifice for the sake of Allah? In how many places around the world have Muslims cried out for help? How can any Muslim think about the situation of the Muslims in Afghanistan, Palestine, India, Philippines, Lebanon, Syria, Eritrea, Ethiopia and not be moved? Where is the *imaan* of the Muslims and their willingness to sacrifice if they are not moved by what they hear and see in the world today? Is there any true *imaan* left in their hearts or have their hearts become hardened? Allah speaks to the believers,

أَلَمْ يَأْنِ لِلَّذِينَ آمَنُوا أَنْ تَخْشَعَ قُلُوبُهُمْ لِذِكْرِ اللَّهِ وَمَا نَزَلَ
مِنْ الْحَقِّ وَلَا يَكُونُوا كَالَّذِينَ أُوتُوا الْكِتَابَ مِنْ قَبْلُ فَطَالَ
عَلَيْهِمْ الْأَمَدُ فَقَسَتْ قُلُوبُهُمْ وَكَثِيرٌ مِنْهُمْ فَاسِقُونَ

"Is not the time ripe for the hearts of those who believe to submit to Allah's reminder and to the truth which is revealed, that they become not as those who received the scripture of old but the term was prolonged for them and so their hearts were hardened, and many of them are evildoers" (*al-Hadeed* 16).

To reiterate, a hatred for jihad or a lack of enthusiasm for sacrificing for the sake of Allah is a characteristic of the hypocrites—especially in conditions like today's; the sincere believers, on the other hand, are anxious to sacrifice their wealth and lives for the sake of Allah and do their best to change the situation of their fellow Muslims.

Exhortation to Take Part in Jihad

Besides commanding believers to take part in jihad, Allah has promised those who sacrifice for His sake great rewards in both this life and the Hereafter. There are many verses and hadith that encourage the believers to take part in this noble duty. The verses from the Quran include:

لَا يَسْتَوِي الْقَاعِدُونَ مِنَ الْمُؤْمِنِينَ غَيْرُ أُوْلِي الضَّرَرِ وَالْمُجَاهِدُونَ فِي سَبِيلِ اللَّهِ بِأَمْوَالِهِمْ وَأَنفُسِهِمْ فَضَّلَ اللَّهُ الْمُجَاهِدِينَ بِأَمْوَالِهِمْ وَأَنفُسِهِمْ عَلَى الْقَاعِدِينَ دَرَجَةً وَكُلاًّ وَعَدَ اللَّهُ الْحُسْنَى وَفَضَّلَ اللَّهُ الْمُجَاهِدِينَ عَلَى الْقَاعِدِينَ أَجْرًا عَظِيمًا دَرَجَاتٍ مِنْهُ وَمَغْفِرَةً وَرَحْمَةً وَكَانَ اللَّهُ غَفُورًا رَحِيمًا

"Those of the believers who sit still, other than those who have a (disabling) hurt, are not on an equality with those who strive in the way of Allah with their wealth and lives. Allah has conferred on those who strive with their wealth and lives a rank above the sedentary. Unto each Allah has promised good, but He has bestowed on those who strive a great reward above the sedentary degrees of rank from Him, and forgiveness and mercy. Allah is ever Forgiving, Merciful" (al-Nisaa 95-96).

أَجَعَلْتُمْ سِقَايَةَ الْحَاجِّ وَعِمَارَةَ الْمَسْجِدِ الْحَرَامِ كَمَنْ آمَنَ
بِاللَّهِ وَالْيَوْمِ الآخِرِ وَجَاهَدَ فِي سَبِيلِ اللَّهِ لا يَسْتَوُونَ عِنْدَ
اللَّهِ وَاللَّهُ لا يَهْدِي الْقَوْمَ الظَّالِمِينَ الَّذِينَ آمَنُوا وَهَاجَرُوا
وَجَاهَدُوا فِي سَبِيلِ اللَّهِ بِأَمْوَالِهِمْ وَأَنْفُسِهِمْ أَعْظَمُ دَرَجَةً
عِنْدَ اللَّهِ وَأُوْلَئِكَ هُمُ الْفَائِزُونَ

"Consider you the quenching of a pilgrim's thirst and tending of the Inviolable Place of Worship as (equal to the worth of him) who believes in Allah and the Last Day, and strives for the sake of Allah? They are not equal in the sight of Allah. Allah guides not wrongdoing folk. Those who believe and have left their homes and striven with their wealth and their lives in Allah's way are of much greater worth in Allah's sight. These are they who are triumphant" (*al-Taubah* 19-20).

إِنَّ اللَّهَ يُحِبُّ الَّذِينَ يُقَاتِلُونَ فِي سَبِيلِهِ صَفًّا كَأَنَّهُمْ بُنْيَانٌ
مَرْصُوصٌ

"Lo Allah loves those who battle for His cause in ranks, as if they were a solid structure" (*al-Saff* 4).

The following hadith touch upon this topic:

Abu Hurairah related that a man came to the Messenger of Allah (peace be upon him) and said, "O Messenger of Allah, show me a deed that is equal to jihad." The Prophet (peace be upon him) told him, "I do not find such a deed." Then he told him, "Can you, while the Muslim fighter is in the battlefield, enter your mosque to perform prayers without cease and fast and never break your fast?" The man said, "Who could do that?" The Prophet (peace be upon him) told him, "The one who makes jihad is rewarded even for the footsteps of his horse while it wanders about for grazing while tied on a long rope." (Recorded by al-Bukhari.)

Abu Saeed al-Khudri narrated that a man came to the Prophet (peace be upon him) and said, "O Allah's Messenger, who is the best among the people?" The Prophet (peace be upon him) said,

مُؤْمِنٌ يُجَاهِدُ فِي سَبِيلِ اللَّهِ بِنَفْسِهِ وَمَالِهِ

"A believer who strives his utmost in Allah's cause with his life and property." (Recorded by al-Bukhari.)

Intimidation Concerning not Performing Jihad

The above should be enough to prove that the willingness to participate in jihad is a sign of one's *imaan* and the lack of such willingness is a sign of hypocrisy. But the following may be added to the above to further demonstrate how important it is for the believer to participate in or be willing to make jihad.[1]

(1) The abandonment of jihad is a source of destruction in both this life and in the Hereafter. With respect to this life, if people do not make an effort to propagate and defend what they believe in, they may be subjugated and despised by others and will not be able to live freely. With respect to the Hereafter, the person who does not perform jihad may not be deserving of Allah's mercy and he may actually be destroying himself. Allah says,

---

[1] Cf., Ali al-Ulyani, *Ahamiyat al-Jihaad* (Riyadh: Daar Taibah, 1985), pp. 247-253. In this section, the stress is on what happens to the individual when he neglects jihad.

وَأَنفِقُوا فِي سَبِيلِ اللَّهِ وَلَا تُلْقُوا بِأَيْدِيكُمْ إِلَى التَّهْلُكَةِ
وَأَحْسِنُوا إِنَّ اللَّهَ يُحِبُّ الْمُحْسِنِينَ

"Spend your wealth for the cause of Allah, and be not cast by your own hands to ruin; and do good. Lo, Allah loves the beneficent" (*al-Baqarah* 195). This verse was explained by the Companion Abu Ayyoob al-Ansaari. When the Muslims were trying to penetrate and throw themselves into the enemy's ranks at Constantinople, some of them said that they were not supposed to kill themselves by their own hands. Abu Ayyoob said, "We are more knowledgeable about this verse. It was revealed concerning us, the Companions of the Prophet (peace be upon him). We participated in the battles with the Prophet and Allah aided us. Then when Islam spread and we were victorious, we said, 'Allah has honored us by being Companions of the Prophet and He aided him until Islam spread and its numbers were many. We sacrificed our time with our families, wealth and children. Now, the burden of war is over and we should return to our families and children and spend our time with them.' Then Allah revealed concerning us, 'Spend your wealth for the cause of Allah, and be not cast by your own hands to ruin; and do good. Lo, Allah loves the beneficent.'"[1] Thus, by abandoning spending in the way of Allah and, therefore, jihad, the person is actually destroying himself by his own hands.

(2) The abandonment of jihad is a reason for humiliation and disdain. The Prophet (peace be upon him) said,

---

[1] Imaad al-Deen Ibn Katheer, *Tafseer al-Quran al-Adheem* (Kuwait: Daar al-Arqam, 1985), vol. 1, pp. 402-403.

لَئِنْ تَرَكْتُمُ الْجِهَادَ وَأَخَذْتُمْ بِأَذْنَابِ الْبَقَرِ وَتَبَايَعْتُمْ بِالْعِينَةِ
لَيُلْزِمَنَّكُمُ اللَّهُ مَذَلَّةً فِي رِقَابِكُمْ لَا تَنْفَكُّ عَنْكُمْ حَتَّى تَتُوبُوا
إِلَى اللَّهِ وَتَرْجِعُوا عَلَى مَا كُنْتُمْ عَلَيْهِ

"If you abandon the jihad, take after the tails of cattle [that is, spend all of your time with your agriculture and wealth] and you deal in *eena*[1], then Allah will make you accompanied with humiliation and you will not get rid of it until you repent to Allah and return to your old state."[2] Al-Ulyani wrote,

> What the Messenger (peace be upon him), who does not speak from his own desires, stated is certainly true. If anyone looks to the situation of the Muslims today, who are heedless of the most important aspects of their religion as they have abandoned the jihad against the unbelievers and taking the *jizyah* from them, he will see that Allah has inflicted them with humiliation as they turn to the unbelievers of the East or the unbelievers of the West, seeking aid and honor from them, and they do not even realize that this humility will never leave them until they return to their religion as the most honest speaker [the Prophet] has stated in this hadith. If they continue in their present state they can be given the same tidings that Allah has given them [when He said], "Bear unto the hypocrites the tidings that for them there is a painful doom; Those who choose disbelievers for

---

[1] This is a type of business deal with implicitly deals with interest although outwardly it seems to be void of interest.

[2] Recorded by Ahmad. Ahmad al-Banna wrote, "I have not found this hadith with such a wording except in Ahmad's collection and its chain is good. Abu Daawood, ibn Maajah and al-Baihaqi related the same hadith with a different wording but with the same meaning... And the hadith has a lot of supporting evidence." Ahmad al-Banna, *Fath al-Rabbaani li-Tarteeb Musnad al-Imam Ahmad* (Cairo: Daar al-Hadeeth, n.d.), vol. 15, pp. 44-45.

their patrons instead of believers. Do they look for power at their hands? Lo, all power appertains to Allah" [*al-Nisaa* 138-139].[1]

(3) The abandonment of jihad is also a source of calamity, affliction and trials. The Prophet (peace be upon him) said,

إِذَا ضن الناس بالدينار والدرهم وتبايعوا بالعينة واتبعوا أذناب البقر وتركوا الجهاد في سبيل الله أنزل الله بهم بلاء فلم يرفعه عنهم حتى يراجعوا دينهم

"If the people become stingy with their *dinars* and *dirhams* [that is, their wealth], begin to participate in *eena*, spend their time with their agriculture and they leave jihad for the sake of Allah, then Allah will inflict them with a trial that will not leave them until they return to their religion."[2]

(4) Under certain conditions, the abandonment of jihad is also a source of punishment from Allah. Allah says in the Quran,

إِلَّا تَنفِرُوا يُعَذِّبْكُمْ عَذَابًا أَلِيمًا وَيَسْتَبْدِلْ قَوْمًا غَيْرَكُمْ وَلَا تَضُرُّوهُ شَيْئًا وَاللَّهُ عَلَى كُلِّ شَيْءٍ قَدِيرٌ

"If you go not forth [for jihad] He will afflict you with a painful doom, and will choose instead of you a folk other than

---

[1] Al-Ulyani, p. 248.

[2] Recorded by Ahmad. Ahmad al-Banna stated, "Recorded by Abu Daawood and al-Tabaraani. The narrators of Ahmad's hadith are all trustworthy and ibn al-Qattaan stated the hadith to be *sahih*. And the hadith has many other hadith and chains supporting and strengthening it." Ahmad Al-Banna, vol. 14, p. 27. Muhammad Naasir al-Deen al-Albaani also says this hadith is *sahih*. Muhammad Naasir al-Deen al-Albaani, *Silsilat al-Ahaadeeth al-Saheehah* (Beirut: al-Maktab al-Islaami, 1979), hadith #11.

you. You cannot harm Him at all. Allah is able to do all things" (*al-Taubah* 39). In Sayyid Qutb's *tafseer* he wrote,

> This verse is addressed to a particular people at a particular time but its message is general and it is directed to anyone who believes in Allah. The punishment that is awaiting them is not just of the hereafter but there is also a punishment in this life. This punishment includes the humiliation that comes to those who stay back from the jihad and facing their enemies. Therefore, their enemies overtake them and prevent them from bounties. Furthermore, they will also lose lives and wealth—much more than what they would have lost if they would have faced their enemies and taken part in jihad.... There is no nation that has left jihad except that Allah has afflicted it with humiliation.[1]

The Reality of Islam and Why Jihad is an Imperative

Two Parties of Humans

Allah has divided this creation into two types of creatures. One type is not free to disobey the natural order of the creation and acts strictly according to "instinct" or divine direction. This first type includes all of the different animal kingdoms. The other type of creature, the humans (and jinn), has a limited free-will. With respect to some things, they have no free-will; for example, they must breathe, blood must circulate through their veins and so on. But in other aspects they are physically free to act in any manner, to some extent, that they wish.

---

[1] Qutb, vol. 3, p. 1655.

But Allah did not leave this second type of creature without any guidance. Instead, He sent them messengers and revealed books for their benefit. Allah has established a proof against mankind by revealing guidance and showing the proper way to act. Allah says,

رُسُلاً مُبَشِّرِينَ وَمُنذِرِينَ لِأَلاَّ يَكُونَ لِلنَّاسِ عَلَى اللَّهِ حُجَّةٌ بَعْدَ الرُّسُلِ وَكَانَ اللَّهُ عَزِيزًا حَكِيمًا

"Messengers of good cheer and of warning, in order that mankind might have no argument against Allah after the messengers. Allah was ever Mighty, Wise" (*al-Nisaa* 165).

In Allah's mercy towards mankind, He continued to send such messengers.

ثُمَّ أَرْسَلْنَا رُسُلَنَا تَتْرَى كُلَّ مَا جَاءَ أُمَّةً رَسُولُهَا كَذَّبُوهُ فَأَتْبَعْنَا بَعْضَهُمْ بَعْضًا وَجَعَلْنَاهُمْ أَحَادِيثَ فَبُعْدًا لِقَوْمٍ لا يُؤْمِنُونَ

"Then We sent Our messengers one after another. Whenever its messenger came unto a nation they denied him; so We caused them to follow one another (to disaster) and We made them just tales. A far removal for folk who believe not" (*al-Muminoon* 44).

The last of these prophets was the Prophet Muhammad (peace be upon him). Like all the other messengers, those who refused to follow the truth opposed his teachings and they will continue to do so until the Day of Judgment.

Hence, mankind became two groups or parties: the party that followed the messengers of Allah (called "the party of Allah") and the party that refused to believe in and follow the messengers that Allah had sent for their own benefit (this group is called "the party of the Satan").

The relations between these two parties is one of enmity. Satan, the leader of the forces of evil, swore to mislead mankind until the Day of Judgment. Allah says,

قَالَ فَبِمَا أَغْوَيْتَنِي لَأَقْعُدَنَّ لَهُمْ صِرَاطَكَ الْمُسْتَقِيمَ ثُمَّ لَآتِيَنَّهُمْ مِنْ بَيْنِ أَيْدِيهِمْ وَمِنْ خَلْفِهِمْ وَعَنْ أَيْمَانِهِمْ وَعَنْ شَمَائِلِهِمْ وَلَا تَجِدُ أَكْثَرَهُمْ شَاكِرِينَ

"He [Satan] said: Now, because you have sent me astray, verily I shall lurk in ambush for them on Your Right Path. Then I shall come upon them, from before them and from behind them and from their right hand's side and from their left hand's side, and You will not find most of them grateful (unto You)" (*al-Araaf* 16-17).

The unbelievers, who are inevitably aligned with Satan, will never be satisfied and will never rest until they eradicate every form of obedience and worship of Allah as they can. Allah clearly states,

وَلَا يَزَالُونَ يُقَاتِلُونَكُمْ حَتَّى يَرُدُّوكُمْ عَنْ دِينِكُمْ إِنْ اسْتَطَاعُوا

"And they will not cease from fighting against you till they have made you renegades from your religion if they are able to" (*al-Baqarah* 217).

Some people, in their ignorance, believe that Muslims may be able to unite and live as brothers with the followers of the earlier prophets, the Jews and Christians. But spite towards the followers of Prophet Muhammad (peace be upon him) also comes from those who claim to follow the earlier messengers. Allah says about them,

وَلَنْ تَرْضَى عَنْكَ الْيَهُودُ وَلَا النَّصَارَى حَتَّى تَتَّبِعَ مِلَّتَهُمْ

"And the Jews will not be pleased with you, nor will the Christians, until you follow their way of life" (*al-Baqarah* 120).

Furthermore, this enmity against Islam not only exists in the lands dominated by churches and synagogues but even in the lands of mosques where the Muslims are fought against and even tortured. In analyzing the situation, Hasan Ayyoob even went so far as to say that the Arabs in Israel are freer than the Muslims in many of their own lands. In Israel (Ayyoob wrote this in 1977), the Arabs are able to protest and yell right in the face of the police while if they tried that in some Muslim countries they would be taken to prison and, perhaps, tortured *en masse*.[1]

Therefore, the only way that Allah's law, justice, right and truth will prevail on this earth is if the believers in Allah sacrifice their time, wealth and souls for the establishment of truth. That is, they must participate in jihad until the Day of Judgment since the ungodly forces will not rest until that time. Allah says,

$$\text{وَلَوْلَا دَفْعُ اللَّهِ النَّاسَ بَعْضَهُمْ بِبَعْضٍ لَفَسَدَتْ الأَرْضُ}$$

"And if Allah had not repelled some men by means of others, the earth would have been corrupted" (*al-Baqarah* 251).

Islam as a Religion and Complete Way of Life

The enmity towards Islam intensifies when the unbelievers and immoral people understand exactly what Islam is about. Maudoodi writes,

> In common terminology "religion" means nothing more than a hotch potch of some beliefs, prayers and

---

[1] Hasan Ayyoob, *Al-Jihaad wa al-Fadaaiyyah fi al-Islaam* (Kuwait: Risaalah al-Masjid, 1977), p. 13. Ayyoob (pp. 20-21) also states that the harm that those who call themselves "Muslims" have done to the true Muslims is greater than that done by the colonial powers.

rituals. If this is what "religion" means, then, it should, indeed, be a private affair.... But the truth is that Islam is not the name of a "religion" [if that is your concept of religion]... In reality Islam is a revolutionary ideology and programme which seeks to alter the social order of the whole world and rebuild it in conformity with its own tenets and ideals.[1]

In fact, this Western understanding of religion is not correct at all. Hasan Ayyoob wrote,

If one studies all of the Messengers he will see that their goal was justice and the removal of *dhulm* (oppression, wrongdoing)— regardless of whether that be *dhulm* committed by the person on himself by disbelief, evil deeds and sinfulness, or *dhulm* to others by harming their persons, family, wealth and honor. That is what is concluded from Allah's saying, "We verily sent Our messengers with clear proofs, and revealed with them the Scripture and Balance, that mankind might observe justice; and He revealed iron, wherein is mighty power and many uses for mankind" [*al-Hadeed* 25].[2]

Therefore, consistent with the mission of all of the Messengers of Allah, Islam is not a religion that seeks to purify its individual members. The purpose of Islam is the correct worship of Allah alone. In its totality, this also includes implementing the law of Allah on this earth. It implies that no one is allowed to put himself as the god or lord of another, as there is just one Lord or God to this creation. This also shows the true purpose or goal of jihad. As al-Almaiy stated, "The goals of jihad for the sake of Allah are: establishing the law of Allah on the earth, establishing truth and justice among

---

[1] Maudoodi, pp. 3-5.
[2] Ayyoob, p. 24.

mankind and making the rule or order for Allah only. And to allow no guidance except for the guidance of Allah and no ruling except by the *shareeah*."[1]

Jihad as an Imperative

Now it can be seen why Jihad is an imperative—a must in the life of the Muslim. As a whole, the unbelievers will not leave the Muslims completely free to follow their religion. They will meddle in the affairs of Muslim communities throughout the world, sometimes in the name of "human rights," "democracy," "freedom" and so forth. The only way a Muslim will be able to stick to his religion would be through jihad—from *jihad al-nafs* (the jihad of struggling against the desires sometimes found in one's soul) all the way to *jihad al-kufaar* (jihad against the disbelievers).

Hasan Ayyoob stated the following characteristics of the battle between the followers of truth and the followers of falsehood:

(1) There will always be a group of humans who oppose the believers—this is part of the plan of Allah for this creation.

(2) This is a natural type of enmity as it is a war between the followers of Allah and the followers of the Satan, and there is no way for the two groups to live in peace.

(3) But it is more than just enmity. The unbelievers will not cease their warfare until they change the followers of Islam into unbelievers. In the verse quoted above, Allah says,

وَلَا يَزَالُونَ يُقَاتِلُونَكُمْ حَتَّى يَرُدُّوكُمْ عَنْ دِينِكُمْ إِنِ اسْتَطَاعُوا

---

[1] Dhaahir al-Almaiy, "Al-Jihad fi Sabeel Allah: Asbaabuhu wa Ahdaafuhu," *Majallat Bahooth al-Islaamiyya* (Vol. 9, 1974), p. 306.

"And they will not cease from fighting against you till they have made you renegades from your religion, if they can" (*al-Baqarah* 217). And,

$$إِنْ يَثْقَفُوكُمْ يَكُونُوا لَكُمْ أَعْدَاءً وَيَبْسُطُوا إِلَيْكُمْ أَيْدِيَهُمْ$$

$$وَأَلْسِنَتَهُمْ بِالسُّوءِ وَوَدُّوا لَوْ تَكْفُرُونَ$$

"If they have the upperhand over you, they will be your foes, and will stretch out their hands and their tongues toward you with evil (intent), and they long for you to disbelieve" (*al-Mumtahanah* 2).[1]

Finally, Ayyoob states, "In conclusion, the enmity between *imaan* and *kufr* is a natural enmity between two conflicting opponents and there is no hope for any peace or agreement between them."[2]

But, furthermore, the job of the believer is not just to safeguard his own religion but his job is to purify and cleanse the whole earth of *kufr* (disbelief) and *dhulm* (wrongdoing and oppression). As Rabee ibn Amir told the emperor of Persia, "We have been sent by Allah to deliver whom He pleases from the lordship of His slaves (that is, humans) to His own lordship, and from the narrow confines of this world to the boundlessness of the next and from the oppressiveness of other ways of life to the fairness and justice of Islam."[3] Allah says about this community,

$$كُنْتُمْ خَيْرَ أُمَّةٍ أُخْرِجَتْ لِلنَّاسِ تَأْمُرُونَ بِالْمَعْرُوفِ وَتَنْهَوْنَ$$

$$عَنِ الْمُنْكَرِ وَتُؤْمِنُونَ بِاللَّهِ$$

---

[1] Ayyub, pp. 29-30.
[2] Ayyub, p. 30.
[3] Imaad al-Deen Ibn Katheer, *Al-Bidaayah wa al-Nihaayah* (Beirut: Daar al-Maktab al-Ilmiyyah, 1985), vol. 7, p. 40.

"You are the best nation raised for mankind; you order the good and you forbid the evil and you believe in Allah" (*ali-Imraan* 110).

Therefore, the only way a believer in Allah can freely and properly worship Allah and the only way for him to fulfill his duties to Allah is through jihad, in all of its comprehensive forms.

Perhaps the importance of jihad in the life of the Muslim is best summarized by Muhammad ibn Abdul Lateef who said, "Jihad is one of the pillars of Islam without which Islam cannot be established and without which the *shareeah* could not be implemented."[1]

Finally, the Messenger of Allah (peace be upon him) himself said,

رَأْسُ الْأَمْرِ الْإِسْلَامُ وَعَمُودُهُ الصَّلَاةُ وَذِرْوَةُ سَنَامِهِ الْجِهَادُ

"The head of the matter is Islam. Its pillar is the prayer. And its apex is jihad."[2]

REFERENCES

al-Albaani. Muhammad Naasir al-Deen. *Silsilat al-Ahaadeeth al-Saheehah.* Beirut. al-Maktab al-Islaami. 1979.

al-Almaiy, Dhaahir. "Al-Jihad fi Sabeel Allah: Asbaabuhu wa Ahdaafuhu." *Majallat Buhooth al-Islaamiyyah.* Vol. 9. 1974.

Ayyub, Hasan. *Al-Jihaad wa al-Fadaaiyyah fi al-Islaam.* Kuwait. Risaalah al-Masjid. 1977.

al-Banna, Ahmad. *Fath al-Rabbaani li-Tarteeb Musnad al-Imaam Ahmad.* Cairo. Daar al-Hadeeth. n.d.

---

[1] Quoted in al-Ulyani, p. 234.
[2] An authentic hadith recorded by Ahmad, al-Tirmidhi and others.

al-Banna, Hassan. "On Jihad," in Hassan al-Banna. *Five Tracts of Hassan al-Banna*. Charles Wendell, tr. Berkeley. University of California Press. n.d.

ibn Humaid, Abdullah ibn Muhammad. "The Call to Jihad in the Holy Quran" in M. M. Khan, trans. *Sahih al-Bukhari*. Chicago. Kazi Publications. 1976.

Jitmoud, Linda Kay. "An Intellectual Historical Study of Islamic Jihad During the Life of Muhammad and in the Twentieth Century." Ph. D. dissertation. Ball State University. 1985.

Ibn Katheer, Imaad al-Deen. *Al-Bidaayah wa al-Nihaayah*. Beirut. Daar al-Fikr. 1978.

-----*Tafseer al-Quran al-Adheem*. Kuwait. Daar al-Arqam. 1985.

Maudoodi, Abul Ala. *Jihad in Islam*. Lahore. Islamic Publications, Ltd. 1976.

al-Nawawi, Yahya. *Sharh Saheeh Muslim*. Beirut. Daar al-Fikr. 1978.

Qutb, Sayyid. *Fi Dhilaal al-Quran*. Beirut. Daar al-Shurooq. 1977.

Saalim, Ibraaheem Ali. *Al-Nifaaq wa al-Munaafiqoon*. Cairo. Daar al-Shaab. 1970.

al-Sawwaaf, Muhammad Mahmood. *Nadhuraat fi Soorah al-Hujuraat*. Beirut. Muasassat al-Risaalah. 1980.

al-Shaukaani, Muhammad ibn Ali. *Fath al-Qadeer*. Cairo. Mustafa al-Baba. 1964.

Siddiqi, Abdul Hameed. *Jihad in Islam*. Lahore. Kazi Publications. 1979.

Siddiqi, Nimat. *Al-Jihad fi Sabeel Allah*. Cairo. Daar al-Itisaam. 1979.

al-Ulyani, Ali. *Ahamiyat al-Jihaad*. Riyadh. Daar Taibah. 1985.

Feature Article:
Islam and Economic Development[1]

Introduction

The subject of this paper is difficult to write about for a number of reasons. But these reasons boil down to the problem of answering these two essential questions: What is the meaning of economic development? And, what does economic development within an Islamic framework entail? The former question I have discussed elsewhere[2], therefore, I will try not to repeat what I have written earlier while offering an extension of that discussion.

It is well-known that Islam is a way of life that is complete. The law and guidance of Islam does not confine itself to self-purification or worship only. Islam is concerned with every aspect of one's social and personal life. It offers its own forms of political, economic and social systems. These systems are unique and derive their basis for existence, and their values and goals from the guidance of Allah as revealed to His Prophet Muhammad (peace be upon him). This implies that an Islamic society is a society which enforces the commandments of Allah in all spheres of activity: penal laws, marital laws, business laws and so on. The sources of these laws are, of course, the Quran and the sunnah.

---

[1] This article appeared in *al-Basheer*, vol. 2, no. 1 (May-June 1988).
[2] Please see my article, "The Need for an Islamic Approach to Economic Development" (*Al-Ittihad*, October-December 1980, pp. 19-26).

Value Judgments and Economics

An Islamic society has certain values that it must abide by and certain goals that it seeks to achieve. These values include virtues such as honesty, modesty, chastity and so on, while the goals are objectives such as justice and brotherhood. Since, as mentioned above, Islam has its own economic system, it also has its own set of "economic values and goals."[1] This is very important to remember when dealing with the question of economic development in Islam.

In the recent past, the nations of the West have been the source of most economic theory, be it development theory or any other field of economic theory. Development theory was derived in the West to be applied to the lesser developed countries of the "South" and the "East". This was done in much the same way as technology was transferred from the Western nations to the lesser developed nations; that is, with very little regard for the environment and specific characteristics of each nation and with very little foresight as to the overall effects on each nation's particular society and

---

[1] Although economists have (or I should say, have tried to) split life into "economic" and "non-economic" aspects, the division is superficial, arbitrary and false. It is impossible from an Islamic point of view to make such divisions in human lives. What is meant here by "economic goals and values" are those values and goals that are most prominently affected by economic dealings. I advise the reader to keep the following in mind while reading this article: "But if anyone thinks it feasible that this [Islamic] economic system can be successfully implemented even if divorced from the complete whole of the ideological, moral and cultural system of Islam, I will humbly request him to get rid of this misunderstanding. This economic system has a deep relationship with the political, judicial, legal, cultural and social system of Islam. And all these branches are fundamentally based on the moral system of Islam... If you do not accept this creed [of Islam], this moral system and the whole of this code of life completely as it is, the economic system of Islam, divorced from its source, cannot be maintained or administered in its purity even for a single day, nor will any appreciable advantage accrue from it if you take it out of its wider context and then seek to apply it to your life." Quoted from Abul Ala Maudoodi, *The Economic Problem of Man and Its Islamic Solution* (Lahore, Pakistan: Islamic Publications, Ltd., 1975), p. 40.

development. For many years, the only object that development economists of the West considered important was what they called "economic development". And what was their definition of economic development? A sustained increase in a nation's per capita income growth; and that was it.[1] As Seers put it, "economic growth *was* development."[2]

Economists always try to describe economics as a positive science and usually demonstrate great hatred for any normative judgments that may have to be made.[3] The above definition of economic development made development seem like a value-free goal that all societies, including Muslim societies, should aspire to; thus, it kept economics positive and avoided any normative aspects.

But was this really the case? Examine what the development economist Dudley Seers wrote as early as 1969,

> The starting point is that we cannot avoid what the positivists disparagingly refer to as "value judgments". "Development" is inevitably a normative concept, almost a synonym for improvement. To pretend otherwise is just to hide one's own value judgments.[4]

---

[1] Cf., W. W. Rostow, *Stages of Economic Growth* (New York: Cambridge University Press, 1960).

[2] See Dudley Seers, "The Meaning of Development" in David Lehman, ed., *Development Theory* (London: Frank Cass, 1979), p. 25.

[3] To paraphrase Lord Lionel Robbins, "Economics is what is and not what ought to be". Note, for example, the Pareto criterion which says, by one definition, that something is Pareto preferred if all the actors are better off. By this criterion, economists avoid any interpersonal comparisons. After all, who could argue with such a criterion? Unfortunately, it does not lead to a complete ordering. See Russell and Wilkinson, *Microeconomics* (New York: John Wiley & Sons, 1979), Chapter 17.

[4] Seers, "Meaning," p. 10.

Growth vs. Development

The basic value judgment made about development, when traditionally defined as above, is that economic growth is good for any and all societies. This seems plausible. Certainly, with an increasingly larger pie there is more to go around and, maybe, after a period of economic growth, all the citizens of a nation will be able to enjoy the benefits of such growth—but the problem concerns how this economic growth is achieved. A very popular approach was the "trickle down" method. This method argues that as economic growth continues, its benefits will continue to spread to more and more people and will reach the poorest sectors of the nation; therefore, after an initial period of most of the benefits accruing to only those in the "modern sector", the benefits should "trickle down" to the poor and the society will be better off in the long run.

This idea came under attack frequently during the 1970s. This was mostly due to empirical findings that showed that in many countries inequality worsened over time and the portion of the population in poverty was not greatly affected even after a decade of constant economic growth. Indeed, this problem was so great that the Institute of Development Studies in Sussex and the World Bank combined efforts to produce a study entitled *Redistribution with Growth*, written to better understand the phenomena of economic growth and growing poverty.

More importantly, for the purposes of this paper, is the recognition that economic growth, or what was equated with "development" earlier, *by itself* may not be a purely beneficial goal after all. There may be other goals considered more important and values that are more cherished by certain societies. Semantically speaking, development has a positive connotation; therefore, work has been done to derive a new definition for the goal called "development."[1] Within the past two decades many new definitions have appeared. For brevity's sake, I will discuss only two.

In the article quoted above, Seers adds three new concepts to the definition of development: reductions in poverty, unemployment and inequality. In his postscript to that article, written ten years later, he adds some new criteria and then concludes,

> If development is now not primarily about per capita income, but also about distribution, and even more about the national capacity to negotiate with trans-national corporations, and to cope with their technological innovations and their cultural impact, then it is not just needed in "developing" countries, but in *all* countries.[2]

Alternatively, Denis Goulet, in his pathbreaking work *The Cruel Choice: A New Concept in the Theory of Development*, defines development as the achievement of "optimum life sustenance, esteem and freedom."[3] (He also concludes that development is also needed in today's "developed" countries.) He related development to the concept of "vulnerability", a society's ability to cope with new situations by using its own values and methods.

These two definitions differ but there is one common notable aspect in these and other recent definitions: a move away from a purely economic definition to one encompassing more aspects of life and society, and the realization that "development" is a normative term. Furthermore, economists began to realize that every society must grapple with

---

[1] "The author of *The Meaning of Development* could have taken the position that to use 'development' as a synonym for growth had so debased the word that it could not longer be used by honest people." Seers, "Postscript," in Ibid., p. 26.
[2] Ibid., p. 27.
[3] Denis Goulet, *The Cruel Choice: A New Concept in the Theory of Development* (New York: Atheneum, 1971), p. 168.

development within the framework of its own social mores and goals.

Islam and Economic Development

This now brings us to the question of Islam and economic development. Muslims must define development, a normative concept, according to Islamic concepts and goals.[1] The question that the Muslim scholars of today must answer is: Does Islam seek economic growth at the cost of any of the other values of Islam?

The Western world is based on a materialistic view of life and has, more or less, sacrificed many values and goals for the achievement of excellent economic performance. (And their development economists have expected other societies to do the same.) One can look at the result of this world view and ask whether or not this is what Islam seeks for the members of its community. Perhaps an example of the result of this world view may be found in Charlie Chaplin's *Modern Times* in which he is arrested for stopping work for a minute to visit with his mother and fiancée. That is an extreme example, no doubt, but the point that I am trying to get across is that a society based on optimum economic achievement may not be optimal according to other non-economic standards, for example, many of the standards and values of Islam.

An example of this divergence may be found in the definition of the concept of "success". In a materialistic society based on the economic life of humans, success would be defined in terms of wealth, money, possessions, economic achievement, and so on. Abul Ala Maudoodi clearly states the different perspectives. In his commentary to verses fifty-five and fifty-six of *Soorah al-Muminoon*,

---

[1] Sayyid Qutb's commentary on *Soorah Abasa* is excellent reading for those who wish to understand the concept of values in Islam. See *In the Shade of the Quran* (London: MWH Publishers, 1979), vol. 30, pp. 40-45.

أَيَحْسَبُونَ أَنَّمَا نُمِدُّهُمْ بِهِ مِنْ مَالٍ وَبَنِينَ نُسَارِعُ لَهُمْ فِي الْخَيْرَاتِ بَل لا يَشْعُرُونَ

"Do they think that to provide them with wealth and children We are solicitous for their welfare? Nay, they do not understand the reality of the matter." Maudoodi stated,

> This question has been posed as a proof of the main theme of the *Soorah*. It is meant to remove their misconception of "success", "welfare" and "prosperity", which the disbelievers had formed to delude themselves. According to them, the one who enjoyed the good things of life and wielded power and influence in the society, had attained "success". On the other hand, the one who was deprived of these things was a "failure". This misconception had involved them in another serious misunderstanding. They thought that the one who had attained "success" was in the right, and the beloved of Allah... One should keep in view the following:.... "Success" is a far higher thing than the material prosperity and the transitory success of an individual, community or nation. It is absolutely wrong to consider "prosperity" and "success" as a criterion of truth and falsehood.[1]

We may, therefore, reason that development in Islam is a process by which the goals of Islam are achieved and the

---

[1] Abul Ala Maudoodi, *The Meaning of the Quran* (Lahore: Islamic Publications, Ltd., 1979), vol. 8, pp. 25-26. The quote is just a small portion of his excellent explanation. I use the example of "success" because it is relevant to economic development, achievement and entrepreneurship. Some economists see entrepreneurship and achievement as the key to economic growth. See David C. McClelland, "The Achievement Motive in Economic Growth" in Finkle and Gable, eds., *Political Development & Social Change* (New York: John Wiley & Sons, 1971).

society has become, to borrow Denis Goulet's term, less vulnerable. That is to say, that any and all events that affect a developed Islamic society can be handled within the values and framework of that society without causing any great crisis within that society. Institutions and values are established within such a society that will lead to the achievement of the goals of Islam.

Islam and Economic Growth Today

In today's world, a number of Islamic goals are being blocked by existing institutions and, therefore, there is a need for development: a change in the institutions and structure of such societies to enable them to achieve the Islamic goals as laid down in the Quran and the sunnah. Note the parallel with the argument below for the establishment of economic development. There exists the goal, economic growth, and societal institutions and values are seen as either blocking or enhancing that goal. If there exist institutions that block that goal, then a development process is needed to change those institutions, to modernize society.

But Islamic goals cover a wide range and touch upon every aspect of human life; thus its definition of development is much broader than the one presented earlier in this paper. Economics is just one aspect of human life. Economic development within Islam is the development of institutions that cater to the goals of Islam with respect to the economic realm of life. Maudoodi states the "economic problem of man" in this way,

> With a view to sustain and advance human civilization, how to arrange economic distribution so as to keep all men supplied of the necessities of existence and to see that every individual in society is provided with opportunities adequate to the

development of his personality and the attainment of the highest possible perfection according to his capacity and aptitude.[1]

A developed economy is one that solves this problem. (Therefore, we are in complete agreement with Seers, Goulet, Illich and others who state that today's "developed" economies are also in need of development.) Islam seeks to solve this problem by the adoption of its guidance for mankind which includes moral exhortations, legal restrictions and penalties and the creation of certain institutions, for example, *zakaat*, that aid society in achieving the goals of Islam.

It is important to realize that Islam seeks to solve this problem within the framework of moral exhortations, legal restrictions and so on. Development economists of the West, who for the most part are the same people who have been advising the Muslim governments of today and of the past, have usually defined economic development (that is, growth) as the sole goal to be achieved; they have looked at Muslim institutions and values as either blocking that goal or enhancing its achievement.[2]

If these economists come to the conclusion that a certain institution or value is an obstacle to economic development, they merely advise the government to try to remove that obstacle. Many unfortunate Muslim governments have been quick to move on the advice of their Western "experts".[3]

What kind of advice might Western advisors, who are ignorant of Allah's guidance, give the Muslim governments?

---

[1] Maudoodi, *Economic*, p. 8.

[2] An excellent article on how development economists have viewed obstacles to development and how ignorant economists really are on this subject is Albert O. Hirschman, "Obstacles to Development: A Classification and a Quasi-Vanishing Act," in Uphoff and Ilchman, eds., *The Political Economy of Development* (Berkeley: University of California Press, 1972).

[3] See my article, op cit., on how many of these governments are run by the elite and have become alienated from Islamic principles.

This can be seen by the types of studies carried out in the West. The January 1979 issue of *World Development* contained the article "Corruption and Development" by Michael Beenstock. In summarizing his article, the author writes,

> A typology of corruption is established drawing the distinction between extortionary, subversive and benign corruption and their effects on allocative efficiency are explored. It is argued that while the economic effects of corruption are likely to be unfavorable there may be circumstances where the converse holds. This discussion does not extend to the moral and social aspects of corruption.[1]

Possible advice: close your eyes to certain types of corruption as they are good for allocative efficiency. Such a discussion, from an Islamic viewpoint, is absurd. The reason Beenstock did not include a moral discussion of the subject is because corruption is morally wrong and this rules out any reason for studying the possible positive economic effects of corruption.

Under one condition only is such a study useful and that is when allocative efficiency is valued greater than the moral character of society, that is, according to this Western approach to economic development which is not development according to Islam.

Let me present another example which may not be so extreme. Islam stresses the brotherhood of the believers, the closeness of family relations and care for the needy of one's community. In 1965, Albert O. Hirschman wrote his *The Strategy of Economic Development*. In this work he discussed ego-focussed and group-focussed images of society. Hirschman concluded that too much stress on ego-focussed

---

[1] Michael Beenstock, "Corruption and Development," *World Development* (January 1979), p. 32.

320

achievement may bring about gains in economic entrepreneurship and innovation but may have negative effects on the spirit of cooperation, consultation, and so on, that are needed for society's development, for example, the need for directing and working within staffs or groups for implementing a project. A totally group-focussed achievement approach may be incompatible with certain aspects of development which need to reward achievement, for example, a reward for capable entrepreneurial activity and the existence of social mobility.[1] Feeding of needy relatives, sharing of one's wealth and closeness of family members may be seen by development experts as being extremely group-focussed and detrimental to the development effort.[2] This may lead economists to conclude that the society should be made more "ego-focussed"; this, of course, may work against many Islamic values. (This once again points to the existence of hidden value judgments. If one takes the meaning of development to be the meeting of people's basic needs, then a group-focussed image of society would probably be considered more beneficial or appropriate. On the other hand, if one understands economic development as meaning economic growth, one would come to the opposite conclusion.)

The real damage that such advice, and its subsequent implementation, has on Islamic societies is great. What is being dealt with, in reality, are the values of the society as a whole. As Maudoodi mentions, quoted in an earlier footnote, the basis of the Muslim society is the moral system of Islam. When foreign economists seek to change the values of Muslim societies, they are striking at the basis of the Islamic way of life.

---

[1] See Albert O. Hirschman, *The Strategy of Economic Development* (New York: Yale University Press, 1965).

[2] Hirschman concludes that only a balanced mix of ego- and group-focussed images will be beneficial to development. Although it is beyond the scope of this paper, such a balanced mix is to be found in the economic and social systems of Islam.

As an example, multinational corporations seek to "sell" new values, ways of life and aspirations to the underdeveloped parts of the world in order to increase their possibilities for profit.[1] Such policies by national or multinational bodies in an Islamic context would lead to the disintegration of Islamic values and would hinder the achievement of Islamic goals. There is no question that such policies would have to constitute what Lebret calls "anti-development" from an Islamic viewpoint. Thus the "experts" who are talking from a different perspective are not benefiting the Muslim societies but are leading them down the road to social conflict only, and not to any real form of development.

The above was written to point out the importance of economic development in Islam being a goal that is to be achieved within the institutions and values of Islam; if it is not to be achieved in this manner, it becomes tantamount to the abandonment of Islam, the adoption of a new way of life and "anti-development". The way of thinking of the early development economists, who are still influential today and whose theories are still being taught in the universities throughout the United States and elsewhere, is backwards according to Islamic thought. Economic development is not an end to which all other goals, values and institutions must yield. Indeed, in Islam, it is the values of the religion that reign supreme and all other aspects have been created to aid in achieving such values and goals. Allah has stated that He made all the material objects of the earth for man's purpose and use; man is the master, matter the slave and not vice-versa. Humans are not to be sacrificed to produce more goods and services. Goods and services are to be used to allow humans to fulfill their potential.

---

[1] Cf., Richard Barnet, "Multinationals and Development" in Jegen and Wilber, eds., *Growth with Equity* (New York: Paulist Press, 1979).

What is Real Development?

Islam, not being derived from man's limited knowledge, seeks true prosperity and felicity for all mankind. This cannot be achieved by the mere attainment of goods and services. This is why economic miracles such as Brazil may be considered disasters when seen in the light of Islam's guidance.

What happened in the country of Brazil?[1] Output doubled in only eight years (1968-74)— an outstanding achievement of economic development according to the orthodox criteria. At the same time, the income share of the wealthiest 20 percent increased from 40 to 48 percent while the share of the poorest 40 percent actually dropped two percentage points, from 11 to 9 percent. Employment was created by forcing persons into the wage earning sector. One explanation of what happened is given by Jameson and Wilber:

> Many persons were forced into the modern sector because of changes in the economy: ejection from share-cropped lands in the Northeast; closing down of informal activity by government power; removal of slum dwelling places from the city which resulted in necessary reliance on costly transport... Davis has provided many examples of the degradation of the Indian way of life and some examples of virtual genocide in the name of progress for Brazil... Persons... are turned into virtual slaves by this new system of economic activity.[2]

---

[1] The following data and analysis are from Kenneth P. Jameson and Charles K. Wilber, "Employment, Basic Human Needs and Economic Development," in Jegen and Wilber, pp. 132-134.

[2] Jameson and Wilber, p. 133. The title of Davis' book is *Victims of the Miracle: Development and the Indians of Brazil* (New York: Cambridge Univ. Press, 1977).

Is that development and progress indeed? We have here a problem that calls for a value judgment. As I alluded to earlier, "traditional economists look on people's values as means. Since the goal is growth, if people's values have to change in order to get growth, then society must affect that change."[1] The following question must be asked: What is more important to life, fulfillment and happiness, the mere production of more goods and services or those noble institutions, deemed as obstacles to economic progress, that must be sacrificed in order to achieve the increase in output?

Whenever an economist deems a certain social or cultural institution an obstacle to development, he is making a value judgment. Islam asks one to look at the institution and to see if it is a necessary part of an Islamic society; that is, does it contribute to human happiness as Islam views it. If it is deemed necessary, then the goal of economic growth will not be enough to eradicate it. As in the example stated earlier, under no circumstances would an Islamic government allow the existence of corruption, no matter how beneficial it may be for development.

Some have suggested that Muslims do a study like Adelman and Morris' *Society, Politics & Economic Development* or Donald Smith's *Religion and Political Development*. What these researchers did was to look at institutions, values and so on and see if they were positively or negatively related to economic and political development. There is a problem with these works, however, when one tries to apply them to development within Islam. For example, Smith has some negative things to say about Islam and political development, but such results are completely determined by how one defines political development. For

---

[1] Charles Wilber and Kenneth Jameson, "Paradigms of Economic Development and Beyond," in Jameson and Wilber, eds., *New Directions in Economic Development* (South Bend: Notre Dame Univ. Press, 1981), p. 33.

example, as is commonly the case[1] if one defines political development or modernization as being the process of becoming more and more like the United States, then one may certainly find many "negative" aspects in Islam. The reason for this is simple. Islam's goal is not a society like that of the United States and, therefore, the results are irrelevant; in fact, it should be expected that Islam will not achieve "modernization" when it is defined in such a manner.

A close analogy may be found in the following quote from a discussion on Cuba by Dudley Seers:

> And then [national income in Cuba] declined in the following three years. The main issue therefore appears to be whether redistribution has inhibited growth. But this is misleading... to discuss the "trade-off" in these terms is theoretically mistaken when elimination of poverty is the central objective.[2]

His point is that if the country is concerned with goal A, why should it be judged on how well it achieved goal B? If our goal is to attain Islamic values and goals, why should we be concerned with whether or not we meet Western criteria or goals?

In Tunisia, the government called for the abolishment of Ramadhaan as it was considered a constraint on production and therefore an obstacle in the country's path to development. Most Western economists, at least those of the orthodox school of thought, would agree with this line of thinking. Again, Muslims must ask themselves what is more important: "economic development" (that is, growth) or an institution that is an act of worship of Allah. Would the increase in

---

[1] Cf., Daniel Lerner, *The Passing of Traditional Society* (Glencoe: The Free Press, 1958).

[2] Dudley Seers, "Cuba" in Hollis Chenery, et al., eds., *Redistribution with Growth* (Oxford: Oxford University Press, 1974), p. 328.

production, if there was any, bestow more benefits on the community than the institution it must abolish?[1]

The above example shows that making the (normative) decision to achieve economic growth at the expense of the values of society may be injurious to the society as a whole.

An Islamic View of Economic Growth

Admittedly, economic growth will be needed to meet the needs of the ever-growing population. I am not arguing that Islam does not value the growth of economic activity. Those of Islam's past, for instance, Sufi ascetics and other extremists who have viewed material things as inherently evil, have been severely criticized by other scholars for their misconceptions in this regard. Asceticism is denounced by Islam. The way of life prescribed by Islam is "the middle or balanced way". This is an apt description of how Islam views economic life and materialism. Islam is neither too materialistic nor too other worldly. Instead, it strikes a perfect accord between the two extremes.

The point is that Islam puts all things in their proper place. Material well-being is not all there is to life. Islam, though, does realize the necessity of meeting people's basic needs.

Many Muslim economists like to state that wealth may lead to immorality while poverty may lead to idolatry. Goulet mentions a widely accepted theory that states that people must have their basic needs met before they can move on to higher "enhancement needs."[2] But even the most impoverished people

---

[1] Note that the question of whether or not the institution, in this case the fast of Ramadhaan, is indeed harmful to production is not discussed here. It is possible that the many spiritual and physical benefits of fasting may be a boon to production.

[2] Denis Goulet, "Strategies for Meeting Human Needs" in Jegen and Wilber, p. 123. The major proponent of the above theory is Maslow.

in the world see more to life than just meeting their "basic needs." Empirical studies have found that many primitive (economically) and impoverished people of the world spend a portion of their wealth on ceremonies and other "wasteful," that is, non-essential, activities while at the same time some of their children may be starving or suffering from malnutrition. In some parts of Africa where cattle are seen as a sign of wealth and prestige, many of the poor refuse to slaughter their cattle for food although starvation and malnutrition may be their lot. These societies value some things more than mere economic growth.

Islam has its own set of priorities, as do the poor referred to above; and these priorities extend into the realm of economics. We should therefore seek to determine what is the purpose of the material things of this life according to Islam. (A complete answer to this question is beyond the scope of this paper and would include many theological questions that do not concern us here.)

The sunnah shows that one of the main purposes for the material objects of this life is to aid society to satisfy the "basic needs" of its members.[1] These basic needs include such things as food, clothing and shelter. (*Ijtihaad* may be made to determine the exact basic needs of the Muslim people today.) Islamic societies have built-in mechanisms to see to it that such needs are met. For example, zakaat is taken from the rich and given to the poor to help them meet these needs and become full participants in society.

Stating that Islam gives the guidelines for development does not mean that one can look to the Quran and hadith and find statements like, "The poor save less, therefore allow inequalities to generate the savings needed for economic development."[2] What is being implied here is that the values of

---

[1] Elsewhere I discuss the differences between an Islamic approach to development and the current "Basic Needs" approach. See Zarabozo, "The Need..."

[2] This is the "trickle-down" theory of growth.

Islam describe their own definition and path of economic development; and that the "economic problem" of man (as quoted earlier from Maudoodi) is solved within the Islamic framework of society.

This leads to an important point which, though tautological, needs to be stated: the values and the institutions of Islam are completely consistent with the goals that Islam seeks to achieve for mankind. Any nation that truly seeks to attain the noble Islamic goals need only apply Islam's values and institutions and not those of the Western nations and advisors. For example, if a Muslim nation seeks to have the basic material needs of its citizens met, they may be met through the establishment of zakaat, exhortations to practice charity, enforcement of the laws of inheritance and so on, and not by the establishment of Western social security systems[1], Western banks based on interest and so on.

It is also important that Islam itself be established and not a mixture of Islam and other ideologies.

We must disagree with Christine Rider Pinches' statement, "the three elements of Islam, Arabism and socialism are interrelated and not incompatible with the types of decision-making required [to achieve development] in these [Muslim] countries."[2] Islam has been mixed with other ideologies on numerous occasions in attempts to achieve development for Muslim countries. Muslim countries should realize that Islam has its own unique definition of development that is not compatible with others currently being presented to the Muslim world.

---

[1] One qualification that is lacking in the United States' requirement for social security is need. See Moosa Ibraaheem Abdel Rahman, "Zakat, Social Justice and Social Security," in *The Proceedings of the MSA Conference on Islamic Economics* (Plainfield: MSA, 1979).

[2] Christine Rider Pinches, "Economic Development: The Need for an Alternative Approach," *Economic Development and Cultural Change* (October 1977), p. 144.

Turning to Islam

In order to come closer to an Islamic society, the Pakistani government decided to enforce the laws of zakaat. The banks automatically took the zakaat from the depositors' account. A friend of mine showed me a bank statement from a bank in Pakistan and it had the following four entries: Amount Deposited, Amount Withdrawn, Zakat Payment and Interest Accrued. A very interesting combination: zakaat and interest.

Article 1 of the Charter of Economic Rights and Duties of States[1], which the United States opposed, states,

> Every state has the sovereign and inalienable right to choose its economic system as well as its political, social and cultural systems in acceptance with the will of its people, without outside interference, coercion or threat in any form whatsoever.

Virtually every Muslim government voted for this resolution. It is amazing that they can vote for such a statement and at the same time be bouncing from one foreign ideology to the next without ever earnestly trying to promote their own native Islamic system.

Perhaps one cannot put all the blame on the Muslim governments of today for taking their nations down roads that lead virtually nowhere. These countries are working in an international setting that definitely works against the interests of Islam and any Islamic movement. Look at the economic freeze on Iran by those who control the international economic system. Any Muslim government that truly seeks to apply Islam may find the IMF and other international organizations giving them a cold shoulder in the future.

---

[1] United Nations General Assembly Resolution 3281 (XXIX), December 12, 1974. Note that the passage above in no way implies a recognition by this author of the resolutions of the United Nations as any kind of guide for Muslims.

On the other hand, the Muslim leaders may not be totally absolved for failing to meet their Islamic responsibilities as they have not shown the will needed for such an effort.

The Muslim people as a whole must also bear some of the responsibility and blame. They have not demanded Islam from their leaders and have, for the most part, allowed the leaders to apply any way of life they wish.

Where are We Headed?

Here is a final note of pessimism for our readers. In 1969, Dudley Seers wrote,

> The prospect of a "second development decade" is daunting; a repetition of the 1960s, with unemployment and inequality rising still further, would be socially, economically and politically disastrous whatever the pace of economic growth![1]

Indeed, the Muslim nations of the world have shown no signs of change. From the sixties, through the seventies and the eighties, the Muslim governments and people have shown no signs of an awakening.

Now to a final note of optimism. Some alert Western minds have even come close to an Islamic view of development. It is hoped that a new force will arrive in the West that will lead to a change in the international setting that has so constrained the lesser developed nations of the world. As two contemporary economists have written:

> Our goal (of development) is to enhance people's core values. Development becomes the means, not the end, for the end is to enhance what people value.

---

[1] Seers, "Meaning," in Lehman, p. 22.

Development or growth is desirable only if it is
consistent with people's deepest values.[1]

And note the conclusion of another development
researcher:

Paradoxically the lesson of greatest importance is
that the best model of development is the one that
any society forges for itself on the anvil of its own
specific conditions.[2]

Let us hope that the Muslims of today will also reach
the same conclusion and stop looking elsewhere for answers
and truly seek to attain development as it is defined by their
religion of Islam.

References

Abdel Rahman, Moosa Ibraaheem. "Zakat, Social Justice and Social
Security," in *The Proceedings of the MSA Conference on
Islamic Economics*. Plainfield: MSA. 1979.

Barnet, Richard. "Multinationals and Development" in Jegen and
Wilber, eds., *Growth with Equity*. New York: Paulist Press.
1979.

Beenstock, Michael. "Corruption and Development," *World
Development*. January 1979.

Goulet, Denis. *The Cruel Choice: A New Concept in the Theory of
Development*. New York: Atheneum. 1971.

-----"Looking at Guinea-Bissau: A New Nation's Development
Strategy. Occasional Paper No. 9." Overseas Development
Council. March 1978.

-----"Strategies for Meeting Human Needs" in Jegen and Wilber,
eds., *Growth with Equity*. New York: Paulist Press. 1979.

---

[1] Wilber and Jameson in Jameson and Wilber, p. 18.
[2] Denis Goulet, "Looking at Guinea-Bissau: A New Nation's Development Strategy"
(Occasional Paper No. 9, Overseas Development Council, March 1978), p. 52.

Hirschman, Albert O. "Obstacles to Development: A Classification and a Quasi-Vanishing Act," in Uphoff and Ilchman, eds., *The Political Economy of Development*. Berkeley: University of California Press. 1972.

-----*The Strategy of Economic Development*. New York: Yale University Press. 1965.

Jameson, Kenneth P. and Charles K. Wilber, "Employment, Basic Human Needs and Economic Development," in Jegen and Wilber, eds., *Growth with Equity*. New York: Paulist Press. 1979.

Lerner, Daniel. *The Passing of Traditional Society*. Glencoe: The Free Press. 1958.

Maudoodi, Abul Ala. *The Economic Problem of Man and Its Islamic Solution*. Lahore, Pakistan: Islamic Publications, Ltd. 1975.

-----*The Meaning of the Quran*. Lahore: Islamic Publications, Ltd. 1979.

McClelland, David M. "The Achievement Motive in Economic Growth" in Finkle and Gable, eds., *Political Development & Social Change*. New York: John Wiley & Sons. 1971.

Pinches, Christine Rider. "Economic Development: The Need for an Alternative Approach." *Economic Development and Cultural Change*. October 1977.

Qutb, Sayyid. *In the Shade of the Quran*. London: MWH Publishers. 1979.

Rostow, W. W. *Stages of Economic Growth*. New York: Cambridge University Press. 1960.

Russell, R. R. and Wilkinson, J. *Microeconomics*. New York: John Wiley & Sons. 1979.

Seers, Dudley. "Cuba" in Hollis Chenery, et al., eds., *Redistribution with Growth*. Oxford: Oxford University Press. 1974.

-----"The Meaning of Development" in David Lehman, ed., *Development Theory*. London: Frank Cass. 1979.

-----"Postscript" in David Lehman, ed., *Development Theory*. London: Frank Cass. 1979.

United Nations General Assembly Resolution 3281 (XXIX), December 12, 1974.

Wilber, Charles and Kenneth Jameson, "Paradigms of Economic Development and Beyond," in Jameson and Wilber, eds., *New Directions in Economic Development*. South Bend: Notre Dame Univ. Press. 1981.

Zarabozo, Jamaal al-Deen M. "The Need for an Islamic Approach to Economic Development." *Al-Ittihad*. October-December 1980.

Index of Quranic Verses Quoted

General Index